Child Life Studies 2HC3

MW00743529

TABLE OF CONTENTS
& ACKNOWLEDGEMENTS

PAGE

Module 3: The Hospitalized Child

Module 4: Therapeutic Interventions

Module 5: Families in Crisis, Culture & Grief

Module 1:
A Child's Hospital Experience

HOSPITALISM

An Inquiry into the Genesis of Psychiatric Conditions in Early Childhood[1]

By RENÉ A. SPITZ, M.D. (New York)

"En la Casa de Niños Expositos el niño se va poniendo triste y muchos de ellos mueren de tristeza."
(1760, *from the diary of a Spanish bishop.*)

1. *The Problem*

The term *hospitalism* designates a vitiated condition of the body due to long confinement in a hospital, or the morbid condition of the atmosphere of a hospital. The term has been increasingly preempted to specify the evil effect of institutional care on infants, placed in institutions from an early age, particularly from the psychiatric point of view.[2] This study is especially concerned with the effect of continuous institutional care of infants under one year of age, for reasons other than sickness. The model of such institutions is the foundling home.

Medical men and administrators have long been aware of the shortcomings of such charitable institutions. At the beginning of our century one of the great foundling homes in Germany had a mortality rate of 71.5% in infants in the first year of life(1).[3] In 1915 Chapin(2) enumerated ten asylums in the larger cities of the United States, mainly on the Eastern seaboard, in which the death rates of infants admitted during their first year of life varied from 31.7% to 75% by the end of their second year. In a discussion in the same

1. Preliminary report.
2. *Hospitalism* tends to be confused with *hospitalization*, the temporary confinement of a seriously ill person to a hospital.
3. Numbers in parentheses refer to the bibliography at the end of the paper.

year before the American Pediatric Association(3), Dr. Knox of Baltimore stated that in the institutions of that city 90% of the infants died by the end of their first year. He believed that the remaining 10% probably were saved because they had been taken out of the institution in time. Dr. Shaw of Albany remarked in the same discussion that the mortality rate of Randalls Island Hospital was probably 100%.

Conditions have since greatly changed. At present the best American institutions, such as Bellevue Hospital, New York City, register a mortality rate of less than 10%(4), which compares favorably with the mortality rate of the rest of the country. While these and similar results were being achieved both here and in Europe, physicians and administrators were soon faced with a new problem: they discovered that institutionalized children practically without exception developed subsequent psychiatric disturbances and became social, delinquent, feeble-minded, psychotic, or problem children. Probably the high mortality rate in the preceding period had obscured this consequence. Now that the children survived, the other disadvantages of institutionalization became apparent. They led in this country to the widespread substitution of institutional care by foster home care.

The first investigation of the factors involved in the psychiatric consequences of institutional care of infants in their first year was made in 1933 in Austria by H. Durfee and K. Wolf(5). Further contributions to the problem were made by L. G. Lowrey(6), L. Bender and H. Yarnell(7), H. Bakwin (4), and W. Goldfarb(8-11). The results of all these investigations are roughly similar:

Bakwin found greatly increased susceptibility to infection in spite of high hygienic and nutritional standards. Durfee and Wolf found that children under three months show no demonstrable impairment in consequence of institutionalization; but that children who had been institutionalized for more than eight months during their first year show such severe psychiatric disturbances that they cannot be tested. Bender, Goldfarb and Lowrey found that after three years of institutionalization the changes effected are irreversible. Lowrey found that whereas the impairment of children hospitalized during their first year seems irremediable, that of children hospitalized in the second or third year can be corrected.

Two factors, both already stressed by Durfee and Wolf, are made responsible by most of the authors for the psychological injury suffered by these children.

First: Lack of stimulation. The worst offenders were the best equipped and most hygienic institutions, which succeeded in sterilizing the surroundings of the child from germs but which at the same time sterilized the child's psyche. Even the most destitute of homes offers more mental stimulation than the usual hospital ward.

Second: The presence or absence of the child's mother. Stimulation by the mother will always be more intensive than even that of the best trained nursery personnel(12). Those institutions in which the mothers were present had better results than those where only trained child nurses were employed. The presence of the mothers could compensate even for numerous other shortcomings.

We believe that further study is needed to isolate clearly the various factors operative in the deterioration subsequent to prolonged care in institutions. The number of infants studied by Bakwin, Durfee, Wolf and Lowrey in single institutions is very small and Bender, Yarnell, and Goldfarb did not observe infants in the first twelve months of life. We are not questioning here whether institutions should be preferred to foster homes, a subject now hardly ever discussed—the decision can by implication be deduced from the results of the studies of the Iowa group in their extensive research on the "Nature Versus Nurture" controversy(13-18). It may seem surprising that in the course of this controversy no investigation has covered the field of the first year of life in institutions. All Iowa investigators studied either children in foster homes or children over one year of age, using their findings for retrospective interpretations. They did not have at their disposal a method of investigation that would permit the evaluation and quantification of development, mental or otherwise, during the first year of life. Their only instrument is the I.Q. which is unreliable(21), and not applicable during the first year. However, the baby tests worked out by Hetzer and Wolf(22) fill the gap, providing not only a quotient for intelligence but also quantifiable data for development as a whole, such as indication of Developmental Age and of a Developmental Quotient. They provide, furthermore, quantifiable data on six distinct sectors of personality, namely development of perception, body mastery, social relations, memory relations to inanimate objects, and intelligence (which in the first

4. Woodworth(19) in discussing the results of the Child Welfare Research Station of the State University of Iowa makes the following critical remarks (p. 71): "The causes of the inferior showing of orphanage children are obviously open to debate... It would seem that a survey and comparative study of institutional homes for children would be instructive...."

5. Jones(20) takes exception to this method as follows: "It seems probable that we shall turn from retrospective surveys of conditions assumed to have had a prior influence and shall prefer to deal with the current and cumulative effects of specific environmental factors. It may also be expected that our interest will shift to some extent from mere statistical studies ... to investigations of the dynamics of the growth process in individuals."

(130 infants). Since the two institutions were situated in different countries of the Western hemisphere, a basis of comparison was established by investigating non-institutionalized children of the same age group in their parents' homes in both countries. A total of 34 of these were observed. We thus have four environments:

TABLE I.

Environment	Institution No. 1	Corresponding private backgrounds	Institution No. 2	Corresponding private background
Number of Children	69	11	61	23

III. Procedure.

In each case an anamnesis was made which whenever possible included data on the child's mother; and in each case the Hetzer-Wolf baby tests were administered. Problems cropping up in the course of our investigations for which the test situation did not provide answers were subjected to special experiments elaborated for the purpose. Such problems referred, for instance, to attitude and behavior in response to stimuli offered by inanimate objects, by social situations, etc. All observations of unusual or unexpected behavior of a child were carefully protocoled and studied.

A large number of tests, all the experiments and some of the special situations were filmed on 16/mm film. A total of 31,500 feet of film preserve the results of our investigation to-date. In the analysis of the movies the following method was applied: Behavior was filmed at sound speed, i.e., 24 frames per second. This makes it possible to slow action down during projection to nearly one-third of the original speed so that it can be studied in slow motion. A projector with additional handdrive also permits study of the films frame by frame, if necessary, to reverse action and to repeat projection of every detail as often as required. Simultaneously the written protocols of the experiments are studied and the two observations compared.

1. Institution No. 1 will from here on be called "Nursery"; Institution No. 2, "Foundling Home".

2. The small number of children observed in this particular environment was justified by the fact that it has been previously studied extensively by other workers; our only aim was to correlate our results with theirs. However, during the course of one year each child was tested at least at regular monthly intervals.

---

year is limited to understanding of relations between and insight into the functions of objects).

With the help of these data ("dimensions"), a profile (personality curve) is constructed from which relevant conclusions can be drawn and with the help of which children can be compared with one another. Averages of development in any one sector or in all of them can be established for given environments. Finally, the relevant progresses of one and the same child in the several sectors of its personality can be followed up. The profiles present a cross-section of infantile development at any given moment; but they also can be combined into longitudinal curves of the developmental progress of the child's total personality as well as of the various sectors of the personality.

The aim of my research is to isolate and investigate the pathogenic factors responsible for the favorable or unfavorable outcome of infantile development. A psychiatric approach might seem desirable; however, infant psychiatry is a discipline not yet existent; its advancement is one of the aims of the present study.

II. Material[7]

With this purpose in mind a long-term study of 164 children was undertaken. In view of the findings of previous investigations this study was largely limited to the first year of life, and confined to two institutions, in order to embrace the total population of both

6. It is interesting to note that independently of our approach to this problem (mapped out and begun in 1936) Woodworth[19] recommends a research program on extremely similar lines as being desirable for the better understanding of the problem of heredity and environment:

"Orphanages. Present belief based on a certain amount of evidence regards the orphanage as an unfavorable environment for the child but the causes are not well understood. Two general projects may be suggested.

(a) A survey of institutional homes for children with a view to discovering the variations in their equipment and personnel and in their treatment of the children, with some estimate of the results achieved.

(b) Experimental studies in selected orphanages which retain their children for a considerable time, with a view to testing out the effects of specific environmental factors. For example, the amount of contact of the child with adults could be increased for certain children for the purpose of seeing whether this factor is important in mental development. It is conceivable that an orphanage could be run so as to become a decidedly favorable environment for the growing child, but at present we do not know how this result could be accomplished."

7. I wish to thank K. Wolf, Ph.D., for her help in the experiments carried out in "Nursery" and in private homes, and for her collaboration in the statistical evaluation of the results.

RENE A. SPITZ

IV. Results.

For the purpose of orientation we established the average of the Developmental Quotients for the first third of the first year of life for each of the environments investigated. We contrasted these averages with those for the last third of the first year. This comparison gives us a first hint of the significance of environmental influences for development.

Type of Environment	Cultural and Social Background	Developmental Quotients	
		Average of first four months	Average of last four months
Parental Home	Professional	199	191
	Village Population	107	108
Institution	"Nursery"	101.5	105
	"Foundling home"	124	72

TABLE II.

Children of the first category come from professional homes in a large city; their Developmental Quotient, high from the start, remains high in the course of development.

Children in the second category come from an isolated fishing village of 499 inhabitants, where conditions of nutrition, housing, hygienic and medical care are very poor indeed; their Developmental Quotient in the first four months is much lower and remains at a lower level than that of the previous category.

In the third category, "Nursery", the children were handicapped from birth by the circumstance of their origin, which will be discussed below. At the outset their Developmental Quotient is even somewhat lower than that of the village babies; in the course of their development they gain slightly.

In the fourth category, "Foundling Home", the children are of an unselected urban (Latin) background. Their Developmental Quotient on admission is below that of our best category but much higher than that of the other two. The picture changes completely by the end of the first year, when their Developmental Quotient sinks to the astonishingly low level of 72.

Thus the children in the first three environments were at the end of their first year on the whole well-developed and normal, whether they were raised in their progressive middle-class family homes (where

obviously optimal circumstances prevailed and the children we[re] well in advance of average development), or in an institution or village home, where the development was not brilliant but st[ill] reached a perfectly normal and satisfactory average. The ch[il]dren in the fourth environment, though starting at almost as high a level as the best of the others, had spectacularly deteriorated.

The children in Foundling Home showed all the manifestations hospitalism, both physical and mental. In spite of the fact th[at] hygiene and precautions against contagion were impeccable, the ch[il]dren showed from the third month on, extreme susceptibility to [in]fection and illness of any kind. There was hardly a child in who[m] case history we did not find reference to otitis media, or morbilli, varicella, or eczema, or intestinal disease of one kind or another. [The] figures could be elicited on general mortality; but during my stay epidemic of measles swept the institution, with staggeringly hi[gh] mortality figures, notwithstanding liberal administration of conval[es]cent serum and globulins, as well as excellent hygienic conditions. [Of] a total of 88 children up to the age of 2½, 23 died. It is strik[ing] to compare the mortality among the 45 children up to 1½ yea[rs] to that of the 43 children ranging from 1½ to 2½ years: usual[ly] the *incidence* of measles is low in the younger age group, but amo[ng] those infected the mortality is higher than that in the older age grou[p] since in the case of Foundling Home every child was infected, t[he] question of incidence does not enter; however, contrary to expectati[on] the mortality was much higher in the older age group. In the young[er] group, 6 died, i.e., approximately 13%. In the older group, 17 di[ed] i.e., close to 40%. The significance of these figures becomes appar[ent] when we realize that the mortality from measles during the first y[ear] of life in the community in question, outside the institution, w[as] less than ½%.

In view of the damage sustained in all personality sectors of [the] children during their stay in this institution we believe it licit [to] assume that their vitality (whatever that may be), their resistance [to] disease, was also progressively sapped. In the ward of the childr[en] ranging from 18 months to 2½ years only two of the twenty-six surv[iv]ing children speak a couple of words. The same two are able [to] walk. A third child is beginning to walk. Hardly any of them can walk alone. Cleanliness habits have not been acquired and all are inco[n]tinent.

In sharp contrast to this is the picture offered by the oldest inmates in Nursery, ranging from 8 to 12 months. The problem here is not whether the children walk or talk by the end of the first year; the problem with these 10-month-olds is how to tame the healthy toddlers' curiosity and enterprise. They climb up the bars of the cots after the manner of South Sea Islanders climbing palms. Special measures to guard them from harm have had to be taken after one 10-month-old actually succeeded in diving right over the more than two-foot railing of the cot. They vocalize freely and some of them actually speak a word or two. And all of them understand the significance of simple social gestures. When released from their cots, all walk with support and a number walk without it.

What are the differences between the two institutions that result in the one turning out normally acceptable children and the other showing such appalling effects?

A. Similarities.[8]

1. Background of the children.

Nursery is a penal institution in which delinquent girls are sequestered. When, as is often the case, they are pregnant on admission, they are delivered in a neighboring maternity hospital and after the lying-in period their children are cared for in Nursery from birth to the end of their first year. The background of these children provides for a markedly negative selection since the mothers are mostly delinquent minors as a result of social maladjustment or feeblemindedness, or because they are psychically defective, psychopathic, or criminal. Psychic normalcy and adequate social adjustment is almost excluded.

The other institution is a foundling home pure and simple. A certain number of the children housed have a background not much better than that of the Nursery children; but a sufficiently relevant number come from socially well-adjusted, normal mothers whose only handicap is inability to support themselves and their children (which is no sign of maladjustment in women of Latin background). This is expressed in the average of the Developmental Quotients of the two institutions during the first 4 months, as shown in Table II.

8. Under this heading we enumerate not only actual similarities but also differences that are of no etiological significance for the deterioration in Foundling Home. These differences comprise two groups: differences of no importance whatever, and differences that actually favor the development of children in Foundling Home.

The background of the children in the two institutions does therefore not favor Nursery; on the contrary, it shows a very marked advantage for Foundling Home.

2. Housing Conditions.

Both institutions are situated outside the city, in large spacious gardens. In both hygienic conditions are carefully maintained. In both infants at birth and during the first 6 weeks are segregated from the older babies in a special newborns' ward, to which admittance is only permitted in a freshly sterilized smock after hands are washed. In both institutions infants are transferred from the newborns' ward after 2 or 3 months to the older babies' wards, where they are placed in individual cubicles which in Nursery are completely glass enclosed in Foundling Home glass enclosed on three sides and open at the end. In Foundling Home the children remain in their cubicles up to 15 to 18 months; in Nursery they are transferred after the 6th month to rooms containing four to five cots each.

One-half of the children in Foundling Home are located in a dimly lighted part of the ward; the other half, in the full light of large windows facing southeast, with plenty of sun coming in. In Nursery, all the children have well-lighted cubicles. In both institutions the walls are painted in a light neutral color, giving a white impression in Nursery, a gray-green impression in Foundling Home. In both, the children are placed in white painted cots. Nursery is financially the far better provided one: we usually find here a small metal table with the paraphernalia of child care, as well as a chair in each cubicle; whereas in Foundling Home it is the exception if a low stool is to be found in the cubicles, which usually contain nothing but the child's cot.

3. Food.

In both institutions adequate food is excellently prepared and varied according to the needs of the individual child at each age; bottles from which children are fed are sterilized. In both institutions a large percentage of the younger children are breast-fed. In Nursery this percentage is smaller, so that in most cases a formula is soon added, and in many cases weaning takes place early. In Foundling Home all children are breast-fed as a matter of principle as long as they are under 3 months unless disease makes a deviation from this rule necessary.

4. Clothing.

Clothing is practically the same in both institutions. The children have adequate pastel-colored dresses and blankets. The temperature in the rooms is appropriate. We have not seen any shivering child in either set-up.

5. Medical Care.

Foundling Home is visited by the head physician and the medical staff at least once a day, often twice, and during these rounds the chart of each child is inspected as well as the child itself. For special ailments a laryngologist and other specialists are available; they also make daily rounds. In Nursery no daily rounds are made, as they are not necessary. The physician sees the children when called.

Up to this point it appears that there is very little significant difference between the children of the two institutions. Foundling Home shows, if anything, a slight advantage over Nursery in the matter of selection of admitted children, of breast-feeding and of medical care. It is in the items that now follow that fundamental differences become visible.

B. *Differences:*

1. Toys.

In Nursery it is the exception when a child is without one or several toys. In Foundling Home my first impression was that not a single child had a toy. This impression was later corrected. In the course of time, possibly in reaction to our presence, more and more toys appeared, some of them quite intelligently fastened by a string above the baby's head so that he could reach it. By the time we left a large percentage of the children in Foundling Home had a toy.

2. Visual Radius.

In Nursery the corridor running between the cubicles, though rigorously white and without particular adornment, gives a friendly impression of warmth. This is probably because trees, landscape and sky are visible from both sides and because a bustling activity of mothers carrying their children, tending them, feeding them, playing with them, chatting with each other with babies in their arms, is usually present. The cubicles of the children are enclosed but the glass panes of the partitions reach low enough for every child to be able at any time to observe everything going on all around. II can see into the corridor as soon as he lifts himself on his elbow. He can look out of the windows, and can see babies in the othe cubicles by just turning his head; witness the fact that whenever th experimenter plays with a baby in one of the cubicles the babies i the two adjoining cubicles look on fascinated, try to participate i the game, knock at the panes of the partition, and often begin t cry if no attention is paid to them. Most of the cots are provided wit widely-spaced bars that are no obstacle to vision. After the age of months, when the child is transferred to the wards of the older babie the visual field is enriched as a number of babies are then together i the same room, and accordingly play with each other.

In Foundling Home the corridor into which the cubicles ope though full of light on one side at least, is bleak and deserted, exce] at feeding time when five to eight nurses file in and look after th children's needs. Most of the time nothing goes on to attract th babies' attention. A special routine of Foundling Home consists i hanging bed sheets over the foot and the side railing of each co The cot itself is approximately 18 inches high. The side railings a about 20 inches high; the foot and head railings are approximate 28 inches high. Thus, when bed sheets are hung over the railing the child lying in the cot is effectively screened from the world. He completely separated from the other cubicles, since the glass panes (the wooden partitions begin 6 to 8 inches higher than even the hea railing of the cot. The result of this system is that each baby lies solitary confinement up to the time when he is able to stand up in h bed, and that the only object he can see is the ceiling.

3. Radius of Locomotion.

In Nursery the radius of locomotion is circumscribed by t space available in the cot, which up to about 10 months provides fairly satisfactory range.

Theoretically the same would apply to Foundling Home. B in practice this is not the case for, probably owing to the lack of stim lation, the babies lie supine in their cots for many months and hollow is worn into their mattresses. By the time they reach tl age when they might turn from back to side (approximately tl 7th month) this hollow confines their activity to such a degree th they are effectively prevented from turning in any direction. As result we find most babies, even at 10 and 12 months, lying on the backs and playing with the only object at their disposal, their own hands and feet.

4. Personnel.

In Foundling Home there is a head nurse and five assistant nurses for a total of forty-five babies. These nurses have the *entire* care of the children on their hands, except for the babies so young that they are breast-fed. The latter are cared for to a certain extent by their own mothers or by wetnurses; but after a few months they are removed to the single cubicles of the general ward, where they share with at least seven other children the ministrations of *one* nurse. It is obvious that the amount of care one nurse can *give* to an individual child when she has eight children to manage is small indeed. These nurses are unusually motherly, baby-loving women; but of course the babies of Foundling Home nevertheless lack all human contact for most of the day.

Nursery is run by a head nurse and her three assistants, whose duties do not include the care of the children, but consist mainly in teaching the children's mothers in child care, and in supervising them. The children are fed, nursed and cared for by their own mothers or, in those cases where the mother is separated from her child for any reason, by the mother of another child, or by a pregnant girl who in this way acquires the necessary experience for the care of her own future baby. Thus in Nursery each child has the full-time care of his own mother, or at least that of the substitute which the very able head nurse tries to change about until she finds someone who really likes the child.

V. Discussion.

To say that every child in Nursery has a full-time mother is an understatement, from a psychological point of view. However modern its reeducative policies, the deprivation it imposes upon delinquent girls is extensive. Their opportunities for an outlet for their interests, ambitions, activity, are very much impoverished. The former sexual satisfactions as well as the satisfactions of competitive activity in the sexual field, are suddenly stopped: regulations prohibit flashy dresses, vivid nail polish, or extravagant hair-do's. The kind of social life in which the girls could show off has vanished. This is especially traumatic as these girls become delinquent because they have not been able to sublimate their sexual drives, to find substitute gratifica-

tions, and therefore do not possess a pattern for relinquishing pleasure when frustrated. In addition, they do not have compensation in relations with family and friends, as formerly they had. These factors, combined with the loss of personal liberty, the deprivation of private property and the regimentation of the penal institution, all add up to a severe narcissistic trauma from the time of admission; and they continue to affect the narcissistic and libidinal sectors during the whole period of confinement.

Luckily there remain a few safety valves for their emotions: (1) the relationship with wardens, matrons and nurses; (2) with fellow prisoners; (3) with the child. In the relationship with the wardens, matrons and nurses, who obviously represent parent figures, much of the prisoner's aggression and resentment is bound. Much of it finds an outlet in the love and hate relationship to fellow prisoners, where all the phenomena of sibling rivalry are revived.

The child, however, becomes for them the representative of their sexuality, a product created by them, an object they own, which they can dress up and adorn, on which they can lavish their tenderness and pride, and of whose accomplishments, performance and appearance they can boast. This is manifested in the constant competition among them as to who has the better dressed, more advanced, more intelligent, better looking, the heavier, bigger, more active—in a word, the better baby. For their own persons they have more or less given up the competition for love, but they are intensely jealous of the attention given to their children by the matrons, wardens, and fellow prisoners.

It would take an exacting experimenter to invent an experiment with conditions as diametrically opposed in regard to the mother-child relationship as they are in these two institutions. Nursery provides each child with a mother to the nth degree, a mother who gives the child everything a good mother does and, beyond that, everything else she has[10]. Foundling Home does not give the child a mother, nor even a substitute-mother, but only an eighth of a nurse.

9. The psychoanalytically oriented reader of course realizes that for these girls in prison the child has become a hardly disguised phallic substitute. However, for the purposes of this article I have carefully avoided any extensive psychoanalytic interpretation, be it ever so tempting, and limited myself as closely as possible to results of direct observations of behavior. At numerous other points it would be not only possible but natural to apply analytic concepts; that is reserved for future publication.

10. For the non-psychoanalytically oriented reader we note that this intense mother-child relationship is not equivalent to a relationship based on love of the child. The mere fact that the child is used as a phallic substitute implies what a large part unconscious hostility plays in the picture.

First of all it should be kept in mind that the nature of the inanimate perceptual stimulus, whether it is a toy or any other object, has only a very minor importance for a child under 12 months. At this age the child is not yet capable of distinguishing the real purpose of an object. He is only able to use it in a manner adequate to his own functional needs(23). Our thesis is that perception is a function of libidinal cathexis and therefore the result of the intervention of an emotion of one kind or another.[12] Emotions are provided for the

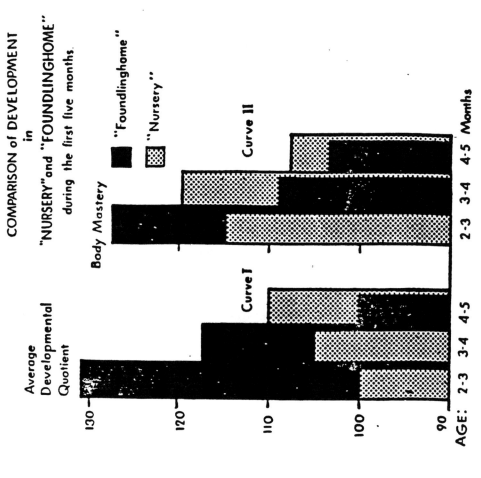

COMPARISON of DEVELOPMENT in "NURSERY" and "FOUNDLINGHOME" during the first five months.

■ "Foundlinghome"

▨ "Nursery"

Average Developmental Quotient — Curve I

Body Mastery — Curve II

130 120 110 100 90

AGE: 2-3 3-4 4-5   2-3 3-4 4-5 Months

We are now in a position to approach more closely and with better understanding the results obtained by each of the two institutions. We have already cited a few: we mentioned that the Developmental Quotient of Nursery achieves a normal average of about 105 at the end of the first year, whereas that of the Foundling Home sinks to 72; and we mentioned the striking difference of the children in the two institutions at first sight. Let us first consider the point at which the developments in the two institutions deviate.

On admission the children of Foundling Home have a much better average than the children of Nursery; their hereditary equipment is better than that of the children of delinquent minors. But while Foundling Home shows a rapid fall of the developmental index, Nursery shows a steady rise. They cross between the 4th and 5th months, and from that point on the curve of the average Developmental Quotient of the Foundling Home drops downward with increasing rapidity, never again to rise (Curve I).

The point where the two curves cross is significant. The time when the children in Foundling Home are weaned is the beginning of the 4th month. The time lag of one month in the sinking of the index below normal is explained by the fact that the Quotient represents a cross-section including all sectors of development, and that attempts at compensation are made in some of the other sectors.

However, when we consider the sector of Body Mastery (Curve II) which according to Wolff is most indicative for the mother-child relationship, we find that the curves of the children in Nursery cross the Body Mastery curve of the Foundling Home children between the 3rd and 4th month. The inference is obvious. As soon as the babies in Foundling Home are weaned the modest human contacts which they have had during nursing at the breast stop, and their development falls below normal.

One might be inclined to speculate as to whether the further deterioration of the children in Foundling Home is not due to other factors also, such as the perceptual and motor deprivations from which they suffer. It might be argued that the better achievement of the Nursery children is due to the fact that they were better provided for in regard to toys and other perceptual stimuli. We shall therefore analyze somewhat more closely the nature of deprivations in perceptual and locomotor stimulation.

11. K. Wolf, "Body Mastery of the Child as an index for the Emotional Relationship between Mother and Child" (in preparation).

12. This is stating in psychoanalytic terms the conviction of most modern psychologists, beginning with Compayré(24) and shared by such familiar authorities in child psychology as Stern(25) and Bühler(26), and in animal psychology, Tolman(27).

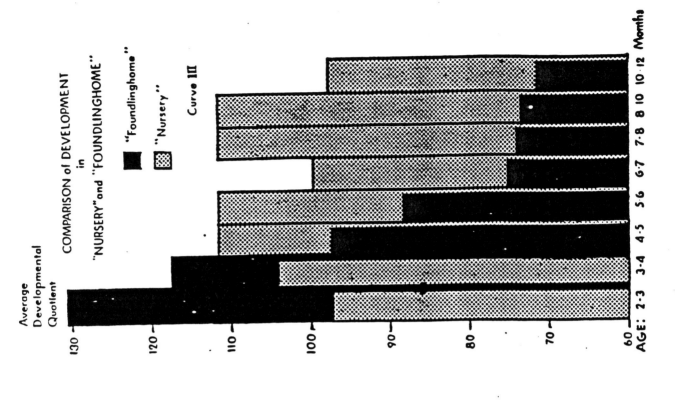

Average
Developmental
Quotient

COMPARISON of DEVELOPMENT in
"NURSERY" and "FOUNDLINGHOME"

Curve III

■ "Foundlinghome"

▨ "Nursery"

130
120
110
100
90
80
70
60
AGE: 2-3   3-4   4-5   5-6   6-7   7-8   8 10   10-12 Months

child through the intervention of a human partner, i.e., by the mother or her substitute. A progressive development of emotional interchange with the mother provides the child with perceptive experiences of its environment. The child learns to grasp by nursing at the mother's breast and by combining the emotional satisfaction of that experience with tactile perceptions. He learns to distinguish animate objects from inanimate ones by the spectacle provided by his mother's face(28) in situations fraught with emotional satisfaction. The interchange between mother and child is loaded with emotional factors and it is in this interchange that the child learns to play. He becomes acquainted with his surroundings through the mother's carrying him around; through her help he learns security in locomotion as well as in every other respect. This security is reinforced by her being at his beck and call. In these emotional relations with the mother the child is introduced to learning, and later to imitation. We have previously mentioned that the motherless children in Foundling Home are unable to speak, to feed themselves, or to acquire habits of cleanliness: it is the security provided by the mother in the field of locomotion, the emotional bait offered by the mother calling her child, that "teaches" him to walk. When this is lacking, even children two to three years old cannot walk.

The children in Foundling Home have, theoretically, as much radius of locomotion as the children in Nursery. They did not at first have toys, but they could have exerted their grasping and tactile activity on the blankets, on their clothes, even on the bars of the cots. We have seen children in Nursery without toys; they are the exception—but the lack of material is not enough to hamper them in the acquisition of locomotor and grasping skills. The presence of a mother or her substitute is sufficient to compensate for all the other deprivations.

It is true that the children in Foundling Home are condemned to solitary confinement in their cots. But we do not think that it is the lack of perceptual stimulation *in general* that counts in their deprivation. We believe that they suffer because their perceptual world is emptied of human partners, that their isolation cuts them off from any stimulation by any persons who could signify mother-representatives for the child at this age.[13] The result, as Curve III shows, is a complete restriction of psychic capacity by the end of the first year.

13. This statement is to be developed further in a forthcoming article on "The Beginning of the Social Relations of the Child".

This restriction of psychic capacity is not a temporary phenomenon. It is, as can be seen from the curve, a progressive process. How much of this deterioration could have been arrested if the children were taken out of the institution at the end of the first year is an open question. The fact that they remain in Foundling Home probably furthers this progressive process. By the end of the second year the Developmental Quotient sinks to 45, which corresponds to a mental age of approximately 10 months, and would qualify these children as imbeciles.

The curve of the children in Nursery does not deviate significantly from the normal. The curve sinks at two points, between the 6th and 7th, and between the 10th and 12th months. These deviations are within the normal range; their significance will be discussed in a separate article. It has nothing to do with the influence of institutions, for the curve of the village group is nearly identical.

VI. Provisional Conclusions.

The contrasting pictures of these two institutions show the significance of the mother-child relationship for the development of the child during the first year. Deprivations in other fields, such as perceptual and locomotor radius, can all be compensated by adequate mother-child relations.; "Adequate" is not here a vague general term. The examples chosen represent the two extremes of the scale.

The children in Foundling Home do have a mother—for a time, in the beginning—but they must share her immediately with at least one other child, and from 3 months on, with seven other children. The quantitative factor here is evident. There is a point under which the mother-child relations cannot be restricted during the child's first year without inflicting irreparable damage. On the other hand, the exaggerated mother-child relationship in Nursery introduces a different quantitative factor. To anyone familiar with the field it is surprising that Nursery should achieve such excellent results, for we know that institutional care is destructive for children during their first year; but in Nursery the destructive factors have been compensated by the increased intensity of the mother-child relationship.

These findings should not be construed as a recommendation for over-protection of children. In principle the libidinal situation of Nursery is almost as undesirable as the other extreme in Foundling Home. Neither in the nursery of a penal institution nor in a foundling home for parentless children can the normal libidinal situation that obtains in a family home be expected. The two institutions have here been chosen as experimental set-ups for the

purpose of examining variations in libidinal factors ranging from extreme frustration to extreme gratification. That the extreme frustration practised in Foundling Home has deplorable consequences has been shown; the extreme gratification in Nursery can be tolerated by the children housed there for two reasons:

(1) The mothers have the benefit of the intelligent guidance of the head nurse and her assistants, and the worst exaggerations are thus corrected.

(2) Children during their first year of life can stand the ill effects of such a situation much better than at a later age. In this respect Nursery has wisely limited the duration of the children's stay to the first twelve months. For children older than this we should consider a libidinal set-up such as that in Nursery very dangerous indeed.

DEVELOPMENT IN NURSERY — DEVELOPMENT IN VILLAGE GROUP
Curve IV — Curve V
Average Developmental Quotient
130　120　110　100　90
AGE: 2-3 3-4 4-5 5-6 6-7 7-8 8-10 10-12　2-3 3-4 4-5 5-6 6-7 7-8 8-10-12 Months

VII. Further Problems.

This is the first of a series of publications on the results of a research project on infancy that we are conducting. As such it is a preliminary report. It is not intended to show more than the most general outline of the results of early institutional care, giving at the same time a hint of the approach we use. The series of other problems on which this investigation has shed some light, as well as the formulation of those problems that could be recognized as such only in the course of the investigation, have not been touched upon in our present study and can only summarily be touched upon; they are headings, as it were, of the chapters of our future program of publication.

Apart from the severe developmental retardation, the most striking single factor observed in Foundling Home was the change in the pattern of the reaction to strangers in the last third of the first year(29). The usual behavior was replaced by something that could vary from extreme friendliness to any human partner combined with anxious avoidance of inanimate objects, to a generalized anxiety expressed in blood-curdling screams which could go on indefinitely. It is evident that these deviant behavior patterns require a more thorough and extensive discussion than our present study would have permitted.

We also observed extraordinary deviations from the normal in the time of appearance and disappearance of familiar developmental patterns; and certain phenomena unknown in the normal child, such as bizarre stereotyped motor patterns distinctly reminiscent of the stereotypy in catatonic motility. These and other phenomena observed in Foundling Home require an extensive discussion in order to determine which are to be classified as maturation phenomena, (which appear even under the most unfavorable circumstances, and which appear with commensurate retardation when retardation is general); or which can be considered as the first symptoms of the development of serious psychiatric disturbances. In connection with this problem a more thorough discussion of the rapidity with which the Developmental Quotients recede in Foundling Home is intended.

Another study is to deal with the problems created by the enormous over-protection practised in Nursery.

And finally the rationale of the one institutional routine as against that of the other will have to be discussed in greater detail. This study will offer the possibility of deciding how to compensate for unavoidable changes in the environment of children orphaned at an early age. It will also shed some light on the social consequences of the progressive disruption of home life caused by the increase of female labor and by the demands of war; we might state that we foresee in the course of events a corresponding increase in asociality, in the number of problem and delinquent children, of mental defectives, and of psychotics.

It will be necessary to take into consideration in our institutions, in our charitable activities, in our social legislation, the overwhelming and unique importance of adequate and satisfactory mother-child relationship during the first year, if we want to decrease the unavoidable and irreparable psychiatric consequences deriving from neglect during this period.

BIBLIOGRAPHY

1. Schlossman, A., "Zur Frage der Säuglingssterblichkeit", Münchner Med. Wochenschrift, 67, 1920.
2. Chapin, H. D., "Are Institutions for Infants Necessary?", Journal of American Medical Association, January, 1915.
3. Chapin, H. D., "A Plea for Accurate Statistics in Infants' Institutions", Archives of Pediatrics, October, 1915.
4. Bakwin, H., "Loneliness in Infants", American Journal of Diseases of Children, 63, 1942, pp. 30-40.
5. Durfee, H. and Wolf, K., "Anstaltspflege und Entwicklung im ersten Lebensjahr", Zeitschrift für Kinderforschung, 42/3, 1933.
6. Lowrey, L. G., "Personality Distortion and Early Institutional Care", American Journal of Orthopsychiatry, X, 3, 1940, pp. 576-585.
7. Bender, L. and Yarnell, H., "An Observation Nursery: a Study of 250 Children in the Psychiatric Division of Bellevue Hospital", American Journal of Psychiatry, 97, 1941, pp. 1158-1174.
8. Goldfarb, W., "Infant Rearing as a Factor in Foster Home Placement", American Journal of Orthopsychiatry, XIV, 1944, pp. 162-167.
9. Goldfarb, W., "Effects of Early Institutional Care on Adolescent Personality: Rorschach Data", American Journal of Orthopsychiatry, XIV, 1944, pp. 441-447.
10. Goldfarb, W., "Effects of Early Institutional Care on Adolescent Personality", Journal of Experimental Education, 12, 1943, pp. 106-129.
11. Goldfarb, W. and Klopfer, B., "Rorschach Characteristics of Institutional Children", Rorschach Research Exchange, 8, 1944, pp. 92-100.
12. Ripin, R., "A Study of the Infant's Feeding Reactions During the First Six Months of Life", Archives of Psychology, 116, 1930, p. 38.
13. Skeels, H. M., "Mental Development of Children in Foster Homes", Journal of Consulting Psychology, 2, 1938, pp. 33-43.
14. Skeels, H. M., "Some Iowa Studies of the Mental Growth of Children in Relation to Differentials of the Environment: A Summary", 39th Yearbook, National Society for the Study of Education, II, 1940, pp. 281-308.
15. Skeels, H. M., Updegraff, R., Wellman, B. L., and Williams, H. M., "A Study of Environmental Stimulation: an Orphanage Preschool Project", University of Iowa Studies in Child Welfare, 15, 4, 1938.
16. Skodak, M., "Children in Foster Homes", University of Iowa Studies in Child Welfare, 16, 1, 1939.
17. Stoddard, G. D., "Intellectual Development of the Child: an Answer to the Critics of the Iowa Studies", School and Society, 51, 1940, pp. 529-536.
18. Updegraff, R., "The Determination of a Reliable Intelligence Quotient for the Young Child", Journal of Genetic Psychology, 41, 1932, pp. 152-166.
19. Woodworth, R. S., "Heredity and Environment", Bulletin 47, Social Science Research Council, 1941.
20. Jones, H. E., "Personal Reactions of the Yearbook Committee", 39th Yearbook, National Society for the Study of Education, I, 1940, pp. 454-456.

Chapter 1

THE STORY OF CHILD LIFE

SUSAN POND WOJTASIK AND CLAIRE WHITE

INTRODUCTION

Discovering the story of childhood and the social and environmental conditions contributing to the health and illness of children is a challenging enterprise. Children are given scant space in the historical record. The modern reader is understandably puzzled and distressed by the indifference, indeed the harshness, with which children have been treated in earlier times. Today, knowledge of children's needs, and efforts to meet those needs, are taken quite seriously. Child life has played, and is continuing to play, a significant role in this new benevolence toward children, especially children in hospitals and other healthcare settings.

The history of how we became a people knowledgeable about and sympathetic to the complexity of childhood, in particular with respect to issues of health and disease, covers a very brief time span. Although theories of the contribution of microbes to the spread of disease and studies leading to improved infant nutrition occurred in the eighteenth century, a specific focus on children's health in the United States did not take hold until the mid-nineteenth century when the first children's hospital began caring for patients in Philadelphia (Brodie, 1986). Some years later scientific interest in the causes and cure of diseases in children, as well as interest in their general welfare, led to the academic institution of pediatric medicine. Nursing schools and social welfare agencies also have their roots in the middle to late nineteenth century and were agents of change in promoting the well-being of children (Dancis, 1972; Brodie, 1986; Colón, 1999).

The Industrial Revolution, which caused the migration of thousands of families from rural areas in this country and thousands more from abroad, caused a crisis in the cities. Men, women and children were paid small wages for long hours of work. Families lived in hovels without access to clean food or water and without even a semblance of sanitation. Disease epidemics were common, and large numbers of babies succumbed to the lethal "summer diarrhea" every year (Colón, 1999).

In the midst of this misery, philanthropists and professionals responded with investigations and programs to help children live and grow. As a deeper understanding of the nature of childhood was probed by professionals interested in the development of intelligence, emotional response, and social relationships, the care of children came to

3

include these elements as well. These aspects of child development have engaged the energies of child life specialists since the early decades of the twentieth century.

"THEY PLAY WITH YOU HERE"

The story of child life begins in the early twentieth century when large numbers of children began to be hospitalized. Children were understandably terrified at being in an unfamiliar place where many children cried and where everyone was a stranger. The children were there, of course, for their own good, for the treatment of illness or accident that would restore them to health.

There was, however, no way for the children to comprehend this. They often faced empty days in which there was nothing to do but wait for the next dreaded examination or treatment. The children were so obviously miserable that in some instances recommendations were made to institute a program of activities to engage the children's interest when they were admitted and while they waited in their cribs for what would happen next.

Some critics of non-medical activities for children argued that a child sick enough to be in the hospital was too sick to play. Surely the hospital, the place where grave illnesses and impending death were the very reasons for being there, was no place for frivolity, for games, for laughter. But children need play like they need air to breathe, no matter what their circumstances.

Play is fundamental to the very structure and meaning of childhood. This is true even in the most onerous of circumstances, perhaps especially in times of great distress. Frank McCourt (1996), in his memoir *Angela's Ashes*, describes his childhood as miserable, immersed in poverty, neglect, the

death of siblings, drunkenness, living conditions of almost unimaginable squalor. He was furious at it. Yet when he and his brothers played at romps and adventures he could say with unbridled enthusiasm, "We had a grand time!"

The preponderance of opinion was ultimately on the side of the child, and programs of play and education were introduced into pediatric hospital care as early as the 1920's (Rutkowski, 1986). Play leaders taught volunteers and nursing students how to communicate with children primarily through play, helped children understand the strange ways of the hospital and the people who work there, and prepared children for what was going to happen to them in their own hospital stay. These play leaders, with their volunteers and students, helped normalize the hospital experience.

There was a sense of urgency in this work based on an understanding that childhood is a time of such rapid development that not a day should go by without attention to the basic imperative to grow. As was noted in an article appearing in 1937:

> Children come to us at a formative period. They are developing rapidly, each day brings vast changes in them. We can do dreadful things to a child during even a twenty-four-hour stay, and we can change his entire outlook on life for better or worse during an eight-months' stay in a hospital. Any program of patient's care naturally begins with excellent medical and nursing care. In addition to that we must safeguard him in every way, physically and mentally. His day should approach the day of a normal child as nearly as is possible under the circumstances. (Smith, 1937, p.1)

By 1950 ten hospitals in the United States and Canada had implemented play programs on their children's wards (Rutkowski, 1986). The stage was set to address systematically the multiple emotional insults experienced by children when they are hospitalized. New scientific discoveries and methods of treatment continually change the face of pediatric medicine, and child life practice has developed to meet the changing needs of sick children. Preparation for medical encounters, supporting family centered care, pain management, coping with grief and loss are as fundamental to child life practice today as is play. Nevertheless, play continues as a central experience in the hospital lives of children. It is a mode of healing.

Play liberates laughter. It blows up and deflates, builds up and knocks down. It takes bits of this and that and makes a new thing. It imitates life and elaborates on it. It can be quite earnest and intense when a child is laboring to come to grips with something important, or it can be as flippant and irreverent as a thumb of the nose.

We value play in the hospital not only for the sheer fun of it, but also for the opportunities it affords for "playing out" emotionally laden hospital experiences in order to come to terms with them. This playing out is analogous to the work we adults do when we think through a problem, play with an idea, imagine a series of scenarios before taking action. It is with this kind of play that we create who we are and who we will become.

THE GROUND WE STAND ON

Humanizing healthcare for children was passionately embraced by its practitioners, but the success of such a revolutionary undertaking depended on validation of its presuppositions by others. Without the scientific enquiries and the advocacy for children's health and well-being by the relatively new division of medicine called "pediatrics," a stable context for child life programs could not exist. The development of

interest in the behavioral aspects of pediatrics opened the way for making hospitalization a more child-friendly experience (Bakwin, 1941; Spitz, 1945). The insights of early to mid-twentieth century developmentalists and child psychologists provided a firm theoretical rationale for child life practice (Erikson, 1963; Winnecott, 1964; Piaget & Inhelder, 1969; Bowlby, 1982), and the structure of the multidisciplinary organization that came to be known as the Association for the Care of Children's Health added the impact of many voices from nursing, social work, pediatric medicine and psychiatry to help sustain and focus the ongoing work of child life specialists (Brooks, 1975).

Pediatrics: Developmental Medicine

In the late nineteenth century a sufficient body of knowledge existed about the health maintenance and the diseases of children for a new division of medical practice devoted exclusively to the care of infants and children to be established. Pediatrics in the United States has a very short history indeed, beginning, officially, when Abraham Jacobi, M.D., became the first Professor of Pediatrics in 1870 at Columbia University in New York City. Although Jacobi remained a general practitioner all his life, he had an unusual interest in and knowledge of the diseases of children and was a great advocate in the field of children's health. His interests were not limited to the diagnosis and treatment of disease but were wide-ranging, taking on issues of proper nutrition, preventive care, and the social aspects of illness. He began a tradition of concern for children's health that has had a profound and enduring effect on the well-being of children (Abt, 1965; Dancis, 1972; Colón, 1999).

In the first half of the twentieth century, city hospitals were filled with children sick from the poverty and filth that corrupted their food and drink just as certainly as they were sick from rheumatic fever, tuberculosis, diphtheria, polio, meningitis and other diseases (Dancis, 1972; Colón, 1999). The advent of pediatrics brought scientific methods to the study of childhood illnesses, but there was still little in the formulary to overcome them. The germ theory was embraced enthusiastically leading to improved standards of cleanliness and the institution of infection control methods (Brenneman, 1931; Bakwin, 1941; Dancis, 1972). However, immunizations were not readily available to children until the outbreak of World War II, and antibiotics were not used in civilian populations in the United States until after that war.

When children became sick from infectious processes, the medical response was an intensification of infection control measures: strict isolation or quarantine, and, in the case of babies, infrequent handling and meticulously aseptic surroundings (Brenneman, 1931). Medical approaches had, however, been dramatically unsuccessful in the care of infants in hospitals and foundling homes. These babies frequently failed to gain weight or to reach normal developmental milestones. They were unusually susceptible to infections. Death rates were high. In a report given before the American Pediatric Society in 1915, H. D. Chapin, a prominent pediatrician and social activist, presented his findings that infant mortality rates in ten urban institutions ranged from thirty-one to seventy-five percent (Spitz, 1945).

"Hospitalism"

René Spitz popularized the term "hospitalism," as a description of this condition of severe physical and developmental decline (1945). Something in the environment was lethal, to be sure, but he didn't think it was primarily pathogens. His solution was the antithesis of the accepted hospital practice of scrupulous asepsis, and this interface of medical and psychological approaches to health and illness fostered the opening of pediatrics to the idea that social and environmental factors, as well as medical management, influence a child's response to treatment.

Spitz made careful observational studies of infants in a foundling home in order to test his hypothesis that it was precisely the absence of mothering and environmental stimulation that led to this alarming susceptibility to disease, physical wasting, and emotional withdrawal. Spitz's studies of the developmental decline in infants raised in even the most well meaning and hygienic foundling home, as compared with those raised in families or in an institution where their prisoner mothers could be with them every day, have been meticulously recorded on film (Spitz, 1947). Pictures of infants in the foundling home must surely be some of the most haunting film footage in the entire library of child studies. The babies raised in the foundling hospital were emaciated, listless, unsmiling, scarcely able to move. Pictures like these are seen these days only where there is social devastation.

Spitz's studies were carried out on babies institutionalized for conditions "other than sickness" (Spitz, 1945). Harry Bakwin, a pediatrician in hospital practice working with sick children, shared Spitz's bias toward humanizing care and was to initiate unlimited parental visits to infants. He also encouraged house staff to develop friendly relationships with the children they treated. The term "T.L.C." (tender loving care) was coined to characterize this relationship (Dancis, 1972).

According to Bakwin (1941), hospitalism "is looked on as a result of repeated infections" (p. 30). Strict infection control policies were instituted which isolated infants from human contact and sensory stimulation.

To lessen the danger of cross infections, the large open ward of the past has been replaced by small, cubicled rooms in which masked, hooded and scrubbed nurses and physicians move about cautiously so as not to stir up bacteria. Visiting parents are strictly excluded, and the infants receive a minimum of handling by the staff. Within recent years attempts at isolation have been intensified, and a short time ago there was devised a box equipped with inlet and outlet valves and sleeve arrangements for the attendants. The infant is placed in this box and can be taken care of almost untouched by human hands. (p. 31)

Bakwin questioned whether these precautions might not be harmful to the child.

Infants confined in hospitals present a fairly well defined clinical picture. A striking feature is their failure to gain properly, despite the ingestion of diets which in the home are entirely adequate for growth. Infants in hospitals sleep less than infants who are at home, and they rarely smile or babble spontaneously. They are listless, apathetic and look unhappy. The appetite is indifferent, and food is accepted without enthusiasm. . . . Infections of the respiratory tract which last only a day or two in a home often persist for months in a hospital. Return home results in defervescence within a few days and a prompt and striking gain in weight. (p. 31)

A satisfactory medical solution never was found for the foundling hospitals. Most were ultimately shut down, and homeless infants were raised in the community by foster families, a solution initially suggested by Chapin (Dancis, 1972). During the struggle to resolve the issues of infant deaths in institutions, however, a great deal was discovered about the needs of infants and, by inference, of all children, for special attention to environmental factors both personal and spatial, in their psychosocial development.

With the exception of infant wards like Bakwin's at Bellevue, which permitted mothers to tend to their children, early twentieth century hospitals were more receptive to the inclusion of volunteers and "play ladies" who could function as "substitute mommies and daddies" than they were to the inclusion of real parents. There were, of course, reasons other than hospital rules that precluded or limited parental visiting, but by many accounts hospitals found parents a nuisance: disruptive of routines and upsetting to children, as well as sources of disease. Even D. W. Winnicott (1964), the champion of mothering on every other count, drew the line at the hospital door. He saw visits as compromising medical care by the practice of parents giving children foods "completely upsetting the investigation on which future treatment is to be based" (p. 222). He was concerned that visiting would undermine the selfless giving of the nurse (sister) who gives all her care and attention to the child only to be usurped by the parent during visiting hour. And there is always a lot of crying when parents come and sad leave-taking when they go.

It would not be so bad if the mothers were contented to go in and see their children for a few minutes and then go out again; but mothers do not feel like this, naturally. As will be expected, they go into the ward and use the whole time that is allowed. Some seem to be almost 'making love' to their child; they bring presents of all kinds, and especially food, and they demand affectionate response; and then they take quite a long time going, standing waving at the door till the child is absolutely exhausted by the effort of saying good-bye. And the mothers are quite liable to go to the Sister on the way out and say something about the child's not being warmly enough clad or not having enough to eat for dinner or something like that. (Winnicott, 1964, p. 223)

Hospitals would look elsewhere, to something less threatening to the hospital system than parents, for help in easing the distress of children.

An Early Play Program

Like a stranger in a foreign land who suddenly hears his own language, the child reaches out to play as an assurance of friendliness in a bewildering situation. (Smith, 1937)

At about the same time that Spitz was carrying out his studies and Bakwin was describing the psychosocial shortcomings of pediatric wards, the first hospital play programs were inaugurated. Although archival material on the origins and early history of child life programs has only recently been accumulated and is still being collected, we have a report on the first years, 1932-1937, of the development of a play program at Children's Memorial Hospital in Chicago written by Anne Smith. Smith does not identify her relationship to the program she describes, but her knowledge of the details of its origins, organization, development and scope might fairly lead one to believe her to be its creator. This was a remarkably vigorous program in which play leaders were asked to respond to the distress of children admitted in large groups for tonsillectomies and to individual children undergoing major surgeries; to provide daily activities for children on the wards, many of them long term patients; to help with parent visiting by setting up toy displays to educate parents on what is suitable to bring to their children; and to set up a program for outpatients receiving bronchoscopies (Smith, 1937).

In addition to their work with patients and parents the director and play leaders taught play techniques to student nurses and nurses on the Children's Memorial staff.

University students and volunteers often joined these classes about play in the hospital and benefited from the clinical supervision of their work with children. To further the normalization of the hospital environment, the play director facilitated the development of a school program for kindergarten and early elementary grades; built and staffed a library; and invited special volunteers to visit with nature projects, handicraft projects and entertainments.

The program was put together by the play director on the basis of clearly identified needs, starting with the most obvious: pandemonium on the days when groups of about fifteen children ages two to twelve were admitted for tonsillectomies. Smith described this scene, noting that "Often their crying and screaming could be heard all down the halls. In their terror, some bit and kicked" (p. 3). The play director engaged these children in simple games, stories and songs immediately after they were admitted and again the next day as they waited to be taken to the operating room, one by one. Because children were said to go easily under anesthesia and to wake up smoothly, the play program was considered a success. As part of their training in play, nurses ran these groups once their efficacy was established.

Group play was highly valued by the play leaders. They saw that children were reassured by the company of each other. Play without equipment was also highly valued, possibly because toys were hard to come by and, in certain of these situations, encumbering. Play was not dependent on toys. Nurses were taught to use play while doing their usual routines and treatments with children. Again, simple finger games, songs, guessing games and stories were planned to engage the child all day long.

Much emphasis was placed on the program's teaching efforts. The entire nursing staff, students and volunteers were all made comfortable with using play as a primary means of communicating good will. The importance of play in the child's daily life was strongly endorsed by Smith, who wrote, "Like a stranger in a foreign land who suddenly hears his own language, the child reaches out to play as an assurance of friendliness in a bewildering situation" (p. 2).

There were no set protocols for this work. Group play was the choice for children newly admitted for surgery and during the waiting time before surgery. Individual projects worked well for some long-term patients. From an eclectic repertoire of activities play leaders could experiment until they found the ones best suited to the task at hand. According to Smith, children were offered opportunities to play in order to prevent their being returned home "marked and scarred psychologically, retarded mentally, or rendered social misfits because of the neglect of stimulating interests and happy co-operation with other children" (p. 9). This sentiment echoes that of the psychoanalytically oriented pediatricians describing the fate of infants who survived long periods of institutional care. As Spitz (1945) states in the opening comments of his article on hospitalism, ". . . physicians and administrators . . . discovered that institutionalized children practically without exception developed subsequent psychiatric disturbances and became asocial, delinquent, feeble-minded, psychotic, or problem children" (p. 54).

Developmental Psychology

Mid-twentieth century concern for the psychological responses of children exposed to war, separation from parents, bodily illness, and confinement in hospital, led to investigations and theoretical constructs about the emotional life of children (Bowlby, 1952; Freud, A., 1952; Prugh, Staub, Kirsch-baum, & Lenihan, 1953). These theories of relationships, perceptions of reality, behaviors, and feelings and how these change over a child's lifetime are of fundamental interest to child life studies.

Observations of his own children's infant activities led to Jean Piaget's elegant theory of the development of intelligence (Piaget & Inhelder, 1969). Piaget's work, together with Erikson's interpretations of psychosocial development, has given us a picture of what and how infants, children and adolescents think and feel. The role of the senses in first learning, the limits of cognition at various ages, the importance of play as an interpretive and problem solving activity have illuminated and made accessible to students of development the physical, mental and emotional lives of children that could only be guessed at in earlier times.

The major themes have been laid down for us by Erikson and Piaget. Erikson (1963) took the ancient "ages of man" model to construct an epigenetic theory of psychosocial development from birth to death. Far from the disinterest of the ancients in the first seven years of life, this period was the most interesting to those clinicians and scholars who were drawn to psychoanalytic interpretations of childhood. Infants and toddlers were especially interesting.

The root meaning of the word *infant* is voiceless, speechless. For much of western history the child was considered virtually speechless until the age of seven. The following is from a medieval manuscript describing the ages of man.

The first age is childhood when the teeth are planted, and this age begins when the child is born and lasts until seven, and in this age that which is born is called an infant, which is as good as saying not talking, because in this age it cannot talk well or form its words perfectly, for its teeth are not yet well arranged or firmly implanted.

... After infancy comes the second age ... and this age lasts until fourteen. (Aries, 1965, p. 21)

We might say that the imperfect speech described here is a metaphor for the persistence of imaginative thought in the speech of young children which to this day confounds adults whose mode of thinking is fully rational. It is at points of dissonance like this that child life becomes the interpreter of the medical system to the child and of the child to his medical caregivers.

Piaget has taught us to listen to children in a new way, to observe their language in play and to tease out the internal logic of their imaginative constructs. We can then see with utmost seriousness and sympathy how children gradually develop the capacity to separate fantasy from reality, to see something from the point of view of another, to manipulate symbols instead of real objects, to distinguish between proximity and causality, to learn that something hidden may not be gone forever.

John Bowlby, James and Joan Robertson

John Bowlby began his work on attachment and separation issues in the early 1950s. Bowlby was interested in the theoretical aspects of the observed reactions of young children to brief separations from their mothers or mother surrogates. These observations provided some of the first clinical evidence for the considerable emotional complexity of infants and toddlers. His work, drawing upon ethological studies as well as clinical research in human bonds, led to his conclusion that human attachment, most commonly seen in mother-infant bonds, but also prevalent throughout the life span, constituted a primary and singular component of human life independent of

other needs or gratifications. This is a fundamental part of the human condition and, as we have seen in the foundling hospital stories, is necessary for life. This innate need for social intimacy has been extraordinarily important to the understanding of human nature. Interruptions in love relationships, particularly the early ones, pose significant challenges to healthy psychological development (Bowlby, 1982).

A close associate of Bowlby's in his early years of research was James Robertson. Robertson and his wife, Joan, filmed children's responses to brief separations from parents under a variety of circumstances. Of special interest to child life studies is the film, *A Two-Year-Old Goes to the Hospital* (1953). A child is hospitalized for several days for a hernia operation. Her parents can make only a few visits, and she expresses the full range of feelings and behaviors associated with separation and the fear of abandonment: protest, despair, detachment. We do not see in this child the marasmic faces of the foundlings, but traces of their distress flicker across the face of this otherwise vivacious toddler. To add the stresses of separation to the stresses inherent in hospitalization is to place a great emotional burden on a very small child. These studies led to the suggestion that elective hospitalizations be postponed until after the age of three years.

THE CHILD LIFE MOVEMENT

Emma Plank: Child Life Speaks Out

In 1962, Emma Plank's publication, *Working with Children in Hospitals*, described the work of the Child Life and Education Department at Cleveland Metropolitan Hospital. She called her staff "child-care workers" and vividly describes the substance of their clinical tasks in the hospital. There is a resistance to generalization in this text. Plank depends on the anecdote to show what the child-care worker can do. One child with no family ties needs an especially close and trusting relationship; a gang of small boys, far from needing the permissive atmosphere usually desired on the ward, are gotten firmly in hand; a child's misunderstanding is untangled; a four-year-old is prepared for amputation of her leg.

She is careful to note the individual differences of children's responses to illness and hospitalization and to stress initial and ongoing assessments of these responses. It is through knowing the child and developing a carefully thought out and continually reviewed plan of care that child-care work will succeed.

There are some general principles here that need to be applied in an individual manner. For very young children, the fear of abandonment is more alarming than the illness itself or its treatment. Plank applauds hospitals which provide rooming in for mothers with very small children. She also applauds the advance of more liberal visiting hours and notes the comforting attention staff members give to children who cry when the time is up. The maintenance of trust in relationships is reinforced by truth-telling, no matter how difficult that may be. Parents are not to sneak away; children are not to be deceived about the possibility of pain or even loss.

The child's day should be as normal as possible with opportunities for play and schooling away from medical interventions. The child's day has a structure and plan, which is basic to his sense of being in a reasonable world even when the day's plan includes going to x-ray or surgery. To illustrate the importance of these arrangements to a child's well-being, Plank (1962) says the following:

> It is nice to have entertainments during holidays or at regular intervals, such as a week-

ly movie or puppet plays, given by a volunteer service. But a healthy child's day is not built around entertainment, and a sick child's should be even less. Children do not need diversion to get well, but rather opportunities to participate with all available emotional and intellectual energy in daily living. (p. 73)

Plank continues by stating the goals of a child life and education program:

1. To provide a setting for children of all ages where they can find play and activities that interest and absorb them, counteract their loneliness and anxiety, and help to turn the passivity of the patient into the activity of the growing child.
2. To give children a chance to interact with others away from their cubicle, to form relationships to adults as well as to other children, to help them work through the basic fears inherent in illness and hospitalization, to reassure them about or prepare them for procedures and surgery.
3. To help school-age children to continue with some of their schoolwork while hospitalized.
4. To arrange specific opportunities for play under direction of a skilled worker where fantasies or traumatic experience in relation to hospitalization can be played out and worked through.
5. To provide an area where parents can visit and play with their child as part of an ongoing program. At the time when parents have to leave, the child finds himself with others and can be more easily reassured.
6. To help children at mealtimes to accept hospital food or limiting diets, by providing food groupings at mealtimes with a chance for conversation and informality. (p. 73)

Plank speaks of the common experiences and special problems that need to be assessed and planned for in each hospital admission by the "staff." She does not mean by this the child life and education staff alone but the whole of pediatrics. She is convinced that the child's needs will be served only when there is a coordinated effort and ease of communication among all professionals working with children. The work of the person on the child-care side of the interface between normalization and medical treatment must be included in the total care of the child.

What's in a Name?

We will speak throughout this document of "child life" as the designated name of the professional service and its practitioners whose goals have been to help children engage and subdue fears, misconceptions, anger and profound sadness that hospital experiences provoke, to protect and enhance their developmental integrity, and, whenever possible, use the experiences of illness and hospitalization to build strengths rather than compromise them. But as Rubin (1992) pointed out, the eclectic nature of the staff and programs, made it hard to find a name inclusive enough to take into account all that child life does. Recreation therapy was too narrow and misleading, so was teacher, so was play lady, although that's what the children often called us.

What the programs and the people who staffed them were called both reflected and determined what people thought of them. For the child the program and its people would always be play providers, sources of pleasure and safety. This is no mean thing. D.W. Winnicott (1964), pediatrician and child analyst, was to go so far as to say, "Play is the continuous evidence of creativity, which means aliveness" (p.144). The child

analysts and psychologists understood play to be both the child's language and means of learning about and interpreting the world. Cut off from play, the young child is lost in an unintelligible environment. But the word "play" is a two-edged sword, appealing to children and people knowledgeable about the intellectual and psychological development of children, but easily denigrated by administrators on tight budgets and medical staff on tight schedules.

Environments

When Doctor F. C. Robbins hired Emma Plank to organize the Child Life and Education Department at Cleveland Metropolitan Hospital, one of his goals was to change the drab, stark spaces in which the children stayed. The huge wards with only utilitarian furnishings provided an efficient environment, but hardly an appealing one. Entrusted with improving the hospital environment for children, Plank carved playrooms out of the available space where children could engage in meaningful activities away from medical care. Here the task of living was fully engaged.

In its 1960 report and recommendations for the care of hospitalized children, the American Academy of Pediatrics stated that all pediatric units should have a playroom stocked with appropriate supplies of toys, games, books. The playroom should be placed near the nurses' station for ease of supervision or, if that wasn't feasible, there should be an effort made to recruit volunteers to supervise the playroom.

We have seen that in the early play program at Children's Memorial Hospital, 1932-1937, play without equipment and play in any setting where the children could be gathered seemed to be the norm. There is no mention of a special room for play. This recommendation for space and supplies indicates an acknowledgement by the Academy of the importance of play in the daily lives of children in the hospital.

It takes, however, both space and equipment and a staff whose full attention can be invested in using the playroom to help children cope effectively with the hospital experience. The state of playrooms that have not been managed by child life has often been a sorry story. Volunteers could seldom take on the full-time responsibility of supervising a playroom. Without supervision, toys were broken or lost. Children felt neither safe nor fulfilled in what could often be a state of chaos, without boundaries or rules. Unsupervised playrooms, some with a dirty doll or two for decoration, stopped being used altogether by children and parents and were sometimes taken over by staff as a place to have lunch or take a break.

As child life matured it assumed responsibility for playrooms and equipment, and in 1985, the Academy, in its chapter on child life, acknowledged playroom management as one of the tasks of child life. A well-stocked and well-managed playroom is far more than a place to play. It offers sanctuary, a safe place away from hospital routines and treatments. It's a safe place to just hang out and fool around or talk it over or play it out.

In the 1980s great emphasis was placed on making the entire pediatric unit feel like a safe and friendly place. Walls were brightened, pictures were hung, the stark, white uniform was no longer required of nurses, treatment rooms were hung with mobiles and instruments were made less conspicuous.

In some institutions quite elaborate efforts were made to bring the huge scale of the hospital down to human size, to child size. Many of these environments were well designed to make children feel both comfortable and pleasurably stimulated. But adults often mistakenly assume that they know what children like and will, for

instance, apply liberal doses of cartoon characters to corridor walls and the windows of nurses' stations. Olds (1986), designer of children's hospital environments, warns that primary colors can become strident if overused in the assumption that "that's what children like."

Child Life and the Founding of ACCH

Child life was formative in the creation of the multidisciplinary organization ultimately known as the Association for the Care of Children's Health (ACCH) whose members where dedicated to promoting and providing developmentally based psychosocial care to sick children. ACCH throughout its history has fostered a veritable explosion of services for children and families in healthcare settings. Principle among these are support for child life programs and the development of family centered care programs.

In 1965 a group of forty professionals working in play and education programs in twenty-three hospitals scattered throughout the United States and Canada gathered in Boston to discuss "Patient Recreation in Pediatric Settings" (Brooks,1975). Although this title would suggest a modest agenda, these participants were in fact inaugurating a revolution in pediatric healthcare. Emma Plank (1962), speaking of her own program at Cleveland Metropolitan General hospital stated, "We asked ourselves how we can best serve the child who is about to enter the hospital; what we can do for him when he is there; and how to help him to return to normal living" (p. 2). This would serve well as the definition of the work we still strive to do.

By the end of this first conference there was a consensus concerning the need to create an organization that would provide a forum for the discussion of experiences and problems in their own program areas and that would promote appropriate attention to the growth and developmental needs of hospitalized children. Representatives from six participating hospitals were chosen as founders, and an interim committee was chosen to study the establishment of a permanent organization and to plan a conference for the following year (Brooks, 1975).

Because their numbers were small and because, although essential to the well-being of children, their work was not central to the mission of medical care, the founders were persuaded that their hope of achieving their goals could best be served by inviting the participation of other pediatric professionals.

At the second conference in 1966 representatives from pediatrics, surgery, nursing and social work joined in the discussions of psychosocial issues and formed, with the original group of recreation, play and education specialists, an association briefly named The Association for the Well-Being of Hospitalized Children and Their Families. Although this first name has the virtue of being an almost perfect description of the organization's purpose, it was a mouthful. After two other failed attempts at naming, the organization became the Association for the Care of Children in Hospitals (ACCH)-- until its mission expanded and it became the Association for the Care of Children's Health (also ACCH).

By the time of the third conference, in Philadelphia, more potential participants applied than could be accommodated. The hard work of the founders and their multidisciplinary colleagues had provided the groundwork for a functional organization, and 1967 saw officers and a board of directors elected, by-laws accepted, and standing committees formed. ACCH membership increased dramatically, and conference sites moved across the continent from their east coast origins to the Midwest and on to record-breaking attendance in San Francisco

in 1970. In 1972, the meetings were held in Canada for the first bilingual conference (Brooks, 1975).

In 1975 ACCH drew members from forty-five states and the District of Columbia, all ten Canadian provinces, and several foreign countries. Membership had grown from 40 in 1965 to 1,200 in 1975. The number of child life programs also increased dramatically during this ten year period from 10 in 1950 to 170 in 1975 (ACCH, 1984).

ACCH as Identity and Context for Child Life

The richly multidisciplinary environment of ACCH, which included nurses, psychologists, social workers, physicians, and, in 1978, parents, was an excellent medium for the work of self-definition for child life. Child life specialists always formed a large percentage of the ACCH membership and consistently held leadership positions in the organization until it ceased operations in 1999.

The rapid growth of ACCH in the sixties and seventies reflected a corresponding growth in child life programs. Because child life practice was the clearest embodiment of the goals of ACCH at this time, its quarterly journal Children's Health Care, annual conference presentations, and local membership chapters were filled with contributions from the ranks of child life professionals. ACCH provided a forum and a publishing house for child life initiatives, and child life benefited from the organization's linkages to the Society of Pediatric Psychology, the Academy of Child Psychiatry (now the American Academy of Child and Adolescent Psychiatry, AACAP), and the American Academy of Pediatrics (AAP). Child life leaders represented ACCH on the Academy of Pediatrics' Hospital Care Committee.

The Child Life Position Statement, 1979

During the 1970s child life began in earnest to develop the philosophical, theoretical and ethical ground of its work, to define the necessary skills and knowledge of its practitioners and to determine educational requirements for practice. In 1979, *The Child Life Position Statement* was drafted and ratified by ACCH. This had been preceded by more than a decade of discussion and debate resulting in the consolidation of the many aspects of child life work into a single statement and the many tasks of child life workers into a many-faceted but single job description.

This position statement was a hard won consensus that rested securely on child life's past and became the cornerstone of all future conceptual developments. It contained a rationale for child life programs based on the observed emotional damage to children caused by stress factors, interruptions of development, regression and the loss of self-esteem. Essential components of child life programs were listed as abundant play opportunities for self-expression, mastery and understanding of medical experiences; familiarization with the hospital milieu; maintaining family relationships and providing empathic support to parents; the provision of essential life experiences; and providing opportunities to retain self-esteem and appropriate independence. It was believed that, with appropriate support, a child's hospital experience might even be a positive one, providing an opportunity for enhanced development.

The *Position Statement* also included staffing standards and job descriptions for child life personnel. To be a child life specialist required a bachelor's degree, supervised experience in a healthcare setting and competencies in growth and development, family dynamics, play and activities, interpersonal communication, developmental observation and assessment, the learning process, group process, behavior management, the reactions of children to hospitalization, to illnesses and to medical terminology, supervisory skills (ACCH, 1979).

The child life program should be autonomous, have a budget for staff and supplies, be given adequate space for activities and storage, and assume responsibility for training and supervising volunteers in its service. Child life staff should be on an equal footing with other clinical team members.

Child Life Speaks for Itself: The Child Life Council

During the sixties and seventies the child life membership met as a study section at ACCH annual meetings to talk among themselves about their mission, identity, policies, and practices. Times allotted for these discussions were short and sometimes in conflict with other study sections that members were interested in attending. Frustration ran high. There was just too much to do at the one time in the year when everyone could get together.

As in the first years of ACCH, child life brought together an interdisciplinary task force to consider the feasibility of establishing a Child Life Council under the auspices of ACCH. Child life felt the need to return to one of its original goals in calling its first meeting in 1965: to provide a forum for the discussion of experiences and problems in their own program areas.

In 1980, Gene Stanford, a leader in the field of child life, challenged the fledgling organization to enter adulthood by achieving three things: a clearly defined role, clearly defined qualifications, and control of who can enter the profession. The Child Life Council was established in 1982 to take on these and other professional issues. At its first meeting the Council elected officers, approved by-laws and held two days of meetings prior to the ACCH annual conference. In order to be eligible for Council membership, child life professionals were required to maintain their membership in ACCH. As an early and highly symbolic act of independence, the Child Life Council revised and reissued the *Child Life Position Statement* under its own imprimatur in 1983.

Child life continued to benefit from the rich mix of disciplines and parents that comprised ACCH, and it was ACCH that secured and administered the grant that made child life's major research project possible. Over time, however, as Council membership increased and the demands of professionalization intensified, the focus on child life issues began to overshadow interest in interdisciplinary issues. In 1992 the Child Life Council (CLC) became incorporated as a free-standing organization. Membership in ACCH was now an option rather than a requirement for Council members.

Academic Programs

As the profession emerged, leaders in the field called for educational programs designed specifically to train child life practitioners. Course offerings related to working with hospitalized children are found in the Wheelock College Catalog in the 1960s. Specific programs of study (or majors) in child life are documented as being formally established in the 1970s. Among the first colleges and universities to offer child life programs were: Wheelock College, Boston, MA, established 1972; Mills College, Oakland, CA, established 1977; and Utica College of Syracuse University, NY, established 1978. Several other academic settings offering formalized training programs were established throughout the 1970s and 1980s.

By the late 1980s the profession still lacked a unified standard of preparation for entrance into the field.

In order to achieve high quality and maximum effectiveness in the profession, standards for the profession were developed over a period of time from 1987 to 1992. *The Standards for Academic and Clinical Preparation Programs in Child Life* was written and approved by the Child Life Council in 1992. The standards were revised in 2001 in order to reflect the growth of the profession and its practitioners. The standards serve as a guide for anyone wishing to pursue academic or clinical training in child life.

It is not the intent for the standards to establish a rigid formula. The standards include curriculum recommendations for academic programs. The child life profession continues to draw practitioners from a variety of educational backgrounds. The Child Life Council currently lists 32 academic programs that offer coursework in child life (S. Clay-Robison, personal communication, August 13, 2003). Some of these programs offer comprehensive child life majors (coursework and integrated internships) and some offer a course on the hospitalized child within another major (e.g., child development, child & family studies, or child psychology).

CHILD LIFE COMES OF AGE

Defining the Tasks

CLC continued work begun in the seventies on creating a core curriculum for academic programs, formulating a theoretical and philosophic base, articulating a code of ethics, defining professional competence, describing a method of program evaluation, and dealing with issues of membership, by-laws, and meeting the standards of regulatory bodies. Much of the material in the *Official Documents of the Child Life Council* published in 1994 was developed in the eighties. These documents *(Standards for Academic and Clinical Preparation Programs in Child Life, Standards for Clinical Practice, Child Life Competencies, Code of Ethical Responsibilities, and Child Life Philosophic Base)* stand as the self-proclaimed authority for holding child life accountable for its actions.

The annual conference agenda expanded to make room for presentations on program development, clinical practice and administrative issues such as documentation in the medical record and data collection. Even as it secured its sense of self, the profession was changing. The conference business meetings were wonderfully exciting. The membership engaged in outspoken and energized discussions of such things as staff/patient ratios, how to conduct program reviews, whether and how to pursue certification, how to continue to welcome people from diverse academic and professional backgrounds into the ranks of child life practitioners.

A collection of articles entitled, *Child Life: An Overview*, published by ACCH in 1986 was both a recapitulation of accomplishments in the second decade of child life's existence and a spur to consolidate and move on. Thompson and Stanford's *Child Life in Hospitals* (1981), which put flesh on the bones of the *Position Statement*, and the first edition of *Guidelines for the Development of Child Life Programs* (1984), which articulated the fundamentals of establishing programs were benchmarks in standardizing practice in a rapidly expanding profession. Although these texts were descriptive rather than prescriptive they provided vivid pictures of best practice in the living, breathing corridors of real hospitals. They would prove invaluable guides to establishing standards.

Descriptive literature was voluminous in this period and included books on such topics as emotional care, parenting in the hospi-

tal, techniques in medical preparation, hospital play, and chronicity. Hospital-based child life programs produced monographs on programming for each developmental stage, on family issues, on outpatient, intensive care, and isolation areas. And as it had from its inception the ACCH journal, *Children's Health Care*, provided a lively forum of ideas.

Credibility

Program Review Guidelines: Self-study and Peer Review

The CLC piloted a set of questions in outline form called the *Program Review Guidelines* in the U.S and Canada in 1985 and published the document in 1987. The process of self-study and peer review which it inaugurated was an important stepping stone toward reaching program standardization. The *Guidelines* were inclusive of a broad spectrum of program elements and helped participants in the self-study determine which of these possible elements were included in their programs and which they would hope to include as their programs developed.

In addition to this self-study, CLC offered hospitals the opportunity to have their child life programs reviewed by experienced child life professionals who could give an outside opinion on strengths and opportunities for growth. This review provided an opportunity for child life to show the hospital leadership what they were doing and what could still be done for children and families.

Credentialing

Certification of child life specialists was highly desired by the Child Life Council membership. The lack of appropriate education and experience could compromise the work of even the most well-meaning practitioner. The establishment of competencies, requirements for completion of a basic curriculum in child studies, and development of properly supervised internships were all geared to assuring that children and families would be well served by the profession.

In 1986 a credentialing tool was approved, and the Child Life Certifying Commission was established to examine the credentials of aspirants to the profession. This was inevitably a cumbersome, time-consuming and somewhat subjective process. In 1998, the credentialing process changed to certification by examination. Successful candidates certified by either method may use the initials, CCLS, (certified child life specialist) in addition to their academic degree as part of their professional designation. However, by 2004 everyone was required to be certified by examination.

Research: The Phoenix Project

The credibility of any practice depends on its demonstrated efficacy. Although there have been innumerable accolades of the good child life does for children and families, to survive in the scientific marketplace of ideas requires more than anecdotal acclaim. Richard Thompson's twenty-year review of the research literature on hospitalized children has both bolstered the idea that psychosocial services were necessary to children in hospitals and shown up the paucity of well-designed studies in this area (Thompson, 1985).

A research project under the auspices of ACCH with John Wolfer, a psychologist, as Principal Investigator was initiated in 1983 to examine the efficacy of child life interventions in reducing stress and accelerating healing. This project was carried out at the newly opened Phoenix Children's Hospital. Control data were collected from children

and families before the child life team began its work. Subsequently, children were provided with a range of child life services, and their responses were compared with those of children hospitalized during the control period. The research focused on "helping children understand and master potentially upsetting health care experiences" (Wolfer, Gaynard, Goldberger, Laidley, & Thompson, 1988). On most measures the children receiving child life interventions responded more favorably than did children who did not have access to child life.

The project also produced a teaching tool for child life staff and students and all audiences interested in children's healthcare. *Psychosocial Care of Children in Hospitals: A Clinical Practice Manual* (Gaynard, Wolfer, Goldberger, Thompson, Redburn, & Laidley, 1990) describes the practices and teaching tools used with children by the researchers.

A Place at the Table

Child life was also making contributions to and getting affirmation from outside organizations. The Joint Commission on the Accreditation of Healthcare Organizations invited the Council to contribute to its developing standards for the psychosocial care of pediatric patients. Members of the Child Life Council were appointed to attend Joint Commission meetings and to represent ACCH as a liaison member of the American Academy of Pediatrics Committee on Hospital Care. This Committee's 1985 recommendations include an entire chapter on child life and describe it as an essential component in the comprehensive care of sick children in pediatric units. The Canadian Pediatrics Society passed a resolution in 1978 recommending that "all hospitals that have pediatric units have organized facilities for play available under the direction of a child life worker for both inpatient and outpatient facilities." And in 1985 the American Academy of Pediatrics commented in its journal, *Pediatrics*, that child life is "one of the most progressive, useful and humane programs to be initiated in recent years" (p. 467).

CHILD LIFE IN THE LONG RUN

The Changing Nature of Children's Healthcare

The AAP Committee on Hospital Care in its 1994 report noted dramatic shifts in the nature of children's healthcare and in healthcare financing over the previous twenty years. Fundamental changes in hospital reimbursement practices by both federal agencies and private insurers brought about significant decreases in hospital funding. At the same time hospital costs were rising, paying for medical and surgical advances that greatly reduce morbidity and mortality. Advances in radiology, nuclear medicine, chemotherapy, dialysis, surgery and many other technologies and pharmaceuticals have produced long remissions and cures for diseases and defects once considered hopeless. These advances are as profound as were the immunizations and antibiotics of a previous generation.

In hospital practice the length of a patient's stay has been shortened, inpatient admissions present more complex and severe medical problems, more beds are filled by chronically ill children hospitalized for episodic treatments, and more surgeries and procedures involving increasingly advanced technologies are done in special outpatient areas.

The kinds of health issues confronting pediatrics today—chronic diseases, congenital and neonatal anomalies, multiple trauma, mental and developmental problems—comprise what is called the *new morbidity*. Success in treating many of the children suffering from these morbidities depends on complex technology and frequent medical interventions. Family life becomes medicalized. The lives of children whose afflictions are not amenable to cure need support and palliation to sustain them through their every day lives. The challenges to families living with the new morbidly are challenges to child life professionals as well.

Parents and Families

The inclusion of parents in the hospital care of their children has been incremental and hard won, with pockets of resistance all along the way. Even when parents were allowed to visit on a fairly open basis, they often felt as dislocated as their children, not knowing what was permitted and what was not. But gradually parents began to take ownership of their rights to be with their children and to be the primary decision makers in their children's care. Indeed the term "visitor" has become virtually obsolete when discussing the presence of parents in the hospital.

In 1978 ACCH opened its membership to parents of sick children. By the 1990s parents were beginning to assume leadership roles in ACCH and were joining as full partners in efforts to change healthcare policies and practices to include consideration of how life is really lived by families with a child with multiple healthcare requirements.

Child life has always made common cause with parents, advocating for extended visiting and overnight sleeping accommodations in the early days, and working with parents and siblings who are living with the new morbidity, whose daughter or brother will live their lives in the context of healthcare. Parents as members of advisory boards and as teachers of medical personnel have raised the consciousness of the medical community to the complex dimensions of raising a chronically ill child at home and at school, as well as in the hospital.

In 1992 ACCH published a set of comprehensive guidelines for the hospital care of children and their families (Johnson, Jeppson, & Redburn, 1992). It undertook to articulate the hospitals' responsibilities in providing psychosocial care for both children and families and is a landmark in the development of family centered care. Initiatives in family centered care continue unabated to enable families to be full participants in their sick child's care and to enable the healthcare system to understand and respond to needs for change in the delivery of that care.

The Changing Role of Child Life in Healthcare

Child life specialists increasingly staff outpatient areas, emergency rooms, and day surgery programs. In large institutions where there are neonatal and pediatric intensive care units, transplant units and special treatment units such as dialysis and burn centers, child life is present. Outreach efforts are addressed to children on home care protocols, in hospice programs, in community-based healthcare centers, in programs addressing school re-entry, and in private practice. Wherever child life is practiced, however, its essential core of service remains the same. As the American Academy of Pediatrics states in its report and recommendations from the Hospital Care Committee (2000), there are three essential responsibilities that child life specialists must undertake:

(1) providing play experiences; (2) presenting developmentally appropriate information about events and procedures; and (3) establishing therapeutic relationships with children and parents to support family

involvement in each child's care. . . . Child Life Programs have become a standard in large pediatric settings and should not be withheld regardless of reimbursement. (p. 1156)

The tasks of meeting the non-medical needs of sick children and their families in the context of the new morbidity may seem overwhelming to the child life specialist whether working in the hospital or the community. It may be helpful to keep firmly in mind the three child life responsibilities stated above. These are our priorities.

Vision to Action

In 1996 a group of child life administrators, clinicians and educators elected from the CLC membership met to grapple with issues of what the future might hold for child life specialists. This process was called *Vision to Action* and the proceedings were shared with the general membership at the Child Life Conference when it was next convened. Conference members were invited to continue the discussion at this meeting. Given the continuing crisis in healthcare costs and the shortened length of in-hospital stays, what was the conventionally trained child life specialist to do?

Child life specialists have adapted in-hospital practice to a broad range of patients and settings (e.g., chronically ill children in multiple settings; children treated at home and at school; children in hospital and community clinics; in special camps, in hospice and in private practice settings). Because of child life's demonstrated adaptability within healthcare, it seemed reasonable that the education, experience and training of child life specialists enabled them to mitigate the distress of children in a number of situations beyond healthcare. What about shelters for homeless families? What about family court?

What about children traumatized by terrorist activity or its threat?

In the spring of 1997, Mission, Vision and Values statements were published in the Child Life Council newsletter (Fenn, 1997). The *Values Statement* basically reaffirms the values child life has endorsed from its inception: an understanding of and respect for infants, children, youth and families, their individuality and complexity, their diversity and community; an understanding of the need for play as an essential part of childhood, as a healing modality in itself and as a method of child life practice; an understanding of the importance of therapeutic relationships; an understanding of communication as a task of interpretation of the child and family to the hospital and the hospital to the child and family; an appreciation of the theoretical foundations of practice, of professional collaboration, of professional standards of practice, of research.

The *Mission Statement* affirms the profession's intent to provide meaningful interventions in traumatic situations involving children and their families which will mitigate the impact of the trauma and preserve basic developmental pathways and family support systems. The Vision Statement reinforces and expands the Mission Statement. "The philosophy and practice of child life will be applicable to any healthcare setting and transferable to other environments or situations in which the potential for infants, children and youth to cope, learn and master is placed at risk" (p. 1).

At its annual conference in the late spring of 2002, the Child Life Council celebrated its twentieth anniversary. Of its 2,400 members, 720 attended the conference to exchange information, to teach and to learn, to sustain and support each other in the professional life we have chosen. Instead of facing diminished opportunities to give service as the number of inpatient pediatric beds declines,

the child life profession has undertaken the challenge to serve the growing number of children and families in other settings who need support and empowerment. In our demonstrated capacity to maintain traditional programs and establish new ones, in our resilience and creativity in overcoming obstacles, in our ability to establish and meet goals, it is clear that child life has evolved into a mature and fruitful profession over its nearly forty-year history.

REFERENCES

Abt, I. (1965). *History of pediatrics.* Philadelphia: W. B. Saunders.

American Academy of Pediatrics. (1960). *Committee on hospital care: Care of children in hospitals.* Evanston: Author.

American Academy of Pediatrics. (1985). Committee on hospital care: Child life programs for hospitalized children. *Pediatrics, 76,* 467-470.

American Academy of Pediatrics. (1993). Committee on hospital care: Child life programs. *Pediatrics, 91,* 671-673.

American Academy of Pediatrics. (2000). Committee on hospital care: Child life services. *Pediatrics, 106,* 1156-1159.

Aries, P. (1965). *Centuries of childhood.* New York: Vintage Books.

Association for the Care of Children's Health. (1984). *Guidelines for the development of child life programs.* Washington, DC: Author.

Association for the Care of Children's Health. (1986). *Child life: An overview.* Washington, DC: Author.

Association for the Care of Children's Health. (1979). *Child life position paper.* Washington, DC: Author.

Bakwin, H. (1941). Loneliness in infants. *American Journal of the Diseases of Children, 63,* 30-40.

Bowlby, J. (1982). Attachment and loss: Retrospect and prospect. *American Journal of Orthopsychiatry, 52,* 664-678.

Bowlby, J. (1952). *Maternal care and mental health.* Geneva: World Health Organization.

Brennemann, J. (1931). The infant ward. *American Journal of the Diseases of Children, 43*, 577-584.

Brodie, B. (1986). Yesterday, today and tomorrow's pediatric world. *Children's Health Care, 14*, 168-173.

Brooks, M. (1975). The growth and development of ACCH. *Journal of the Association for the Care of Children in Hospitals, 4*, 1-7.

Canadian Pediatric Society. (1978). *Resolution passed on the child in hospital.* Ottawa, Ontario: Author.

Child Life Council. (1983). *Child life position paper.* Rockville, MD: Author.

Child Life Council. (2001). *Child life position paper.* Rockville, MD: Author.

Child Life Council. (2001). *Directory of child life programs.* Rockville, MD: Author.

Child Life Council. (1994). *Official documents of the child life council.* Rockville, MD: Author.

Child Life Council. (1997). *Operating principles: Mission, vision and values.* Rockville, MD: Author.

Child Life Council. (1987). *Program review guidelines.* Rockville, MD: Author.

Child Life Council. (2001). *Standards for the academic and clinical practice programs in child life.* Rockville, MD: Author.

Colon, A. R. (1999). *Nurturing children.* Westport, CT: Greenwood Press.

Dancis, J. (1972). *History of a pediatrics department.* New York: New York University School of Medicine, Department of Pediatrics, Bellevue Medical Center.

Erikson, E. (1963). *Childhood and society.* New York: Norton Press.

Fenn, L. (1997). Mission, vision and values statements for the child life profession. *Child Life Council: Bulletin, 14*, 1-2.

Freud, A. (1952). The role of bodily illness in the mental life of children. In *The psychoanalytic study of the child.* New York: International Universities Press.

Gaynard, L., Wolfer, J., Goldberger, J., Thompson, R. H., Redburn, L., & Laidley, L. (1990). *Psychosocial care of children in hospitals: A clinical practice manual.* Bethesda, MD: ACCH.

Johnson, B., Jeppson, E., & Redburn, L. (1992). *Caring for children and families: Guidelines for hospitals.* Bethesda, MD: ACCH.

McCourt, F. (1996). *Angela's ashes.* New York: Simon and Schuster.

Olds, A. (1986). Psychological considerations in humanizing the physical environment of pediatric outpatient and hospital settings. In *Child life: An overview.* Washington, DC: ACCH.

Piaget, J., & Inhelder, B. (1969). *The psychology of the child.* New York: Basic Books.

Plank, E. (1962). *Working with children in hospitals.* Cleveland: Western Reserve Press.

Prugh, D., Staub, E., Sands, H., Kirschbaum, R., & Lenihan, E. (1953). A study of the emotional reactions of children and families to hospitalization and illness. *American Journal of Orthopsychiatry, 23*, 70-106.

Robertson, J. (1958). *A two-year-old goes to the hospital: A scientific film record.* (film). Nacton, UK: Concord Film Council.

Robertson, J. (1958). *Young children in hospitals.* New York: Basic Books.

Rubin, S. (1992). What's in a name? Child life and the play lady legacy. *Children's Health Care, 21*, 4-13.

Rutkowski, J. (1986). A survey of child life programs. In *Child life: An overview.* Washington, DC: ACCH.

Smith, A. (1937). *They play with you here, The Modern Hospital, Report on the development of play at the Children's Memorial Hospital, Chicago, IL.* Unpublished paper.

Stanford, G. (1980). Now is the time: The professionalization of child life workers. *Children's Health Care, 8*, 55-59.

Spitz, R. (1945). Hospitalism: An inquiry into the genesis of psychiatric conditions in early childhood. *Psychoanalytic Study of the Child, 1*, 53-74.

Spitz, R. (1947). *Grief: A peril in infancy.* (film). New York: New York University Film Library.

Thompson, R. (1985). *Psychosocial research on pediatric hospitalization and health care.* Springfield, IL: Charles C Thomas.

Thompson, R. H. & Stanford, G. (1981). *Child life in hospitals: Theory and practice.* Springfield, IL: Charles C Thomas.

Winnecott, D. W. (1964). *The child, the family and the outside world.* London: Penguin Books.

Wolfer, J., Gaynard, L., Goldberger, J., Laidley, L., & Thompson, R. (1988). An experimental evaluation of a model child life program. *Children's Health Care, 16*, 244-254.

Module 2:
Theoretical Background

86 The Child's Cognitive Understanding of Illness

David J. Schonfeld, M.D.

Physicians realize how difficult it is to provide adequate and effective explanations of illness and proposed treatment to their adult patients. Medical education has left the physician with a qualitatively different way of understanding illness, both physical and mental, that is beyond the grasp of the lay public. Explanations must be translated by the physician so that the patient can understand. This is not a simple process of merely replacing unfamiliar medical terminology with words from the patient's own vocabulary, but often involves the much more difficult task of restructuring the explanation to comply with a conceptual framework that is comprehensible to the patient. When the patient is a child, the clinician is confronted with a broad range of conceptual frameworks, some of which may initially seem idiosyncratic. The challenge of ensuring effective communication therefore becomes far greater, but is of no less importance.

The prospect of determining each child's unique conceptual framework for understanding illness may at first seem difficult. Fortunately, systematic research has been conducted that provides important insights into the developmental process by which children obtain an understanding of the fundamental concepts of physical illness, such as causality, prevention, and treatment. These cognitive-developmental studies (Burbach and Peterson, 1986) demonstrate that there is a systematic and predictable sequence by which these concepts of illness are acquired, and that this process is comparable to that of the acquisition of causal understanding as described by Piaget (Piaget, 1929). According to Piaget's model (Brewster, 1982; Ginsburg and Opper, 1969; Perrin and Gerrity, 1981; Piaget and Innhelder, 1969), as the result of biologic maturation and the accumulation of experience, the child progresses through four sequential stages of cognitive development: the sensorimotor period (infancy), the preoperational period (early childhood, roughly 2 to 7 years), the concrete operational period (middle to late childhood, roughly 7 to 11 years), and the formal operational period (adolescence and adulthood). Although experience has shown that children often progress through these stages at a faster rate than was initially predicted by Piaget, the nature and sequence of these stages, described by Piaget as invariate, have been confirmed by extensive research. Children in the preoperational period rely on direct personal experiences and have little ability to generalize to related situations or to appreciate multiple aspects of one situation; their thought processes tend to be empirical rather than logical. Later stages involve an increasing ability to utilize logical thought processes, with abstract thought attained only during the formal opera-

tional period. Later stages also are characterized by the child's increasing ability to differentiate self from others and to distinguish internal wishes, needs, and thoughts from the realities of the external world.

Efforts to promote the child's adjustment to physical illness and its treatment requires an appreciation of this developmental process. Effective support and assistance is predicated on an understanding of not only the child's feelings but also the child's beliefs about being ill (Bibace and Walsh, 1980). For example, it is often assumed that children fear blood drawing because of the pain associated with the procedure, and reassurances thereby take the form of "It will only hurt a little." In reality, the child's feeling of fear may be related to a belief that the phlebotomist will remove too much blood and the child will die (Licamele, 1987). In this situation the reassurances offered will be ineffective, and the child will be left to deal, alone, with a terrifying misconception about the treatment process. Efforts to facilitate the child's adjustment to physical illness and its treatment must therefore be based on an appreciation of the child's knowledge of the relevant concepts of illness. Otherwise the ill child will be left, as depicted by Anna Freud, "to submit uncomprehendingly, helplessly and passively" to both the illness and the treatment process (Freud, 1977, p. 2).

The child's knowledge and understanding of the concepts of illness can thereby be viewed as vital determinants of the child's adjustment to illness. The focus of this chapter will be to review what is known of the developmental process by which children acquire an understanding of the concepts related to illness, and the implications of this knowledge for clinicians.

PRIOR RESEARCH

On the basis of a review of the cognitive-developmental literature on children's concepts of physical illness, Burbach and Peterson (1986) concluded that there exists a positive relationship between level of understanding of the concepts of illness and the child's chronologic age/cognitive maturity that is consistent with Piaget's theories of cognitive development. Wide variability in children's understanding as a function of age was noted across studies; similar but somewhat lesser variation persisted when analysis was conducted as a function of cognitive-developmental level (frequently measured in terms of Piagetian tasks). Global estimates of a child's cognitive abilities are thereby often inaccurate predictors of the level of understanding of concepts about illness; on average, the understanding of the causality of illness typically lags behind that of general causality (Perrin and Gerrity, 1981).

949

Children bring their own personal experiences to bear on their understanding of illness; some of these experiences may promote understanding of the concepts for a particular child, whereas others may have been negative experiences that only serve to heighten anxiety and interfere with the acquisition of knowledge. It is not surprising, then, that it is still unclear what role personal experience with illness plays in the process by which children develop an understanding of the concepts of illness (Burbach and Peterson, 1986). For this reason, in the sections to follow, the focus will not be on what "a typical child" knows or thinks at a particular age. When possible, generalizations about representative age ranges will be provided, but the emphasis will be on an overview of the process and not a time line. Clinicians are advised not to rely on age-based normative data but to develop instead an appreciation of the process of cognitive development in this area. Simple inquiry into the child's views and understanding will then identify the child's level of comprehension and lead to an appreciation of the child's unique misconceptions and concerns.

IMMANENT JUSTICE, GUILT, AND SHAME

With increasing cognitive maturity (and age), children's understanding of the causality of illness increases in a predictable manner. Younger children, lacking an adequate explanation for the cause of illness, are apt to resort to explanations that attribute the cause of illness to immanent justice, "the belief that a form of natural justice can emanate from inanimate objects," wherein misdeeds will be automatically punished. Such a belief leads to the acceptance of personal guilt and shame for the etiology of illness. It is hypothesized that magical thinking and immanent justice concepts are employed by the young child in preference to the concept of chance, thereby allowing the child to retain the illusion of order and personal control in what would otherwise appear to be a random and often unfair world (Wilkinson, 1988, p. 60). Freud also appreciated the child's tendency to assume guilt for personal illness: "[Illness] appears to the child as a confirmation of the belief that wrongdoing, however secretly performed, is open to punishment, and that other, still undetected misdeeds, whether actually carried out or merely contemplated in fantasy, will likewise be followed by retribution of some kind" (Bergmann and Freud, 1965, p. 138). As one 11-year-old boy related about his diagnosis of polio 2 years prior: "I was charged with having polio. I had to plead guilty, and my sentence was life imprisonment in a wheel chair" (Bergmann and Freud, 1965, p. 96).

Research has shown that explanations based on immanent justice are more persistently utilized for ailments for which the child has limited personal experience and for which another explanation is not readily available (Siegal, 1988). With increasing cognitive maturity and with the accumulation of experience with illness, the child will more likely reject the notion that illness and misbehavior are linked, and instead acquire more accurate perceptions of personal control over illness and recovery (Burbach and Peterson, 1986). It is hoped that by providing the child with more appropriate explanations for the cause of illness, the child will be able to abandon immanent justice explanations at an earlier age (Kister and Patterson, 1980). Such immanent justice explanations can only be expected to result in guilt and/or shame, impede competent understanding of the etiology of disease and thereby hinder attempts to promote compliance with preventive health measures and treatment regimens, and impair adjustment and coping to illness of self and significant others. Recently, it has been demonstrated that even preschoolers will dismiss immanent justice as an explanation for familiar ailments with which they have had personal experience (e.g., colds) while retaining this concept in their explanations of causality for ailments with which they are less familiar (e.g., toothaches) (Siegal, 1988). Such findings lend support for the role of personal experience, and indirectly education, in advancing the child's understanding of the causality of illness.

FURTHER UNDERSTANDING OF ILLNESS CAUSALITY

As children begin to develop an understanding of the true causes of physical illness, the concept of contagion appears in their explanations for the causality of disease. Younger children (preoperational stage) initially tend to overextend the concept of contagion to include noncontagious illness; the concept is applied most appropriately by children reaching the later stages of cognitive development (concrete and formal operational stages) (Kister and Patterson, 1980; Potter and Roberts, 1984). Yet in appropriate circumstances, proper discriminant application of the concept of contagion is within the grasp of children as young as the preschool level. Siegal (1988) demonstrated that most preschool children in his study (the mean age for study participants was 4 and $^{11}/_{12}$ years) were able to accurately attribute contagion to the common cold and to differentiate this from certain noncontagious ailments (e.g., a scraped knee). As such, it was concluded that knowledge of the causes of illness is within the cognitive grasp of very young children, offering support for the incorporation of causal knowledge into health education efforts for children even at the preschool level.

Subsequent to the acquisition of the knowledge that illness can be contagious, an understanding of the physical process by which this can occur must be developed by the child. Such an understanding typically takes the form of a germ theory. In a study of Scottish nursery children (3 to 5 years in age), Wilkinson (1987) describes the early stages of children's understanding of the role of germs in the spread of disease. Initially, the child is unfamiliar with the word and will often confuse germ with bug (and thereby insect) in addition to other terms—"I don't know what a germ is but I have heard of a German person." They view germs within their own magical and egocentric context: "Germs are not there all the time. They come when mummies go away." And they attempt to draw on concrete experiences to explain what they look like. Many children in Wilkinson's study stated that germs were blue and 1 to 9 inches in diameter, and although they had not seen one, they claimed "I think I will see one one day." Discussion with parents disclosed that the children were drawing these images from a television commercial for a cleaner wherein hidden imaginary blue germs were destroyed by the application of the product. Little understanding is seen at this age as to how germs are transmitted or cause illness. One mother, attempting to have her son describe the nature of germs, inquired, "Why are you made to wash your hands before eating?" His reply illustrated his lack of comprehension: "So my plate doesn't get dirty."

Perrin and Gerrity (1981) found that by about 9 or 10 years

cf age, children generally believe that illness is caused by germs but still have little understanding of how this is accomplished once the germ is internalized. By about 12 or 13 years of age, illness is seen as the result of multiple causes; with this comes an appreciation of the role of host factors and the beginning of an understanding of the subtle interactions between host and agent in the causality of disease and the recovery from illness. It is therefore not until at least adolescence that the child can associate apparently unrelated symptoms (e.g., headache and rash) and view them as belonging to one illness, and can identify and relate the various phases of an illness into a coherent progression of one disease process. During the formal operational period, children also develop an increased understanding of their bodies, which allows an appreciation of internal physiologic structures and functions that is demonstrated in the emergence of physiologic explanations for the causality of illness in early adolescence (Bibace and Walsh, 1980). Only at this stage, with this improved understanding of internal physiology and the causality of illness, can the child be expected to comprehend many of the simplest treatment regimens that adults take for granted, such as the use of oral antibiotics to treat an ear infection or the use of injections of insulin in diabetes.

IMPLICATIONS

Knowledge of what children understand about illness and its treatment at various stages of cognitive development has practical implications for child psychiatry consultations to clinicians. It provides a framework for offering guidance on how to approach discussions about illness and its treatment with children, both to advance their understanding and coping skills and to promote their attainment of an active role in the decision-making process for their health care. As children acquire increasing knowledge about the concepts related to illness and the cognitive skills to process this information, they become more able to accurately report symptoms of illness, comply with the treatment regimens prescribed, adjust to the illness and its treatment, and make informed decisions regarding preventive health measures.

THE CHILD'S ABILITY TO REPORT SYMPTOMS

Young children, with their immature understanding of disease processes, may fail to report important symptoms of serious illness. This may be due, in part, to a lack of sensitivity to the relevant internal cues and objective signs of even serious illness (Pidgeon, 1985). But even when aware of their symptoms, egocentrism and magical thinking may lead them to withhold this information from caregivers, preferring instead to rely on internal mechanisms of dealing with the illness. They may assume that if they do not wish to be ill, then they will not be ill; they may worry that the mere vocalization of their concerns may be sufficient to bring their fears to reality. Children who persist with immanent justice explanations for the causality of illness may also be disinclined to voice their symptoms out of shame or fear of retribution. These issues are particularly relevant for children with chronic illnesses that require prompt recognition and management of often subtle internal symptoms, such as hypoglycemia in the child with diabetes.

THE CHILD'S COMPLIANCE WITH TREATMENT

Attempts to communicate effectively with children about illness and its treatment will also maximize efforts to enlist the child's cooperation in the treatment process. Such efforts should maintain as a long-term goal the child's attainment of an active role in the decision-making process in the child's own health care. In times of frustration it is easy to lose sight of this goal, such as when a child with asthma is noncompliant with treatment and is warned, "If you don't take your medicine, you'll have to go to the emergency room and get a needle" but is not provided with a developmentally appropriate explanation of the treatment process. Parents will need help in appreciating that such threats may yield temporary compliance, but at the expense of reinforcing maladaptive concepts of illness, that may, in the long run, lead to decreased compliance. This approach might be justifiable if it were shown that the concepts of illness were beyond the grasp of children and that illness in the child could be effectively prevented through compliance with recommendations. Both assumptions are incorrect. First, the preceding discussions illustrate that an understanding of the concepts of illness is possible even in very young children, if given appropriate explanations and provided with constructive learning experiences. Second, even if children were able to fully comply with all the numerous restrictions and requirements placed on them by their parents in the hopes of preventing illness (e.g., to get enough sleep, to eat the right food, to dress correctly), many will still get ill. If the only explanations provided about the causality of illness reinforce immanent justice, then the child is left with no other recourse but to accept self-blame for personal illness. Hospitalization and increasingly invasive medical management, when required, is then not perceived as a result of the natural process of the disease but instead as a personal failure on the part of the child. The child feels he or she has failed and is being punished; in addition to feeling ill and frightened, the child is now apt to feel angry and rejected. As one child remarked about his failure to be discharged from the hospital: "I did everything the doctors told me to do, and now they won't let me go home." He had been told in simple terms what he needed to do to get better but had not been given explanations that he could understand of how these procedures would influence his illness. After complying fully with the requirements placed on him and failing to become well and be discharged, he was understandably hurt and angry.

THE CHILD'S ADJUSTMENT TO ILLNESS AND THE TREATMENT PROCESS

Explanations for children about their illness and treatment should seek not only to achieve compliance but also to promote the child's understanding. The explanations should be presented in a manner that is consistent with the current level of understanding of the child, or perhaps slightly advanced (Bibace and Walsh, 1980; Brewster, 1982). These explanations should aim to replace frightening misconceptions and supply constructive information in a manner that will promote coping and adjustment. This is, of course, an ongoing process. Children need to be questioned about their understanding of the explanations provided, thereby allowing the discussion to become a true dialogue. Vocabulary used should be simple and direct. Indeed, even adult patients misinterpret terminology at a rate that exceeds the expectations of most physicians. In one study of women attending a public health clinic, 80% of patients confused "anemia" with "enema," and over 50% defined "well-nourished" as "nervous body" (Collins, 1955).

When under stress, such as during an acute illness, children often regress in their developmental abilities and are least amenable to techniques to advance their developmental progress. Even in this setting, recognition of children's current level of functioning will still have practical implications for efforts to restructure their thinking and provide support during the illness. For example, when constructing a plan to help control pain for a child in the preoperational period, the connection between the medication taken orally and the relief of the pain can be emphasized, but more concrete measures that will be reassuring to the child (e.g., application of a heating pad for abdominal pain) should also be employed. As much as possible, the use of intramuscular pain medication should be avoided, realizing the child's tendency to associate treatment with punishment and to fail to comprehend the logic of giving a painful intramuscular injection to treat abdominal pain. And in selecting the oral medication to be given, knowledge of the child's cognitive abilities regarding comprehension of quantity and number may have further practical implications; it may be preferable when the dose of pain medication is to be adjusted to give two 15-mg pills instead of one 30-mg pill, or to use elixir instead, because of the even clearer concrete representation of increasing dose with increasing amount (Clark, 1985). Appreciation of children's understanding of their illness and its treatment and knowledge of their cognitive abilities can thereby provide guidance not only in the selection of explanations but also in the selection of the most appropriate techniques for the delivery of health care.

Research also has shown that parallel to the process of conceptual development wherein children acquire an understanding of the causes of illness, children also develop increasing appreciation for the intent of medical procedures. Brewster (1982) describes three stages in this process: The child initially views the procedures as punishment, is subsequently able to understand the intent of the procedures but feels that the staff will only be empathetic if the child outwardly expresses pain, and, finally, is able to infer both empathy and intention. In order to enlist their cooperation and to decrease their anxiety and fear surrounding the procedures, it is important that children be prepared for procedures with information and explanations that are consistent with their level of understanding of the relevant concepts. Preoperative teaching for the child in the preoperational period, for example, might focus on acquainting the child with what the concrete experiences will be (e.g., what the room will look like, who will be there), whereas preparation for the child in the formal operational period might also include a more detailed discussion of the procedure, including mention of anatomical and physiologic principles within the cognitive grasp of the more mature child (Perrin and Gerrity, 1981).

Programs to prepare children psychologically for procedures have been shown to be effective in helping them cope with the associated anxiety. A recent study (Edwinson, 1988) demonstrated that such programs are effective in reducing anxiety, even in the setting of emergency surgical procedures (e.g., acute appendectomy), when compared with standard, unstructured preoperative preparation. Recent research is also just beginning to empirically demonstrate that preparation programs for hospitalization and medical procedures that are consonant with the child's cognitive-developmental level are more effective in decreasing distress and anxiety in response to procedures when compared to preparations that are not designed with these concepts in mind (Rasnake and Linscheid, 1989).

PREVENTIVE HEALTH EDUCATION FOR CHILDREN

Health education only at the time of illness or hospitalization may not be the most effective means of advancing the child's understanding of illness. During times of illness, as in other stressful periods, children will often regress in their developmental abilities. At these times they will be least prepared to understand the situation confronting them, least able to benefit from educational efforts to promote this understanding, but most in need of this information to facilitate adjustment and successful coping. This observation provides a strong argument for the need to promote the acquisition of these concepts prior to the time they are needed to deal with acute crisis in the form of illness. Health education efforts, then, should begin when the child is well, with the aim of promoting increased understanding, knowledge, and skills in this area. Children should be taught to do more than "just say no" to bad health decisions; they should be helped to understand the rationale behind these choices and to acquire the skills to make informed and responsible health decisions that affect them in the future. For health education to be effective, it must be developmentally based so that discussions coincide with the child's level of understanding.

Physicians should utilize preventive health visits during the pediatric years to educate not only the parents but also the child. Unfortunately, research has shown that little time is spent by the pediatrician during pediatric visits talking directly to the child. In one study of children 4 to 7 years of age attending private pediatric practices for routine health maintenance visits or visits for minor illness, only about 5% of the discussion during these visits was directed by the physician toward the child. Interviews of the children after the visits illustrated that most of them desired more information about their medical problems; their concerns were well formed and relevant to the reason for the current visit, yet these concerns were not addressed by either the parent or physician. In fact, explanations about treatment and symptoms were not provided to the children in this setting, and the children were treated instead as passive recipients of health care (Perlman and Abramovitch, 1987).

Other studies have shown similarly low rates of communication between physicians and child patients. This is unfortunate, as children are interested in clinical information even at a young age and are capable of comprehending the information if it is presented in an appropriate manner. Pediatricians should take advantage of this opportunity to advance the child's understanding of the concepts of physical illness in a salient and relevant context—that of the child's own medical visit. One reason for this oversight may relate to the observation that pediatricians, and other health care professionals who work with children, are unfamiliar with the developmental stages of children's understanding of illness: "Professionals do not operate nan intuitive sense about cognitive development. . . . They lack an understanding of the important qualitative differences in the very basic ways in which children at different stages of development see, interpret, and understand the world around them" (Perrin and Perrin, 1983).

CONCLUDING REMARKS

The focus of this chapter has been on the cognitive process by which children develop an understanding of their illness and treatment, and on the implications of this for health care professionals. It should be emphasized that such a cognitive-developmental approach to viewing the child's understanding of illness is not in conflict with other theories that aim to explain the child's psychological reaction and behavioral response to the illness experience. Conscious understanding (cognitive factors) is only one component of the child's response to illness. Unconscious developmental fantasies, too, may alter the child's perceptions of the illness and treatment process, despite the presence of mature cognitive abilities. For example, a fear of surgery may be heightened by underlying castration anxiety (Lewis, 1982). Even adolescents who have reached the formal operational stage of cognitive development may still be overwhelmed by anxiety from unconscious developmental conflicts. These conflicts may distort their perceptions and result in misconceptions and fears out of proportion to what would be predicted by a purely cognitive-developmental approach. An integrated approach to viewing the ill child that incorporates both the child's cognitive abilities and an appreciation of the psychological factors pertinent to his or her personality development is therefore likely to yield the most insight into the complex process by which the child comes to understand, accept, and respond to both the illness and treatment process.

Subsequent chapters will highlight the child's unique response to specific illnesses and components of the treatment process (such as hospitalization and surgery). An increased appreciation of the stages of children's understanding of illness will allow the physician to communicate more effectively with children, in order to improve their medical care, minimize their anxiety and fear, and promote their adjustment to illness and its treatment. Health care professionals will thus be able to assist the children to acquire the requisite skills to become increasingly active and effective partners in their health care management.

REFERENCES

Bergmann T, Freud A: *Children in the Hospital.* New York, International Universities Press, 1965.

Bibace R, Walsh M: Development of children's concepts of illness. *Pediatrics* 66:912–917, 1980.

Brewster A: Chronically ill hospitalized children's concepts of their illness. *Pediatrics* 69:355–362, 1982.

Burbach D, Peterson L: Children's concepts of physical illness: A review and critique of the cognitive-developmental literature. *Health Psychol* 5:307–325, 1986.

Clark E: Pain assessment, intervention and evaluation. In: Milch R, Freeman A, Clark E (eds): *Palliative Pain and Symptom Management for Children and Adolescents.* Alexandria, Virginia, Children's Hospice International and Division of Maternal and Child Health, 1985.

Collins G: Do we really advise the patient? *J Fla Med Assoc* 42:111, 1955.

Edwinson M: Psychologic preparation program for children undergoing acute appendectomy. *Pediatrics* 82:30–36, 1988.

Freud A: The role of bodily illness in the mental life of children. In: Eissler R, Freud A, Kris M, et al (eds): *Physical Illness and Handicap in Childhood.* New Haven, CT, Yale University Press, 1977, pp. 1–12.

Ginsburg H, Opper S: *Piaget's Theory of Intellectual Development.* Englewood Cliffs, NJ, Prentice-Hall, 1969.

Kister M, Patterson C: Children's conceptions of the causes of illness: Understanding of contagion and use of immanent justice. *Child Dev* 51:839–846, 1980.

Lewis M: *Clinical Aspects of Child Development: An Introductory Synthesis of Developmental Concepts and Clinical Experience* (2nd ed). Philadelphia, Lea & Febiger, 1982.

Licamele W, Goldberg R: Childhood reactions to illness and hospitalization. *Am Fam Physician* 36:227–232, 1987.

Perlman N, Abramovitch R: Visit to the pediatrician: Children's concerns. *J Pediatr* 110:988–990, 1987.

Perrin E, Gerrity S: There's a demon in your belly: Children's understanding of illness. *Pediatrics* 67:841–849, 1981.

Perrin E, Perrin J: Clinicians' assessments of children's understanding of illness. *Am J Dis Child* 137:874–878, 1983.

Piaget J: *The Child's Conception of the World.* New York, Harcourt Brace Jovanovich, 1929.

Piaget J, Innhelder B: *The Psychology of the Child.* New York, Basic Books, 1969.

Pidgeon V: Children's concepts of illness: Implications for health teaching. *MCN* 14:23–35, 1985.

Potter P, Roberts M: Children's perceptions of chronic illness: The roles of disease symptoms, cognitive development, and information. *J Pediatr Psychol* 9:13–27, 1984.

Rasnake L, Linscheid T: Anxiety reduction in children receiving medical care: Developmental considerations. *J Dev Behav Pediatr* 10: 169–175, 1989.

Siegal M: Children's knowledge of contagion and contamination as causes of illness. *Child Dev* 59:1353–1359, 1988.

Wilkinson S: *The Child's World of Illness: The Development of Health and Illness Behavior.* Cambridge, Cambridge University Press, 1988.

Wilkinson S: Germs: Nursery school children's views on the causality of illness. *Clin Pediatr* 26:465–469, 1987.

Research in Review

Vygotsky's Theory:
The Importance of Make-Believe Play

Laura E. Berk

I n most theories of cognition and cognitive development, the social and the cognitive make contact only minimally. Rather than being truly joined and interactive, they are viewed as separate domains of functioning. At best, the social world is a surrounding context for cognitive activity, not an integral part of it. Early childhood educators have a long tradition of regarding what the young child knows as personally rather than socially constructed—a tradition that follows from the massive contributions of Piaget's cognitive-developmental theory to our field.

The ideas of the Russian developmental psychologist Lev Vygotsky, who early in this century forged an innovative theory granting great importance to social and cultural experience in development, have gained increasing visibility over the past decade. In Vygotsky's ([1933] 1978) sociocultural theory, the "mind extends beyond the skin" and is inseparably joined with other minds (Wertsch 1991, p. 90). Social experience shapes the ways of thinking and interpreting the world available to individuals. And language plays a crucial role in a socially formed mind because it is our primary avenue of communication and mental contact with others, it serves as the major means by which social experience is represented psychologically, and it is an indispensable tool for thought (Vygotsky [1934] 1987). A basic premise of Vygotsky's theory is that all uniquely human, higher forms of mental activity are jointly constructed and transferred to children through dialogues with other people.

Vygotsky's ideas are stimulating a host of new ways to educate young children that emphasize opportunities for discussion and joint problem solving. A central Vygotskian concept that has played a formative role in these efforts is the *zone of proximal development*, which refers to a range of tasks that the child cannot yet handle alone but can accomplish with the help of adults

Laura E. Berk is professor of psychology at Illinois State University. Her research interests include Vygotsky's theory on children's private, or self-directed, speech and applications of Vygotsky's ideas to education. She has been NAEYC's Research in Review editor for the past three years.

and more skilled peers. As children engage in cooperative dialogues with more mature partners, they internalize the language of these interactions and use it to organize their independent efforts in the same way (Berk 1992). According to sociocultural theory, supportive guidance from adults that creates a *scaffold* for children's learning is essential for their cognitive development. Such communication sensitively adjusts to children's momentary progress, offering the necessary assistance for mastery while prompting children to take over more responsibility for the task as their skill increases (Wood & Middleton 1975; Wood 1989). Furthermore, *cooperative learning*—in which small groups of peers at varying levels of competence share responsibility and resolve differences of opinion as they work toward a common goal—also fosters cognitive maturity (Forman 1987; Tudge 1992).

The vast literature on children's play reveals that its contributions to child development can be looked at from diverse vantage points.

These Vygotskian ideas about teaching and learning have largely been implemented in academically relevant early childhood contexts, such as literacy, mathematics, and science (Moll 1990; Forman, Minick, & Stone 1993); but a close look at Vygotsky's writings reveals that they recur as major themes in his view of play. Although Vygotsky's works contain only a brief 12-page statement about play, his discussion is provocative, innovative, and ahead of his time. In accord with his emphasis on social experience and language as vital forces in cognitive development, Vygotsky ([1933] 1978) emphasized representational play—the make-believe that blossoms during the preschool years and evolves into the games with rules that dominate middle childhood. Vygotsky

Social and cultural experience are very important in development. Children learn a lot through the social activity we call play, where communication—the sharing of information and ideas—abounds. This is especially true if children are of different backgrounds and ages. Of course children learn a lot through discussions and conversations with adults, too.

accorded fantasy play a prominent place in his theory, granting it the status of a "leading factor in development" (p. 101), as the following frequently quoted remarks reveal:

Play creates a zone of proximal development in the child. In play, the child always behaves beyond his average age, above his daily behavior; in play it is as though he were a head taller than himself. As in the focus of a magnifying glass, play contains all developmental tendencies in a condensed form and is itself a major source of development. (p. 102)

As we discuss Vygotsky's theory and the research stimulated by it, we will see that he situated play squarely within a sociocultural context. Adults and peers scaffold young children's play, nurturing the transition to make-believe and its elaboration throughout the preschool years. Representational play serves as a unique,

broadly influential zone of proximal development within which *children advance themselves* to ever-higher levels of psychological functioning. Consequently, Vygotsky's theory has much to say to teachers about the importance of promoting make-believe in preschool and child care programs.

Development and significance of make-believe play

Vygotsky began his consideration of the importance of play by suggesting that if we can identify its defining features, we can gain insight into its functions in development. To isolate the distinctiveness of play, Vygotsky explored characteristics regarded by other theorists as central to playful activity and found them wanting. For example, the common assumption that play is pleasurable activity is not specific to play. Many other experiences, such as eating a favorite treat, being granted the undivided attention of a parent, or listening to an exciting story, are at least as gratifying and sometimes more so than is play. Furthermore, certain playful experiences—games that can be won or lost—are not pure fun for the child when they result in disappointing outcomes.

A second way of understanding play is to highlight its symbolic features, as Piaget ([1945] 1951) did in his characterization of make-believe as a means through which children practice representational schemes. Yet symbolism is another feature that is not exclusive to play. Both Piaget and Vygotsky noted that it also characterizes language, artistic, and literacy activities during the preschool years.

Vygotsky concluded that play has two critical features that, when combined, describe its uniqueness and shed light on its role in development. First, all representational play *creates an imaginary situation* that permits the child to grapple with unrealizable desires. Vygotsky pointed out that fantasy play first appears at a time when children must learn to postpone gratification of impulses and accept the fact that certain desires will remain unsatisfied. During the second year, caregivers begin to insist that toddlers delay gratification (e.g., wait for a turn) and acquire socially approved behaviors involving safety, respect for property, self-care (e.g., washing hands), and everyday routines (e.g., putting toys away) (Gralinski & Kopp 1993).

The creation of an imaginary situation in play, however, has often been assumed to be a way in which children attain immediate fulfillment of desires not satisfied in real life. Vygotsky pointed out that this commonly held belief is not correct. A second feature of all representational play is that it *contains rules for behavior* that children must follow to successfully act out the play scene. Games that appear in the late preschool period and flourish during the school years are clearly rule based. Even the simplest imaginative situations created by very young children proceed in accord with social rules, although the rules are not laid down in advance. For example, a child pretending to go to sleep follows the rules of bedtime behavior. Another child, imagining himself to be a father and a doll to be a child, conforms to the rules of parental behavior. Yet a third child playing astronaut observes the rules of shuttle launch and space walk. Vygotsky ([1933] 1978) concluded, "Whenever there is an imaginary situation, there are rules" (p. 95). A child cannot behave in an imaginary situation without rules.

These attributes of play—an imaginary situation governed by rules—provide the key to its role in development. According to Vygotsky, play supports the emergence of two complementary capacities: (a) the ability to separate thought from actions and objects, and (b) the capacity to renounce impulsive action in favor of deliberate, self-regulatory activity.

Separating thought from actions and objects

In creating an imaginary situation, children learn to act not just in response to external stimuli but also in accord with internal ideas. Infants and very young children, Vygotsky ([1933] 1978) explained, are reactive beings; momentary perceptions trigger their behavior. A baby who sees an attractive toy grabs for it without delay. A toddler runs after a ball that has rolled into the street without considering consequences. "[I]n play, things lose their determining force. *The child sees one thing but acts differently in relation to what he sees. Thus, a condition is reached in which the child begins to act independently of what he sees*" (p. 97).

Just how does imaginative play help children separate thought from the surrounding world and rely on ideas to guide behavior? According to Vygotsky, the object substitutions that characterize make-believe are crucial in this process. When children use a stick to represent a horse or a folded blanket to represent a sleeping baby, their relation to reality is dramatically changed. The stick becomes a pivot for separating the meaning "horse" from a real horse; similarly, the blanket becomes a pivot

for distinguishing the meaning "baby" from a real baby. This adjustment in thinking occurs because children change the substitute object's real meaning when they behave toward it in a pretend fashion.

Vygotsky emphasized that young children have difficulty severing thinking—or the meaning of words—from objects; they do so only gradually. Indeed, such research reveals that object substitutions become more flexible as children get older. In early pretense, toddlers use only realistic objects—for example, a toy telephone to talk into or a cup to drink from. Around age 2, children use less realistic toys, such as a block for a telephone receiver. Sometime during the third year, children can imagine objects and events without any direct support from the real world, as when they say to a play partner, "I'm calling Susie on the phone!" while pretending to dial with their hands or without acting out the event at all. By this time, a play symbol no longer has to resemble the object or behavior for which it stands (Bretherton et al. 1984; Corrigan 1987).

According to Vygotsky ([1930] 1990), in helping children separate meaning from objects, the pretending of early childhood serves as vital preparation for the much later development of abstract thought, in which symbols are manipulated and propositions evaluated with-

©Nancy P. Alexander

Vygotsky concluded that play has two critical features that, when combined, describe its uniqueness and shed light on its role in development. First, all representational play creates an imaginary situation that permits the child to grapple with unrealizable desires. Games that appear in the late preschool period and flourish during the school years are clearly rule based. Even the simplest imaginative situations created by very young children proceed in accord with social rules, although the rules are not laid down in advance. A second feature of all representational play is that it contains rules for behavior that children must follow to successfully act out the play scene.

> Psychoanalytic theorists have highlighted the emotionally integrative function of pretense, pointing out that anxiety-provoking events—such as a visit to the doctor's office or discipline by a parent—are likely to be revisited in the young child's play but with roles reversed so that the child is in command and compensates for unpleasant experiences in real life.

out referring to the real world. And in detaching meaning from behavior, make-believe also helps teach children to choose deliberately from among alternative courses of action. This capacity to think in a planful, self-regulatory fashion is also strengthened by the rule-based nature of play, as we will see in the following section.

Renouncing impulsive action

Vygotsky pointed out that the imaginative play of children contains an interesting paradox. In play, children do what they most feel like doing, and to an outside observer, the play of preschoolers appears free and spontaneous. Nevertheless, play constantly demands that children act against their immediate impulses because they must subject themselves to the rules of the make-believe context or the game they have chosen to play. According to Vygotsky ([1933] 1978), free play is not really "free"; instead, it requires self-restraint—willingly following social rules. As a result, in play the young child displays many capacities that "will become her basic level of real action and morality" in the future (p. 100). By enacting rules in make-believe, children come to better understand social norms and expectations and strive to behave in ways that uphold them. For example, a child occupying the role of parent in a household scene starts to become dimly aware of parental responsibilities in real situations and gains insight into the rule-governed nature of the parent–child relationship (Haight & Miller 1993).

When we look at the development of play from early to middle childhood, the most obvious way in which it changes is that it increasingly emphasizes rules. The greater stress on the rule-oriented aspect of play over time means that children gradually become more conscious of the goals of their play activities. Vygotsky ([1933] 1978) summarized, "The development from games with an overt imaginary situation and covert rules to games with overt rules and a covert imaginary situation outlines the evolution of children's play" (p. 96). From this perspective, the fantasy play of the preschool years is essential for further development of play in middle childhood—specifically, for movement toward game play, which provides additional instruction in setting goals, regulating one's behavior in pursuit of those goals, and subordinating action to rules rather than to impulse—in short, for becoming a cooperative and productive member of society. Play, in Vygotsky's theory, is the preeminent educational activity of early childhood.

Impact of imaginative play on development

Was Vygotsky correct in stating that make-believe serves as a zone of proximal development, supporting the emergence and refinement of a wide variety of competencies? A careful examination of his theory reveals that the benefits of play are complex and indirect; they may take years to be realized (Nicolopoulou 1991). Still, considerable support exists for Vygotsky's view that play contributes to the development of a diverse array of capacities in the young child.

Sociodramatic play, the coordinated and reciprocal make-believe with peers that emerges around age 2½ and increases rapidly until age 4 to 5, has been studied thoroughly. Compared to social nonpretend activities (such as drawing or putting together puzzles), during social pretend activities, preschoolers' interactions last longer, show more involvement, draw larger numbers of children into the activity, and are more cooperative (Connolly, Doyle, & Reznick 1988). When we consider these findings from the standpoint of Vygotsky's emphasis on the social origins of cognition, it is not surprising that preschoolers who spend more time at sociodramatic play are advanced in general intellectual development and show an enhanced ability to understand the feelings of others. They are also seen as more socially competent by their teachers (Burns & Brainerd 1979; Connolly & Doyle 1984).

> Piaget underscored the opportunities that make-believe affords for exercising symbolic schemes.

A growing body of research reveals that make-believe play strengthens a variety of specific mental abilities. For example, it promotes memory. In a study in which 4- and 5-year-olds were asked either to remember a set of toys or to play with them, the play condition produced far better recall. Rather than just naming or touching the objects (strategies applied in the "remember" condition), children who played with the toys engaged in many spontaneous organizations and uses of the materials that enabled them to memorize effortlessly (Newman 1990). In this way, play may provide a vital foundation for more sophisticated memory strategies mastered during middle childhood that depend on establishing mean-

'ingful relationships among to-be-remembered information. Other research confirms that opportunities to engage in fantasy play promote children's storytelling and story memory (Saltz, Dixon, & Johnson 1977; Pellegrini & Galda 1982).

Language is also greatly enriched by play experiences. As children engage in play talk, they often correct one another's errors, either directly or by demonstrating acceptable ways to speak. For example, in enacting a telephone conversation, one kindergartner said, "Hello, come to my house please." Her play partner quickly countered with appropriate telephone greeting behavior: "No, first you've get to say 'what are you doing?'" (Ervin-Tripp 1991, p. 90). Vocabulary expands during make-believe as children introduce new words they have heard during recent experiences. One 4-year-old playing nurse remarked to an agemate, "I'm going to give you a temperature" (p. 90). Although her first use of the term was not correct, active experimentation increases the chances that she will notice more about the context in which "temperature" is applied and move toward correct usage. Furthermore, the linguistic skills required to express different points of view, resolve disputes, and persuade peers to collaborate in play are numerous. Play offers an arena in which all facets of conversational dialogue can be extended.

Make-believe also fosters young children's ability to reason about impossible or absurd situations—a finding highly consistent with Vygotsky's emphasis that fantasy play assists children in separating meanings from the objects for which they stand. A repeated finding in the cognitive development literature is that through much of early and middle childhood, thinking is tied to the here and now—to concrete reality; but under certain conditions, young children attain a "theoretical" mode of reasoning.

Consider the following syllogism: All cats bark. Rex is a cat. Does Rex bark? Researchers had a group of 4- to 6-year-olds act out problems like this with toys. A second group of children were told that the events were taking place on a pretend planet rather than on Earth. A control group merely listened and answered the question. Children in the two "play" conditions gave more theoretical than factual responses and were also able to justify their answers with theoretical ideas—for example, "In the story, cats bark, so we can pretend they bark" (Dias & Harris 1988, 1990). Entering the pretend mode seems to enable children to reason with contrary facts as if they were true—findings that provide striking verification of Vygotsky's ([1933] 1978) assumption that in play, the child is well "beyond his average age, above his daily behavior" (p. 102).

Finally, young children who especially enjoy pretending or who are given encouragement to engage in fantasy play score higher on tests of imagination and creativity. When children use play objects in novel ways, the objects seem to stimulate the discovery of new relationships and enhance children's ability to think flexibly and inventively (Dansky 1980; Pepler & Ross 1981).

In sum, fantasy play contributes to social maturity and the construction of diverse aspects of cognition. For people who have questioned whether play activities, so indigenous and absorbing to children, must be curbed in favor of more "productive" activities or whether play constitutes a powerful zone of proximal development, the findings just reviewed clearly grant play a legitimate and fruitful place in children's lives.

Scaffolding children's make-believe play

The Piagetian view, dominant for the past three decades, claims that make-believe emerges spontaneously when children become capable of representational thought. Piaget and his followers assumed that children lack the cognitive competencies to share play symbols with others—both adults and peers—until well into the preschool period (e.g., Fein 1981). Not until recently have researchers seriously addressed the social context of children's play experiences. Their findings challenge the notion that fantasy play is an unprompted phenomenon arising solely from tendencies within the child. Instead, new evidence suggests that make-believe, like other higher mental functions, is the product of social collaboration.

Adult–child play

Twenty-four-month-old Elizabeth is being carried upstairs for a diaper change by her mother.

Elizabeth: My going Sherman Dairy. (Sherman Dairy is the family's favorite dessert restaurant.)

Mother: You're going to Sherman Dairy?

Elizabeth: Yeah.

Mother: Is Andrew the cook? (Andrew is a 4-year-old friend who is playing with Elizabeth's sister.)

Elizabeth: Yep. (Pause) *My* cook.

Mother: (Putting Elizabeth on the changing table and beginning to change her) You're the cook? You can cook with your dishes, right? Do you have some pots and pans?

Elizabeth: Yep. (Adapted from Haight & Miller 1993, p. 46)

In the play sequence above, 2-year-old Elizabeth initiates a make-believe scenario in which a trip upstairs for a diaper change is transformed into a journey to buy

---

All theorists recognize that pretense permits children to become familiar with social role possibilities in their culture, providing important insights into the link between self and wider society.

---

ice cream. Her mother encourages her to expand the imaginative theme and act it out with toys. The play episode is elaborated and sustained as her mother asks questions that help Elizabeth clarify her intentions and think of new ideas.

Vygotskian-based research on play emphasizes that make-believe is, from its beginnings, a social activity (El'konin 1966; Garvey 1990). In Western industrialized societies, play first appears between caregivers and children; children initially learn pretense and games under the supportive guidance of experts. From these interactions, children acquire the communicative conventions, social skills, and representational capacities that permit them to carry out make-believe on their own.

In the most extensive study of caregiver scaffolding of make-believe, Haight and Miller (1993) followed the development of pretend play at

© Cheryl Namkung

The fantasy play of the preschool years is essential for further development of play in middle childhood—specifically, for movement toward game play, which provides additional instruction in setting goals, regulating one's behavior in pursuit of those goals, and subordinating action to rules rather than to impulse— in short, for becoming a cooperative and productive member of society. Play, in Vygotsky's theory, is the preeminent educational activity of early childhood.

home of nine middle-class children between 1 and 4 years of age. Social make-believe was common across the entire age span, consuming from 68 to 75% of children's total pretend time. Furthermore, mothers were the children's principal play partners until 3 years of age. By age 4, children played approximately the same amount with their mothers as they did with other children (siblings and peers). Children's pretending with mothers, however, was not caused by a lack of child playmates at the youngest ages. Several investigations reveal that 1- and 2-year-olds who have fairly continuous access to other children prefer to play with their mothers (Dunn & Dale 1984; Miller & Garvey 1984). These findings confirm the Vygotskian view that play with caregivers gradually gives way to play with peers as children's competence increases.

Further evidence that caregivers teach toddlers to pretend stems from Haight and Miller's observation that at 12 months, make-believe was fairly one sided: almost all play episodes were initiated by mothers. From age 2 on, when pretending was better established, mothers and children displayed mutual interest in getting make-believe started; half of pretend episodes were initiated by each. At all ages, mothers typically followed the child's lead and elaborated on the child's contribution. Thus, although pretense was first introduced to 12-month-olds by their mothers, it quickly became a joint activity in which both partners participated actively in

an imaginative dialogue and in which the adult gradually released responsibility to the child for creating and guiding the fantasy theme.

Children's object substitutions during make-believe are also largely traceable to episodes in which their mothers showed them how to engage in object renaming or suggested a pretend action to the child (Smolucha 1992). By the time their children are 2 years old, mothers talk more about nonexistent fantasy objects, a change that may prompt children to widen the range of object substitutions in their play (Kavanaugh, Whittington, & Cerbone 1983). Furthermore, many parents and early childhood teachers surround children with toys designed to stimulate pretend themes. By offering an array of objects specialized for make-believe, caregivers communicate to children that pretense is a valued activity and maximize opportunities to collaborate with them in integrating props into fantasy scenes.

Consequences of supportive caregiver–child play

In their longitudinal study, Haight and Miller (1993) carefully examined the play themes of mother–child pretense and found that it appeared to serve a variety of functions, including communicating feelings, expressing and working through conflicts, enlivening daily routines, and teaching lessons. These diverse social uses of caregiver–child play suggest that adult support and

Vygotsky's special emphasis on the imaginative and rule-based nature of play adds an additional perspective to the viewpoints just mentioned—one that highlights the critical role of make-believe in developing reflective thoughts, as well as self-regulatory and socially cooperative behavior.

expansion of preschoolers' make-believe should facilitate all the developmental outcomes of play already discussed, although as yet, no systematic research on the topic exists.

Accumulating evidence does show that children's make-believe play with their mothers is more sustained and complex than is their solitary make-believe play. One- to 3-year-olds engage in more than twice as much make-believe while playing with mothers than while playing alone. In addition, caregiver support leads early make-believe to include more elaborate themes (Dunn & Wooding 1977; O'Connell & Bretherton 1984; Zukow 1986; Slade 1987; Fiese 1990; Tamis-LeMonda & Bornstein 1991; Haight & Miller 1993; O'Reilly & Bornstein 1993). In line with Vygotsky's zone of proximal development, very young children, for whom make-believe is just emerging, act more competently when playing with a mature partner than they otherwise would. In Haight and Miller's study, suggestive evidence emerged that mother–child play promotes effective child–child play. Children whose mothers ranked high in pretending when their children were 1 year old ranked high in peer play at 4 years. And children of the most enthusiastic and imaginative parents were among the most highly skilled preschool pretenders.

Critical features of adult–child play

Although mother–child play has been granted considerable research attention, a search of the literature revealed no studies of teachers' participation in young children's play. Yet evidence on the effect of adult–child play suggests that it is vital for teachers in preschool and child care programs to engage in joint play with children.

Teachers' effective playful involvement with children requires early childhood environments that are developmentally appropriate. Especially important are generous adult–child ratios, a stable staff that relates to children sensitively and responsively, and settings that are richly equipped to offer varied opportunities for make-believe. These factors are critical because they ensure that teachers have the necessary time, rapport, and play props to encourage children's imaginative contributions and to scaffold them toward social pretend play with peers.

At the same time, adults walk a fine line in making effective contributions to children's pretense. The power of adult–child play to foster development is undermined by communication that is too overpowering or one-sided. Fiese (1990) found that maternal questioning, instructing, and intrusiveness (initiating a new activity unrelated to the child's current pattern of play) led to immature, simple exploratory play in young children. In

contrast, turn taking and joint involvement in a shared activity resulted in high levels of pretense. Furthermore, adult intervention that recognizes children's current level of cognitive competence and builds on it is most successful in involving children. Lucariello (1987) reported that when 24- to 29-month-olds were familiar with a play theme suggested by their mother, both partners displayed advanced levels of imaginative activity and constructed the scenario together. When the theme was unfamiliar, the mother took nearly total responsibility for pretense.

Promoting social pretend play with peers

At preschool, Jason joins a group of children in the block area for a space shuttle launch. "That can be our control tower," he suggests to Vance, pointing to a corner by a bookshelf.

"Wait, I gotta get it all ready," states Lynette, who is still arranging the astronauts (two dolls and a teddy bear) inside a circle of large blocks, which represent the rocket.

"Countdown!" Jason announces, speaking into a small wooden block, his pretend walkie-talkie.

"Five, six, two, four, one, blastoff!" responds Vance, commander of the control tower.

Lynette makes one of the dolls push a pretend button and reports, "Brrm, brrm, they're going up!" (Berk 1993, p. 311)

When pretending with peers, children make use of the many competencies they acquire through their play with adults. Yet pretend play with peers must also be responsive and cooperative to result in satisfying play experiences and to serve as a zone of proximal development in which children advance their skills and understanding. According to Göncü (1993), social play with peers requires *intersubjectivity*—a process whereby individuals involved in the same activity who begin with different perspectives arrive at a shared understanding. In the play episode just described, the children achieve a high level of intersubjectivity as they coordinate several roles in an elaborate plot and respond in a smooth, complementary fashion to each other's contributions.

The importance of intersubjectivity for peer social play is suggested by the work of several major theorists.

A basic premise of Vygotsky's theory is that all uniquely human, higher forms of mental activity are jointly constructed and transferred to children through dialogues with other people.

Piaget ([1945] 1951) notes that for children to play together, they must collectively construct play symbols. Likewise, Vygotsky ([1933] 1978) claimed that in pretense with peers, children jointly develop rules that guide social activity. And Parten (1932) labeled the most advanced form of peer social participation *cooperative play*, in which children orient toward a common goal by negotiating plans, roles, and divisions of labor.

Recent evidence indicates that intersubjectivity among peer partners increases substantially during the preschool years, as the amount of time children devote to sociodramatic play rises. Between 3 and 4-½ years, children engage in more extensions and affirmations of their partners' messages and fewer disagreements, assertions of their own opinions, and irrelevant statements during play (Göncü 1993). Interestingly, preschoolers have much more difficulty establishing a cooperative, shared framework in "closed-end" problem solving, in which they must orient toward a single correct solution to a task (Tudge & Rogoff 1987). Here again is an example of how children's competence during play is advanced compared to other contexts. By middle childhood, the social skills mastered during sociodramatic activities generalize to nonplay activities.

When we look at the features of harmonious child-child play, the relevance of warm, responsive adult communication for encouraging such play becomes even clearer. Even after sociodramatic play is well underway and adults have reduced their play involvement, teachers need to guide children toward effective relations with agemates. Observational evidence indicates that teachers rarely mediate peer interaction except when

---

For teachers who have always made sure that play is a central feature of the early childhood curriculum, Vygotsky's theory offers yet another justification for play's prominent place in programs for young children.

---

intense disagreements arise that threaten classroom order or children's safety. When teachers do step in, they almost always use directive strategies, in which they tell children what to do or say (e.g., "Ask Daniel if you can have the fire truck next") or solve the problem for them (e.g., "Jessica was playing with that toy first, so you can have a turn after her") (File 1993, p. 352).

A Vygotskian-based approach to facilitating peer interaction requires that teachers tailor their intervention to children's current capacities and use techniques that help children regulate their own behavior. To implement intervention in this way, teachers must acquire detailed knowledge of individual children's social skills—the type of information teachers typically gather only for the cognitive domain. When intervening, they need to use a range of teaching strategies because (like

cognitive development) the support that is appropriate for scaffolding social development varies from child to child and changes with age. At times the adult might model a skill or give the child examples of strategies (e.g., "You could tell Paul, 'I want a turn'"). At other times, she might ask the child to engage in problem solving ("What could you do if you want a turn?") (File 1993, p. 356). In each instance, the teacher selects a level of support that best matches the child's abilities and momentary needs and then pulls back as the child acquires new social skills.

Vygotsky's ideas are stimulating a host of new ways to educate young children that emphasize opportunities for discussion and joint problem solving.

Children can be socialized into sociodramatic play by a variety of expert partners. In a recent comparison of the make-believe play of American and Mexican siblings, Farver (1993) found that American 3-½- to 7-year-olds tended to rely on intrusive tactics; they more often instructed, directed, and rejected their younger siblings' contributions. In contrast, Mexican children used more behaviors that gently facilitated—invitations to join, comments on the younger child's actions, suggestions, and positive affect. In this respect, Mexican older siblings were similar to American mothers in their scaffolding of play, a skill that appeared to be fostered by the Mexican culture's assignment of caregiving responsibilities to older brothers and sisters.

These findings suggest that multi-age groupings in early childhood programs offer additional opportunities to promote make-believe and that older siblings from ethnic-minority families may be particularly adept at such scaffolding—indeed, they may be as capable as adults! Because of their limited experience with the caregiving role and their more conflictual relationships with siblings, children from ethnic-majority families may need more assistance in learning how to play effectively with younger peers. In classrooms with a multicultural mix of children, children of ethnic minorities who are skilled at scaffolding can serve as models and scaffolders for agemates, showing them how to engage young children in pretense.

Conclusion

The vast literature on children's play reveals that its contributions to child development can be looked at from diverse vantage points. Psychoanalytic theorists have highlighted the emotionally integrative function of pretense, pointing out that anxiety-provoking events—such as a visit to the doctor's office or discipline by a parent—are likely to be revisited in the young child's play but with roles reversed so that the child is in command and compensates for unpleasant experiences in real life. Piaget underscored the opportunities that make-believe affords for exercising symbolic schemes. And all theorists recognize that pretense permits children to become familiar with social role possibilities in their culture, providing important insights into the link between self and wider society.

Vygotsky's special emphasis on the imaginative and rule-based nature of play adds an additional perspective to the viewpoints just mentioned—one that highlights the critical role of make-believe in developing reflective thought as well as self-regulatory and socially cooperative behavior. For teachers who have always made sure that play is a central feature of the early childhood curriculum, Vygotsky's theory offers yet another justification for play's prominent place in programs for young children. For other teachers whose concern with academic progress has led them to neglect play, Vygotsky's theory provides a convincing argument for change—a powerful account of why pretense is the ultimate activity for nurturing early childhood capacities that are crucial for academic as well as later-life success.

References

Berk, L.E. 1992. Children's private speech: An overview of theory and the status of research. In *Private speech: From social interaction to self-regulation*, eds. R.M. Diaz, & L.E. Berk. 17–53. Hillsdale, NJ: Erlbaum.

Berk, L.E. 1993. *Infants, children, and adolescents*. Boston: Allyn & Bacon.

Bretherton, I., B. O'Connell, C. Shore, & E. Bates. 1984. The effect of contextual variation on symbolic play: Development from 20 to 28 months. In *Symbolic play and the development of social understanding*, ed. I. Bretherton. 271–98. New York: Academic.

Burns, S.M., & C.J. Brainerd. 1979. Effects of constructive and dramatic play on perspective taking in very young children. *Developmental Psychology* 15: 512–21.

Connolly, J.A., & A.B. Doyle. 1984. Relations of social fantasy play to social competence in preschoolers. *Developmental Psychology* 20: 797–806.

Connolly, J.A., A.B. Doyle, & E. Reznick. 1988. Social pretend play and social interaction in preschoolers. *Journal of Applied Developmental Psychology* 9: 301–13.

Corrigan, R. 1987. A developmental sequence of actor-object pretend play in young children. *Merrill-Palmer Quarterly* 33: 87–106.

Dansky, J.L. 1980. Make-believe: A mediator of the relationship between play and associative fluency. *Child Development* 51: 576–79.

Dias, M.G., & P.L. Harris. 1988. The effect of make-believe play on deductive reasoning. *British Journal of Developmental Psychology* 6: 207–21.

Dias, M.G., & P.L. Harris. 1990. The influence of the imagination on reasoning by young children. *British Journal of Developmental Psychology* 8: 305–18.

Dunn, J., & N. Dale. 1984. I a daddy: 2-year-olds' collaboration in joint pretend with sibling and with mother. In *Symbolic play*, ed. I. Bretherton. 131–58. New York: Academic Press.

Dunn, J., & C. Wooding. 1977. Play in the home and its implications for learning. In *Biology of play*, eds. B. Tizard, & D. Harvey. 45–58. London: Heinemann.

El'konin, D. 1966. Symbolics and its functions in the play of children. *Soviet Education* 8: 35–41.

Ervin-Tripp, S. 1991. Play in language development. In *Play and the social context of development in early care and education*, eds. B. Scales, M. Almy, A. Nicolopoulou, & S. Ervin-Tripp. 84–97. New York: Teachers College Press.

Farver, J.M. 1993. Cultural differences in scaffolding pretend play: A comparison of American and Mexican mother–child and sibling–child pairs. In *Parent-child play*, ed. K. MacDonald. 349–66. Albany, NY: State University of New York Press.

Fein, G. 1981. Pretend play: An integrative review. *Child Development* 52: 1095–118.

Fiese, B. 1990. Playful relationships: A contextual analysis of mother-toddler interaction and symbolic play. *Child Development* 61: 1648–56.

File, N. 1993. The teacher as guide of children's competence with peers. *Child & Youth Care Forum* 22: 351–60.

Forman, E.A. 1987. Learning through peer interaction: A Vygotskian perspective. *Genetic Epistemologist* 15: 6–15.

Forman, E.A., N. Minick, & C.A. Stone. 1993. *Contexts for learning*. New York: Oxford University Press.

Garvey, C. 1990. *Play*. Cambridge, MA: Harvard University Press.

Göncü, A. 1993. Development of intersubjectivity in the dyadic play of preschoolers. *Early Childhood Research Quarterly* 8: 99–116.

Gralinski, J.H., & C.B. Kopp. 1993. Everyday rules for behavior: Mothers' requests to young children. *Developmental Psychology* 29: 573–84.

Haight, W.L., & P.J. Miller. 1993. *Pretending at home: Early development in a sociocultural context*. Albany, NY: State University of New York Press.

Kavanaugh, R.D., S. Whittington, & M.J. Cerbone. 1983. Mothers' use of fantasy in speech to young children. *Journal of Child Language* 10: 45–55.

Lucariello, J. 1987. Spinning fantasy: Themes, structure, and the knowledge base. *Child Development* 58: 434–42.

Miller, P., & C. Garvey. 1984. Mother-baby role play: Its origins in social support. In *Symbolic play*, ed. I. Bretherton. 101–30. New York: Academic.

Have You Read These Articles?

Blau, R., A. Zavitkovsky, & D. Zavitkovsky. 1989. Play Is . . . . *Young Children* 45 (1): 30–31.

Chenfeld, M.B. 1991. "Wanna play?" *Young Children* 46 (6): 4–6.

Elkind, D. 1988. From our president. Play. *Young Children* 43 (5): 2.

Myhre, S.M. 1993. Enhancing your dramatic-play area through the use of prop boxes. *Young Children* 48 (5): 6–11.

Nourot, P.M., & J.L. Van Hoorn. 1991. Research in review. Symbolic play in preschool and primary settings. *Young Children* 46 (6): 40–50.

Trawick-Smith, J. 1988. "Let's say you're the baby, OK?" Play leadership and following behavior of young children. *Young Children* 43 (5): 51–59.

You may obtain copies of these or any other *Young Children* articles.

- For articles from the past 5 years, contact the Institute for Scientific Information, 3501 Market St., Philadelphia, PA 19104; phone 215-386-0100; fax 215-386-6362.
- For articles more than 5 years old, send $5, your address, and the title of the article to NAEYC's Editorial Department.

Moll, L.C. 1990. *Vygotsky and education.* New York: Cambridge University Press.

Newman, L.S. 1990. Intentional versus unintentional memory in young children: Remembering versus playing. *Journal of Experimental Child Psychology* 50: 243–58.

Nicolopoulou, A. 1991. Play, cognitive development, and the social world. In *Play and the social context of development in early care and education,* eds. B. Scales, M. Almy, A. Nicolopoulou, & S. Ervin-Tripp. 129–42. New York: Teachers College Press.

O'Connell, B., & I. Bretherton. 1984. Toddler's play alone and with mother: The role of maternal guidance. In *Symbolic play,* ed. I. Bretherton. 337–68. New York: Academic.

O'Reilly, A.W., & M.H. Bornstein. 1993. Caregiver–child interaction in play. In *New directions for child development,* eds. M.H. Bornstein, & A.W. O'Reilly. 55–66. San Francisco: Jossey-Bass.

Parten, M. 1932. Social participation among preschool children. *Journal of Abnormal and Social Psychology* 27: 243–69.

Pellegrini, A.D., & L. Galda. 1982. The effects of thematic-fantasy play training on the development of children's story comprehension. *American Educational Research Journal* 19: 443–52.

Pepler, D.J., & H.S. Ross. 1981. The effect of play on convergent and divergent problem solving. *Child Development* 52: 1202–10.

Piaget, J. [1945] 1951. *Play, dreams, and imitation in childhood.* New York: Norton.

Saltz, E., D. Dixon, & J. Johnson. 1977. Training disadvantaged preschoolers on various fantasy activities: Effects on cognitive functioning and impulse control. *Child Development* 46: 367–80.

Slade, A. 1987. A longitudinal study of maternal involvement and symbolic play during the toddler period. *Child Development* 58: 367–75.

Smolucha, F. 1992. Social origins of private speech in pretend play. In *Private speech: From social interaction to self-regulation,* eds. R.M. Diaz, & L.E. Berk. 123–41. Hillsdale, NJ: Erlbaum.

Tamis-LeMonda, C.S., & M.H. Bornstein. 1991. Individual variation, correspondence, stability, and change in mother and toddler play. *Infant Behavior and Development* 14: 143–62.

Tudge, J.R.H. 1992. Processes and consequences of peer collaboration: A Vygotskian analysis. *Child Development* 63: 1364–79.

Tudge, J.R.H., & B. Rogoff. 1987. Peer influences on cognitive development: Piagetian and Vygotskian perspectives. In *Interaction in human development,* eds. M.H. Bornstein, & J.S. Bruner. 17–40. Hillsdale, NJ: Erlbaum.

Vygotsky, L.S. [1933] 1978. The role of play in development. In *Mind in society,* eds. M. Cole, V. John-Steiner, S. Scribner, & E. Souberman. 92–104. Cambridge, MA: Harvard University Press.

Vygotsky, L.S. [1934] 1987. Thinking and speech. In *The collected works of L.S. Vygotsky: Vol. 1. Problems of general psychology,* eds. R. Rieber & A.S. Carton, trans. N. Minick. 37–285. New York: Plenum.

Vygotsky, L.S. [1930] 1990. Imagination and creativity in childhood. *Soviet Psychology* 28: 84–96.

Wertsch, J.W. 1991. A sociocultural approach to socially shared cognition. In *Perspectives on socially shared cognition,* eds. L.B. Resnick, J. M. Levine, & S.D. Teasley. 85–100. Washington, D.C: American Psychological Association.

Wood, D.J. 1989. Social interaction as tutoring. In *Interaction in human development,* eds. M.H. Bornstein, & J.S. Bruner. 59–80. Hillsdale, NJ: Erlbaum.

Wood, D.J., & D. Middleton. 1975. A study of assisted problem solving. *British Journal of Psychology* 66: 181–91.

Zukow, P.G. 1986. The relationship between interaction with the caregiver and the emergence of play activities during the one-word period. *British Journal of Developmental Psychology* 4: 223–34.

52

Parental Presence during Pediatric Invasive Procedures

Latasha M. Pruitt, RN, BSN, CPN, Arlene Johnson, PhD, RN, CPNP, J. Carol Elliott, PhD, APRN, BC, & Kevin Polley, MD

ABSTRACT

Parental presence during pediatric invasive procedures is becoming more common, yet it remains a controversial issue related to providing family-centered care. A literature review related to this important issue was performed. Credible arguments supporting parental presence during invasive procedures as well as opposing arguments were discussed. One must consider both views in order to create a nonbiased analysis of the issue. Parental presence during invasive procedures raises critical debates related to maintaining or altering the continuum of holistic patient care. Additional research would provide an objective approach to the problem. Development of an evidence-based protocol would provide a framework for this issue. J Pediatr Health Care. (2008) 22, 120-127.

Latasha M. Pruitt is MSN Nursing Student, Clemson University, Clemson, SC.

Arlene Johnson is Assistant Professor, Clemson University School of Nursing, Clemson, SC.

J. Carol Elliott is Assistant Professor, Clemson University School of Nursing, Clemson, SC.

Kevin Polley is Associate Medical Director, Children's Emergency Center, Greenville Hospital System Children's Hospital, Greenville, SC.

Correspondence: Latasha Pruitt, 1328 Memorial Drive Extension, Greer, SC 29651; e-mail: Latashajones1@juno.com.

0891-5245/$34.00

doi:10.1016/j.pedhc.2007.04.008

Parental presence during pediatric invasive procedures is an important issue in family-centered care. Health care professionals are hesitant to allow parental presence during pediatric invasive procedures for a variety of reasons, ranging from the tradition of not doing so to the assumption that the parent truly will hinder the care process. The resistance to parental presence has been challenged by the parents, as consumers of health care who are taking on a more proactive role in their children's health care. This revolution of change has created manifestations of insecurity and uneasiness among pediatric health care providers, creating a need for evidence-based research to validate such processes.

A comprehensive literature review was necessary to gather evidence related to family presence during pediatric invasive procedures and to provide an unbiased analysis of the issue. The literature review provides an overview of the current knowledge base related to parental presence during pediatric invasive procedures, identification of gaps in knowledge, the role of the advanced practice pediatric nurse, and indications for future research that would be imperative to ensure a continuum of holistic health care for the pediatric population.

Hospitalized children experience threatening events that provoke responses that are either adaptive or ineffective. Children are more likely to exhibit adaptive rather than ineffective responses to stress if the people surrounding them are calm and supportive. Therefore, having a trusted family member present to provide protection, comfort, guidance, and encouragement may help alleviate fear and anxiety (Romino, Keatley, Secrest, & Good, 2005). Riehl and Roy (1980) wrote, "Nursing is seen as a unique profession in that it is concerned with all of the variables

Family-centered care is one of the basic principles of pediatric nursing, yet many health care professionals remain hesitant to allow for parental presence during times when the family support system is most needed— during anxiety-provoking times instigated by invasive procedures.

affecting an individual's response to stressors" (p. 119). Family-centered care is one of the basic principles of pediatric nursing, yet many health care professionals remain hesitant to allow for parental presence during times when the family support system is most needed—during anxiety-provoking times instigated by invasive procedures. As early as 1993, the Emergency Nurses Association (ENA) responded to the demands of family members to allow them to be present during their child's resuscitation and invasive procedures (ENA, 2005). Consumerism has been a major driving force behind the movement supporting family presence (Halm, 2005). Recent evidence has indicated that families want to be present during invasive procedures and, if given the choice, would choose to do so again. The concept of parents being present is controversial and prompts much debate from both sides of the issue (Halm).

Pediatric patients often are unable to maintain their own independence, and thus they are reliant on the family for that support. When considering this issue, several important questions arise. Should family members be allowed, or even encouraged, to stay with the child during an invasive procedure? Does the family's presence decrease the anxiety that the child experiences? Does the family's presence affect the quality of care rendered by the

health care team? All these questions need to be answered when considering the issue of parental presence during pediatric procedures.

Family-centered care acknowledges the role of the family in the health and well being of a child, because it is characterized by collaboration among the patient, family, and health care professionals and recognizes that the family is a constant in the patient's life (Eckle, 2001; Eckle & MacLean, 2001). Family-centered care provides an opportunity for pediatric patients to benefit from the presence of their social support system during very stressful situations, such as invasive and many times painful procedures. The core principles of family-centered care include treating patients and families with dignity; respect; open communication; patient and family participation in care; and collaboration in the delivery of care (Eckle; Eckle & MacLean).

Caregivers usually are the primary source of support to their children. Caregivers are defined as whoever provides continued care to the child and to whom the child

has attached as a social support figure. Invasive procedures include intravenous access, laceration repair, lumbar puncture, conscious sedation, and resuscitation efforts. Despite a growing support of family presence, many health care professionals continue to resist adopting the practice (Mason, 2003). Family presence allows the development of a strong bond between patients' family members and the health care staff (Meyers et al., 2000). The formation of this bond results in a continuum of holistic care for the patient. The child is usually under the family's constant care; therefore, incorporating the family into the plan of care for the child is essential to the child's well being.

LITERATURE REVIEW

A variety of research studies were compared in the review of the literature. Each article provided unique information related to the discussion of parental presence during pediatric invasive procedures. A comparison of the studies is noted in the Table 1. The review of the literature related to parental presence during pediatric invasive procedures identified several important issues. First, family members often were not given the option to stay with their child during an invasive procedure. They might not have been given the option for a variety of reasons, such as the assumption that the event may have been too traumatic for the family, care may have been negatively influenced, a family member may have been too emotionally affected by the event, the family's presence would create added

Recent evidence has indicated that families want to be present during invasive procedures and, if given the choice, would choose to do so again.

stress for the health care staff, and the increased chance of liability (ENA, 2005). The American Academy of Pediatrics and the American College of Emergency Physicians (2006) support the recognition of the patient and family as primary decision makers in their medical care and support encouragement of family presence.

Another issue that was revealed was the fact that as the invasiveness of the pediatric procedures increases, the belief of the physicians and nurses that the family should be present decreases (Beckman et al., 2002). One study concluded that pediatricians with more contact with seriously ill children are more likely to support parental presence and that those who witnessed parental presence during resuscitation were more likely to allow parental presence in future resuscitation efforts (O'Brien, Creamer, Hill, & Welham, 2002). Manifestations of anxiety in children can be detrimental, such as during anesthesia induction, in which this type of response can result in a problematic anesthesia induction. It is essential for the advanced practice nurse to be able to identify effective measures to decrease this anxiety, including the possibility of having a parent present for the induction of anesthesia (Romino et al., 2005). There also was a debate about whether families' staying with the patient during invasive procedures interfered with the delivery of care. It was concluded that family members staying with their child during invasive procedures did not disrupt care (Sacchetti, Paston, & Carraccio, 2003). Even though health care professionals often were confronted with the request for a family member to be present during a child's invasive procedure, often there was no written policy that provides for parental presence at the health care facility (MacLean et al., 2003). The findings of a study conducted by Mangurten and colleagues (2006) indicated

that the development of a family presence protocol in the emergency department setting was effective in facilitating uninterrupted patient care.

Several studies recommended family presence during invasive procedures, while others supported the alternative view. There was an argument that there is not enough research to support parental presence, yet there is not sufficient research to support the proposal of keeping the family out of the room during these procedures (Mason, 2003). As reported by Mason, some have argued that the family's presence during procedures may increase the probability of a family filing legal action against the institution, even though the opposite has been found to be true. Mason also reported that the presence of the family during invasive procedures creates a bond be-, tween the family and the health care team, which makes the possibility of a lawsuit less likely. "No evidence supports the notion that litigation occurs as a result of family presence during resuscitation" (Halm, 2005, p. 506). Parental presence also allows family members to see that the health care staff did everything they could to help the patient (Meyers et al., 2000). Health care providers continue to debate the issue of parental presence. A lack of compelling evidence exists to determine if the family's presence during invasive procedures affects the clinical outcome. In addition, not enough research supports the decision that this practice should be discontinued until such research is compiled (Mason).

A concern about the psychosocial impact of presence on the family before, during, and after the experience also was a concern. Halm (2005) proposed that concerns that having a patient's family present during resuscitation would be disruptive and traumatic for the families were unsubstantiated. Melnyk et al. (2004) evaluated the effects of a preventive educational-behavioral intervention program called Creat-

ing Opportunities for Parent Empowerment (COPE), in which it was concluded that COPE mothers reported significant less stress and were more involved in their child's physical and emotional care while on the pediatric unit. Children are considered the "silent consumers of health care" (Carter, 1998, p. 57). Therefore, one also must consider the ethical dilemmas that arise because their views often are obtained by proxy, via adult accounts such as those of teachers and parents (Coyne, 1998). The ENA provided recommendations including maintaining that the family's presence is by desire, not by expectation, screening the family members' readiness for presence, continued availability of support to the family, and continuing to support the family should they choose not to be present (ENA, 2005). Such recommendations also might include preparing and debriefing the family in relation to their presence during invasive care.

A limited amount of information regarding the presence of family during invasive procedures exists, although there is a positive response when families are polled. Boie, Moore, Brummett, and Nelson (1999) concluded that most parents surveyed wanted to be present during invasive procedures performed on their children; yet, as the invasiveness of the procedure increased, the desire of the parent to be present also decreased. Piira, Sugiura, Champion, Donnelly, and Cole (2005) wrote that there was no evidence of increased complications or increased anxiety among the staff for situations in which parents were present, compared with the times when parents were not present. One study indicated that as a child's distress increased, the parent(s) took on an active role to redirect support to the child and that the nurse's role in advocating parent involvement during procedures resulted in a decrease in distress and discomfort for the child (Naber, Halstead, Broome, & Rehwaldt, 1995). Most children

TABLE 1. Comparison of referenced articles

Author(s)/year	Design/instrument	Sample size	Key findings
AAP and the American College of Emergency Physicians (2006)	Policy statement	None	Support family presence during procedures in the ED
American Association of Critical Care Nurses (2005)	Evidence-based informative memorandum	None	Benefits of family presence, need for written policies and educational programs
Beckman et al. (2002)	Survey of physicians and nurses regarding attitude related to parental presence in the ED; anonymous written survey with 6 clinical scenarios	10 EDs in the United States routinely caring for children	Majority surveyed believed parents should be present; as invasiveness increased, fewer physicians and nurses believed parents should be present
Boie et al. (1999)	Large descriptive survey regarding parental views related to presence during invasive procedures; written survey with 5 pediatric scenarios	400 parents in ED waiting areas	Most parents want to be present and desire to help make the decision related to their family's care
Eckle & MacLean (2001)	Validation study of an instrument used to assess family-centered care in the ED; self-assessment inventory of family-centered practice in the pediatric ED	9 EDs (5 pediatric, 4 adult) after published in ENA requesting participation	Tool was easy to use, useful, and helpful; there was slight repetition; there was also a need to test on larger sample size
Eichhorn et al. (2001)	Qualitative design; questioned patient experiences related to family presence using a family presence patient interview guide	9 patients (8 related to presence during invasive procedures and 1 during resuscitation	Themes: comfort, personhood, "right"; it was noted that there was an increase in benefit and a decrease in risk
ENA (2001)	Informative position statement with evidence/rationale	None	ENA supports option for family presence; need collaborative guidelines, written policies, educational programs, and continued research
Halm (2005)	Quantitative vs. qualitative using subgroups and charts; review of literature related to family presence during resuscitation	28 articles with specific criteria	Increase in limitations and gaps in knowledge
MacLean et al. (2003)	Descriptive survey that questioned attitude of ED/critical care nurses related to family presence; 30-item survey: mailed to random sample of 1500-member nursing organization; zero reliability testing of instrument; content validity present	984 nurses (46% ED nurses and 48% critical care nurses with a response rate of 33%)	5% with written policy, split results for preference of written policy, one third have taken family to bedside, one fourth would do again. Recommend written policies
Mangurten et al. (2006)	Survey regarding family presence protocol in the ED	64 family presence events; 92 providers and 22 parents completed the survey	Positive effect of pediatric ED family presence protocol in facilitating uninterrupted patient care
Mason (2003)	Evidence versus tradition editorial regarding parental presence	None	Suggests following research and development of written policies
Melnyk et al. (2004)	A randomized, controlled trial with follow-up assessments 1, 3, 6, and 12 months after hospitalization	163 mothers and 99 children	COPE mothers reported significantly less parental stress and participated more in their children's physical and emotional care on the pediatric unit compared with control mothers, as rated by nurses who were blinded with respect to study group
Meyers et al. (2000)	Descriptive survey that used a Likert scale with qualitative questions added to investigate attitudes of families/staff related to family presence	39 family members and 96 health care providers	Family presence preferred; written procedures needed

56

TABLE 1. Continued.

Author(s)/year	Design/instrument	Sample size	Key findings
Naber et al. (1995)	Qualitative, ethological observations used to observe children/caregiver interaction during painful procedures; videotaped observation with follow-up analysis	17 children aged 4-18 years; 44 painful procedures	As pain increased, child-centered interaction increased and parents became actively involved in verbal support and pain management techniques for child
O'Brien et al. (2002)	10-question survey was distributed to attendees of the AAP annual Pediatric Seminar meeting	245 respondents	65% indicated that they would not allow parental presence; although in the minority, one third of the pediatricians surveyed are comfortable allowing parental presence during cardiopulmonary resuscitation
Piira et al. (2005)	Comprehensive literature search that provided a systematic review regarding parental presence	28 studies (1256 children with parents and 1025 children without parents)	Mixed findings regarding effect of parental presence on child's distress; no increase in complications for health professionals
Robinson et al. (1998)	Pilot study with control/variable groups and follow-up survey; questioned relatives view on family presence and psychological effects; questionnaire related to decision to stay/absent and 5 psychological issues	25 patients with 1 family member each; 13 in the witnessed group and 12 in the control group	Zero reported adverse effects of staying, all satisfied with choice to stay; positive benefits in allowing family to stay, therefore the trial was stopped
Romino et al. (2005)	Literature review	Unknown sample size	Reviews the literature regarding parental presence and pediatric anesthesia and the effect on children and parents; suggestions for appropriate parent preparation techniques are given
Sacchetti et al. (2003)	Prospective observational study used to determine whether families that stay with the child during procedure(s) interfere with delivery of care; 6 categories: stood quietly, asked questions, soothed patient, helped restrain, interfered w/care, and other	54 family members of 37 patients	71 behaviors recorded: 31% soothed, 30% asked questions, 16% helped restrain, 7% interfered w/care (minor), 15% other

AAP, American Academy of Pediatrics; COPE, Creating Opportunities for Parent Empowerment; ED, emergency department; ENA, Emergency Nurses Association.

wanted their parent to be present during procedures because the children believed their parent's presence was the most beneficial intervention in controlling their pain (American Association of Critical Care Nurses [AACN], 2006). Patients also have indicated that having their family present during such procedures provided them comfort, increased their coping capacity and pain control, maintained their bond, and served as a reminder to the health care staff that the patient was a person with a family who deserved dignity and respect (Eichhorn et al., 2001; Robinson, MacKenzie-Ross, Campbell-Hewson, Egleston, & Prevost, 1998). One

study performed revealed findings that supported the increased use of family presence and showed that most physicians thought family presence was helpful to families (Gold, Gorenflo, Schwenk, & Bratton, 2006).

GAPS IN KNOWLEDGE

The review of the literature related to parental presence during invasive procedures revealed that a multitude of variables can be present in a pediatric setting, including: (a) How does one determine the anxiety level of a child who cannot speak? (b) Is there a reliable study technique available to test parental presence? (c) What is the ef-

fect of parental presence on the clinical results as opposed to lack of presence? and (d) Are the opposing views based on evidence or tradition? Often these children are too sick to have a "voice," making them reliant on their parents' voice. Although the patient's "voice" is mentioned several times in the literature, Halm (2005) proposed that the largest gap in the literature is the lack of studies focusing on the patient's "voice." The gaps that were identified in the literature review could be studied through future research.

DISCUSSION

Several issues related to the family's presence during invasive proce-

57

dures were identified in the review of the literature. Health care facilities' policies regarding parental presence during invasive procedures are recommended (MacLean et al., 2003). "Although a third of nurses take patients' families to the bedside during resuscitation, only five percent of these nurses work in a unit with a family presence policy" (Halm, 2005, p. 506). Sacchetti et al. (2003) found that family members staying during an invasive procedure did not disrupt patient care. Mason (2003) found that nurses' comments made powerful statements that mimic the 1990s trend in support of patient-centered and family-centered care. Piira et al. (2005) proposed that it seems appropriate that health care professionals offer parents the opportunity to be present during their child's procedure. All patient care units should have written documentation for presenting the option of family presence during CPR and invasive procedures (AACN, 2006). Educational programs need to be in place for health care staff to include the benefits of the family's presence for the patient and family, criteria for assessing the family, the role of the individual assigned as the family support person, family support methods, and contraindications for family presence (AACN).

Proficiency standards to ensure patient, family, and staff safety, as well as compliance checks, should be utilized. Improvement techniques could include (a) developing a task force to brainstorm compliance ideas, (b) re-education of staff, falling back on the evidence-based practice front, (c) incorporation of family-centered care tactics into orientation programs, (d) development of communication strategies as reminders/alerts, and (e) development of documentation standards (AACN, 2006). The ENA supports giving the family an option to stay during invasive procedures and resuscitation because the patient and family members have the most interest in-

vested in the outcomes. The ENA (2005) also encouraged additional research related to the presence of the family during invasive procedures and resuscitation and the impact on the family, patient, and health care team.

One of the strengths of the studies reviewed was that the issue of parental presence during invasive procedures was approached from a variety of viewpoints, including the (a) patient perspective, (b) family perspective, and (c) health care professionals' perspectives. The varying points of view created an unbiased depiction of the issue. It was noted that there is a lack of objective data, which could be remedied through additional research on this very important topic. Another weakness identified was the small population samples

that were used in each study. One also must take into consideration the variables present during any given situation that may or may not be controllable, including ethnicity, student presence, cultural issues, and location.

RECOMMENDATIONS

The majority of the pediatric population cannot communicate effectively for themselves, which creates a stressful situation for them. Pediatric clients often are unable to function independently. The client in pediatric care includes the patient and the family because the patient often is incapable of assuming full responsibility for his or her own care.

As stated previously, one of the major hindrances to a framework of family-centered care is the lack

of policies that would act as a guide for the staff to follow when confronted with the issue of family presence during an invasive procedure. Several different formats could be used when developing a protocol, but the development of such a model should be a collaborative effort among the health care team members. It should reflect the needs and issues of the specific institution and its origin. Numerous variables must be considered when developing a family-centered protocol that provides for parental presence during invasive procedures. Implementing a uniform plan intended for universal use would not be feasible.

A recommendation using the universal nursing care planning process of assessment, plan, implementation, and evaluation was described by Le-

The lack of evidence to support parental presence during invasive procedures hinders resolution of this very important issue.

Roy et al. (2003). The AHA guidelines are directed toward children having cardiac procedures, but the basic format could be applied to most pediatric settings and serves as an appropriate framework to begin protocol development. The assessment includes the child, family, and institution. The child is assessed for developmental stage, temperament and coping style, and previous health care experiences. The family is assessed according to family composition/roles, support networks, family stressors, parental coping, and knowledge of support techniques for the child. The assessment of the institution includes available resources, protocols, and policies for the specific procedure being performed. The plan includes who, what, when, where, and other. "Who" describes the personnel who are responsible for care, such as advanced practice nurse, social worker, and parents. "What" describes the educational needs/methods being utilized. "When" describes the optimal time to present the information related to the specific procedure being performed. "Where" describes the location for the intervention. "Other" describes other variables such as language, culture, and special needs children. The implementation includes a plan to enhance the positive influence of having the family present during invasive procedures. The evaluation segment is one of the most important areas of the protocol because it allows for quality improvement, which is essential to providing effective and consistent family-centered care. The expected outcomes include: reduced child and parent anxiety, cooperation of child and parent during procedure, enhanced post-procedure recovery, positive short-term and long-term adjustments, increased sense of self-control, and enhanced trust (LeRoy et al.). All of these outcomes are directed toward the child and parent and do not reflect the inclusion of the health care team.

IMPLICATIONS FOR THE ADVANCED PRACTICE NURSE

The lack of evidence to support parental presence during invasive procedures hinders resolution of this very important issue. The traditional view prevails when there is a lack of evidence-based information on the development and implementation of a protocol for parental presence during pediatric invasive procedures. Interventions could include written policies regarding family presence during invasive procedures, staff educational programs, proficiency standards, and compliance checks. An advanced practice nurse could serve as the coordinator for quality checks on such a process. It is imperative that, once the protocol is implemented, there is utilization of a systematic assessment and review process, which would ensure that the protocol would continue to be beneficial to

patients and their families. Advanced practice nurses could conduct additional research on the topic of parental presence during pediatric invasive procedures. The family is an integral part of the care process in the pediatric setting. Therefore, the family's wishes should be taken into consideration when developing a plan of care for the child. Providing families with the option to be present during care opens the door to communication and collaboration, thereby facilitating a holistic plan of care.

As revealed in this review of the literature, a significant debate surrounding the issue of parental presence during pediatric invasive procedures continues. The family unit deserves and expects respect from the health care arena. The field of health care is changing to incorporate family-centered care; yet some institutions are reluctant to implement family-centered policies and procedures. Further research related to parental presence during pediatric invasive procedures is needed to better incorporate the family into the plan of care and to promote positive patient outcomes.

REFERENCES

American Academy of Pediatrics, Committee on Pediatric Emergency Medicine, American College of Emergency Physicians and Pediatric Emergency Medicine Committee. (2006). Patient and family centered care and the role of the emergency physician providing care to a child in the emergency department. *Pediatrics, 118,* 2242-2244.

American Association of Critical Care Nurses. (2006). *Practice alert: Family presence during CPR and invasive procedures.* Retrieved September 23, 2005, from http://www.aacn.org.

Beckman, A., Sloan, B., Moore, G., Cordell, W., Brizendine, E., Boie, E., et al. (2002). Should parents be present during emergency department procedures on children, and who should make that decision? A survey of emergency physician and nurse attitudes. *Academic Emergency Medicine, 9,* 154-158.

Boie, E., Moore, G., Brummett, C., & Nelson, D. (1999). Do parents want to be present during invasive procedures performed on their children in the emergency department? A survey of 400

parents. *Annals of Emergency Medicine, 34,* 70-74.

Carter, B. (1998). Silent consumers of health care. *Journal of Child Health Care, 2,* 57.

Coyne, I. T. (1998). Researching children: Some methodological and ethical considerations. *Journal of Clinical Nursing, 7,* 409-416.

Eckle, N. (2001). *Presenting the option of family presence* (2nd ed.). Des Plaines, IL: Emergency Nurses Association.

Eckle, N., & MacLean, S. (2001). Assessment of the family-centered care for pediatric patients in the emergency department. *Journal of Emergency Nursing, 27,* 238-245.

Eichhorn, D. J., Meyers, T. A., Guzzetta, C. E., Clark, A. P., Klein, J. D., Taliaferro, E., et al. (2001). Family presence during invasive procedures and resuscitation: Hearing the voice of the patient. *American Journal of Nursing, 101,* 26-33.

Emergency Nurses Association. (2005). *Family presence at the bedside during invasive procedures and resuscitation.* Retrieved May 30, 2006, from http://www.ena.org.

Gold, K. J., Gorenflo, D. W., Schwenk, T. L., & Bratton, S. L. (2006). Physician experience with family presence during cardiopulmonary resuscitation in children. *Pediatric Critical Care Medicine, 7,* 428-433.

Halm, M. A. (2005). Family presence during resuscitation: A critical review of the literature. *American Journal of Critical Care, 14,* 494-511.

LeRoy, S., Elixson, M., O'Brien, P., Tong, E., Turpin, S., & Uzark, K. (2003). AHA Scientific Statement: Recommendations for preparing children and adolescents for invasive cardiac procedures: A statement from the American Heart Association Pediatric Nursing Subcommittee of the Council on Cardiovascular Nursing in collaboration with the Council on Cardiovascular Diseases of the Young. *Circulation, 108,* 2550-2564.

MacLean, S., Guzzetta, C., White, C., Fontaine, D., Eichhorn, D., Meyers, T., et al. (2003). Family presence during cardiopulmonary resuscitation and invasive procedure: Practices of critical care and emergency nurses. *American Journal of Critical Care, 12,* 246-257.

Mangurten, J., Scott, S. H., Guzzetta, C. E., Clark, A. P., Vinson, L., Sperry, J., et al. (2006). Effects of family presence during resuscitation and invasive procedures in a pediatric emergency department. *Journal of Emergency Nursing, 32,* 225-233.

Mason, D. J. (2003). Guest editorial. Family presence: Evidence versus tradition. *American Journal of Critical Care, 12,* 190-192.

Meyers, T. A., Eichhorn, D. J., Guzzetta, C. E., Clark, A. P., Klein, J. D., Taliaferro, E., et al. (2000). Family presence during invasive procedures and resuscitation: The experience of family members, nurses, and physicians. *American Journal of Nursing, 100,* 32-42.

Melnyk, B. M., Alpert-Gillis, L., Feinstein, N. F., Crean, H. F., Johnson, J., Fairbanks, E., et al. (2004). Creating opportunities for parent empowerment: Program effects on the mental health/coping outcomes of critically ill young children and their mothers. *Pediatrics, 113,* 597-607.

Naber, S., Halstead, L., Broome, M., & Rehwaldt, M. (1995). Communication and control: Parent, child, and health care professional interactions during painful procedures. *Issues in Comprehensive Pediatric Nursing, 18,* 79-90.

O'Brien, M. M., Creamer, K. M., Hill, E. E., & Welham, J. (2002). Tolerance of family presence during pediatric cardiopulmonary resuscitation: a snapshot of military and civilian pediatricians, nurses, and residents. *Pediatric Emergency Care, 18,* 409-413.

Piira, T., Sugiura, T., Champion, G., Donnelly, N., & Cole, A. (2005). The role of parental presence in the context of children's medical procedures: A systemic review. *Child: Care, Health and Development, 31,* 233-243.

Riehl, J. P., & Roy, C. (1980). *Conceptual models for nursing practice* (2nd ed.). New York: Appleton-Century-Crofts.

Robinson, S., MacKenzie-Ross, S., Campbell-Hewson, G., Egleston, C., Prevcost, A. (1998). Psychological effect of witnessed resuscitation on bereaved relatives. *Lancet, 352,* 614-617.

Romino, S. L., Keatley, V. M., Secrest, J., & Good, K. (2005). Parental presence during anesthesia induction in children. *Association of Operating Room Nurses, 81,* 780-792.

Sacchetti, A., Paston, C., & Carraccio, C. (2003). Family members do not disrupt care when present during invasive procedures. *Academic Emergency Medicine, 12,* 477-479.

60

Module 3:
The Hospitalized Child

APPENDIX D

STATEMENTS OF POLICY
FOR THE CARE OF CHILDREN
AND FAMILIES IN HEALTH CARE SETTINGS*

Preamble

Advancement of technology and medical science has permitted more children to live, to live longer and in most cases, to live more fully. In the process, other dangers to children's healthy development have arisen or come to light. These problems have in turn stimulated the current progress in the behavioral sciences.

Threats posed to the emotional security and development of many children and their families by serious illness, disability, disfigurement, treatment, interrupted human relationships and nonsupportive environments have been clearly demonstrated by worldwide research studies. The outcomes can range from temporary but frequently overwhelming anxiety and emotional suffering to long-standing or permanent developmental handicaps. Such interference with the fullest possible development and expression of individual potential is an unacceptable price to pay.

Closer contact with the emotional life of children, increased parent involvement and communication amongst professionals have also contributed to greater understanding as well as to improvements of care. Whereas there is still much to learn regarding the inter-relatedness of such factors as age, type of illness, length of hospitalization, critical developmental periods and vulnerability, sufficient knowledge now exists to direct action toward both minimizing and preventing such harm.

The Association for the Care of Children in Hospitals endorses the following policies:

All pediatric health care settings should:

1. have a stated philosophy of care which is specific, easily understood by, and made available to patients and families, and which applies in a coordinated manner to all disciplines and departments.

2. Assist or provide programs of prevention and restorative care which respond to emotional, social and environmental causal factors of accidents and illness.

3. Create and maintain a social and physical environment which is as welcoming, unthreatening and supportive as possible, and which fosters open communication, encourages human relationships, and invites involvement of children, their families and the community in decisions affecting their care.

4. Avoid hospitalizing children whenever possible through the development of alternatives.

5. Develop and utilize ambulatory, day and home care programs which are financially and geographically accessible.

6. Minimize the duration of unavoidable hospital stays, while recognizing discharge planning needs.

7. Provide for and encourage the presence and participation in the hospital of persons most significant to the child, to approximate supportive home patterns of interactions and routines.

8. Provide consistent, emotionally supportive nurturing care for young children during the absence of their parents.

9. Respect the unique care-taking role of parents as well as their individual responses, and provide ongoing understandable information and support which will enable them to utilize their strengths in supporting their child.

10. Provide a milieu which is responsive to the uniqueness of each child and adolescent, their ethnic and cultural backgrounds and developmental needs.

11. Provide readily accessible, well designed space, equipment and programs for the wide range of play, educational and social activities which are essential to all children and adolescents, particularly those who have been deprived of normal opportunities for development.

12. Provide child care professionals who are skilled at assessing emotional, developmental and academic needs, communicating with and fostering the involvement of patients and their families in activities appropriate to their needs.

13. Ensure that children and their parents are informed, understand and are supported prior to, during, and following experiences which are potentially distressing.

14. Carefully select all staff and volunteers according to their commitment to the foregoing policies. Those in direct contact, however limited, with children, youth, and families should be sensitive, perceptive, and compassionate. Professionals involved in more extended, intimate, and responsible positions of child care should have special training in child development, family dynamics and the unique psychological needs of children when ill and under stress.

15. Facilitate orientation, continued learning, and consultation in relation to all of the above, and provide support which recognizes the emotional demands on staff.

16. Encourage and foster the inclusion of the above educational focus in

---

*From the Association for the Care of Children in Hospitals

the basic curriculum and field experiences of the various professional and technical personnel preparing for careers in pediatric settings.

17. Support the evolvement of resources for early detection, and of attitudes and facilities for ongoing care of children with health and/or developmental problems.

18. Provide for ongoing evaluation of policies and programs by the recipients of care and staff at all levels.

19. Support and disseminate research which clarifies and pertains to the above.

20. Promote education within the community about the health and developmental needs of children.

Battling a Fear of Hospitals

"Nothing in life is to be feared. It is only to be understood."
Marie Curie

Without a doubt, the hospital can be a scary place, and it's natural to feel anxious about being hospitalized. Not only are the surroundings unfamiliar, but you may also be facing medical tests and procedures that are painful and frightening. While you're at the hospital, you'll probably see people who are very sick, which can cause you to feel worried and alone. One way to deal with hospitalization is to remember that hospitals are very supportive places where you'll be taken care of by trained people who want to help you get better. Another good way to cope with your fears is to face them. Following are seven of the most common fears about hospitalization and how you can cope.

Fear #1: Pain

One of the scariest things about being in the hospital is pain. *What will it feel like to have an IV? What kinds of tests and procedures will the*

167

doctor have to perform? Will the surgery hurt? Whenever possible, your doctor will tell you beforehand about tests, procedures, and surgery. You may feel that the less you know about these things, the less you'll have to fear. Actually, the opposite is true. It's scarier *not* knowing what's going to happen to you because you'll most likely imagine the worst. Once you know and understand the procedures and how they can help you, you may be less afraid. Unfortunately, being aware of what's going to happen won't *prevent* pain, but the doctors and nurses will try their best to make you comfortable. Your short-term pain is meant to help bring long-term relief from pain and other symptoms.

You may be scared (even terrified) of shots and IVs. Maybe you have a general fear of needles. Needles aren't any fun, but some needles (like those used for blood tests) are so small that the pain is minimal and doesn't last long. If you're going to be stuck with a bigger needle, a nurse may first give you a tiny shot or smear of numbing cream to help deaden the pain when the needle is inserted. When it comes to having an IV, understanding how one works can help ease your fears. An IV is inserted into a vein in your body (usually in your arm) with a needle that's taped in place for as long as you need the IV. The needle is connected to a tube and an IV bag full of medication, liquid nutrition, or blood—whatever your body needs. A computer attached to the IV regulates the amount of liquid that's pumped from the bag into your body. When the needle is first inserted, you may feel some pain for a few seconds, but it soon disappears; if it doesn't, ask a nurse to move the IV to another spot so you'll be more comfortable.

Many people hold their breath during painful procedures, but this isn't a good idea because when you feel fear, you tend to clench and tighten the muscles, making the pain even worse. To manage your pain, instead of holding your breath and tightening up, try to relax and breathe deeply—in through your nose for five seconds and out your mouth for five more seconds. Another way to deal with pain is to squeeze someone's hand, which helps release tension.

Reach out to a family member or friend, or even the nurse or technician, as the test or procedure is performed, and continue your deep breathing so you don't end up holding your breath. If you don't want to hold someone's hand, you can substitute a pillow, blanket, or favorite stuffed animal—anything that's soft and easy to grip. (I've decided that you're never too old to need a stuffed animal. Every time I go to the hospital, my friend Dietrich—a stuffed dog that my parents gave me for my tenth birthday—comes with me. Whenever I'm in pain, I hold on to Dietrich, and sometimes I even take him with me for X-rays and other tests.) One last way to deal with pain is to distract yourself. Hum a tune, picture yourself in an island paradise, or think of anything to get your mind off your discomfort. The more you focus on the pain, the more it will hurt. Remember that the pain is only temporary and tell yourself, "In just a little bit, this will all be over."

For many complicated procedures, including surgery, you'll be given anesthesia to make you sleep. Often, the anesthesia will be injected right into your IV tube, and you won't even feel it going in. If you're having a procedure or test, you may be given light anesthesia, which should numb you and make you feel very happy. For surgery, you'll most likely be given enough anesthesia to make you unconscious. During surgery, the anesthesiologist will monitor you to make sure that you're receiving just enough to keep you from waking up during the surgery or prevent you from falling into too deep of a sleep. After surgery, you'll wake up in a recovery room, and you may be sleepy, confused, and sick to your stomach. Surgery and other procedures can tire you out for a number of days, weeks, or sometimes even months, while your body adjusts to the changes that have occurred.

If you're nervous about surgery (and who isn't?), keep in mind that when you wake up, it will all be over. While you're asleep, an experienced team of surgeons, nurses, and an anesthesiologist will be taking care of you. Once you wake up, the worst is over, and you can focus on getting better.

Fear #2: Being Surrounded by Strangers

You'll meet many new people in the hospital, including doctors, nurses, and technicians (people who take X-rays, draw blood samples, and perform other tests). These strangers will be in and out of your hospital room day and night, and all this activity can be unsettling. The good news is, these people are trained to take care of you—they understand that you're sick, and their job is to help you get better.

Your regular doctor will probably come to visit you in the hospital to monitor your progress and talk about how you're feeling. If your doctor can't get to the hospital every day, another doctor will check on you and report to your doctor. If you're going to have surgery, your surgeon will visit you, too. Occasionally, a doctor may want to bring in one or two medical students because they're an important part of their education. Take advantage of these doctor visits to ask questions about your treatment and hospital stay.

Nurses are the people you'll see most often. Hospitals usually have three groups of nurses—those who work in the morning, in the afternoon, and through the night. You'll probably be treated by the same nurses every day (except for weekends). Nurses provide constant care, and they'll be in and out of your room all the time, checking on you, taking your temperature and blood pressure, and giving you your medication. In my experience, most nurses will do as much as possible to make your hospital stay comfortable, and they'll take the time to talk with you and help you in any way they can.

At some point during your stay, you may also meet a dietitian, who will make sure that you're getting the nutrition you need. If you're able to eat solid foods, you may be able to select your meals from a pre-planned menu—it's not homecooking, but it's supposed to be good for you.

Unless you're in intensive care, a section of the hospital reserved for people who are very sick and need a lot of attention,

you'll probably have a roommate. Your roommate may have the same illness or one completely different from yours. More often than not, roommates are the same gender, so you probably won't share a room with someone of the opposite sex. If you're in the pediatric section, your roommate will be another young person; if you're in another section of the hospital, your roommate may be an adult. There's a curtain between the beds that you can close when you want privacy and open when you and your roommate want to visit. You and your roommate can be a source of strength for each other, but if you really don't want a roommate, you may be able to get a single room (they're usually more expensive, so talk to your parents about whether your insurance company covers the additional costs).

While you're at the hospital, you're going to run into other patients besides your roommate. It can be scary, not to mention depressing, to be around so many strangers who are sick. They probably don't want to be in the hospital any more than you do, and they may feel just as uncomfortable about being surrounded by others who are ill. While this may sound strange, I've found that the hospital can be a good place to meet people. I don't mean that you should hang out there on Friday nights, but if you're in the hospital for more than a few days, talking to other patients your age can make you feel less lonely and bored.

Fear #3: Being Away from Friends, Family, and Pets

It's hard to be away from the people you love. Luckily, hospitals have visiting hours so your friends and family can come to see you, and once the doctor says it's okay for you to have visitors, anyone can drop by. Your visitors can bring a deck of cards, puzzles, a photo of your pet, or anything else to get your mind off your hospital stay. It's not a good idea, though, to have a whole bunch of people in your hospital room all at once because you'll probably get worn out.

In some hospitals, parents can visit whenever they want, and family members usually are allowed longer visiting hours. If your room is big enough, the nurses may be able to provide a fold-up bed so you can have a parent stay overnight. You'll feel a lot better just knowing someone you love is close by.

When you're in the hospital, you may want to have a parent spend *every* night with you, but, depending on your family situation, this may not always be possible. If you don't like being alone at night, do something to keep your mind occupied (read, watch TV, play a hand-held video game, write letters, do homework, or work on puzzles).

You may discover that some of your friends aren't comfortable visiting you in the hospital. While this may hurt your feelings, try to understand. Perhaps their only experiences in the hospital have been negative, or maybe they associate hospitals with death. If your friends are too young to drive, they may not be able to visit you for transportation reasons. You'll most likely have a phone in your room, so you can make and receive calls whenever you want. Long distance calls are added to your hospital bill, so check with your parents first.

Remind yourself that your stay is temporary. You won't be in the hospital forever, and soon you'll be back at home with the people you love. Take this time to relax, regain your strength, and get better.

Fear #4: Loss of Control

One of the things I hated most about being in the hospital was not being able to take care of myself. For a while, I couldn't even sit up or roll over without someone helping me. It's very frustrating to have to rely on others for everything, but you can't help it. Instead

of worrying about not being in control, focus on your recovery (and enjoy being waited on hand and foot!).

Don't feel embarrassed about asking the nurses for help—they understand that you can't do everything on your own while you're recovering. I know how humiliating it can be to call a nurse because you have to go to the bathroom and need help, but nurses deal with that kind of thing every day. No one is going to laugh at you because you can't walk to the bathroom by yourself or need to use a bedpan. At the hospital, more than anyplace else, people understand your limitations.

You may feel more comfortable having a family member, rather than a nurse, help you wash yourself. If a parent isn't present at the time a nurse comes in, you can say you'd like to wait because someone else is going to help you. Don't worry that you're offending the nurses because they understand the discomfort of having a stranger help you do personal things.

If you have an emergency while you're at the hospital, the nurse is just a call button away. The call button will be an easy reach from your bed, and all you have to do is push it when you need something.

Fear #5: Being Bored and "Missing Out"

There you are in your hospital bed, looking at the sunshine outside, feeling bored, and wondering what all your friends are doing at school. It's hard to be stuck indoors, especially when you don't have all of your personal belongings to help keep you occupied. You may worry that you're missing out on all the fun (after-school activities, parties, athletic events) and that everyone will forget you. They won't, though. To pass the time, make the hospital your "home away from home." Ask your family to bring your favorite books, your mail, CDs, board games, pictures of your pets, or anything else that reminds you of home and of your friends. If you don't already use a journal, you might want to start because you'll have lots of free time to write.

If you have a chance to pack before you go to the hospital, I recommend that you bring your pillow and favorite blanket, cozy pajamas, socks, a bathrobe, and some slippers or other footwear that's comfortable. If you have to make an emergency trip to the hospital and don't have time to pack, ask a family member to bring the things you need later. You'll most likely have a small table by your bed, and you can use it to display pictures, cards, flowers, and gifts that you receive while you're in the hospital. Having familiar things in plain view will help make your surroundings more comfortable.

As you begin to recover, you'll be able to move around in the hospital, so you can check out the activity rooms or lounges. Activity rooms often have toys, games, movies, reading materials, and sometimes arts and crafts projects. Being in the hospital can be an opportunity to make new friends—you can meet a lot of cool people just like you who also happen to be patients. Some hospitals have child-life specialists and recreational therapists who are trained to help young people relax in the hospital, so use them as a resource when you're lonely or bored.

Fear #6: Falling Behind in School

At first, you may think, "Hurrah, no school!" Then reality sinks in, and you realize how much school work you'll have to make up after your hospital stay. If you have the energy, you can try to complete some assignments in the hospital, but don't put too much pressure on yourself (no one expects you to come back from a hospital stay with all of your school work completed). Your primary goal should be to recover and to take the best possible care of yourself.

Some hospitals offer tutors for young people who have to stay in the hospital for an extended time. These tutors can help you

keep up with your classes while you continue to receive care for your illness. If you need to spend time recovering at home after you leave the hospital, find out if your school has a homebound program so a teacher can work with you one-on-one to help you catch up. If this type of program doesn't exist at your school, you may want to see if your teachers can offer suggestions for getting back on track with your homework, tests, and other assignments.

Fear #7: Going Home

Wait, isn't going home the best part of your hospital stay? Not necessarily. It's common to have mixed feelings about leaving the hospital, especially after you've gotten used to the routines and the constant care. You may worry that you won't be able to handle your recovery on your own, and you may miss the nurses, doctors, and other caregivers who helped you. These feelings probably won't last long. Once you get home, you'll be happy to be in your familiar surroundings with your family close by.

The thought of seeing your friends again can make you anxious. You may wonder if they'll think you look different or if they won't know what to say to you. Although it can be a little awkward at first, seeing your friends is a great way to lift your spirits and make you feel at home again. When you're up to it, plan an informal welcome-back party for yourself and invite a few of your closest friends—they'll be glad that you're back.

Child Life Council Evidence-Based Practice Statement

Child Life Assessment: Variables Associated with a

Child's Ability to Cope with Hospitalization

Submitted by:

Donna Koller, PhD

Associate Professor, Ryerson University Early Childhood Education

Adjunct Scientist, Research Institute, Hospital for Sick Children, Toronto, Ontario, Canada

Approved by the Child Life Council Executive Board August 2008

Rebecca Mador, Wendy Lee, and Michelle Gibson, research assistants at the Hospital for Sick Children, are gratefully acknowledged for their contributions in the preparation of this statement.

1

Preamble

The purpose of this statement is to identify key variables associated with children's ability to cope with hospitalization. Based on the best empirical evidence, this statement can inform child life practice by serving as a guide for initial assessments of hospitalized children. The goal of an initial assessment is to determine a child's risk for negative psychological outcomes due to hospitalization and to plan appropriate interventions.

This statement is based on an exhaustive search of the literature, which was conducted on i) PsycINFO, which records the literature from psychology and related disciplines such as medicine, psychiatry, nursing, sociology, and education; ii) MEDLINE, which focuses on biomedical literature; and iii) CINAHL, the Cumulative Index to Nursing & Allied Health Literature, which covers literature relating to nursing and allied health professions. A variety of keywords and combinations such as "hospitalized children," "coping," "psychological adaptation" and "stress" were used to conduct the search (See Table 1 for a list of search terms). The search was completed in March 2007 with the assistance of a medical librarian. Searches revealed approximately 150 articles regarding coping and adjustment. After the results were sorted to exclude repeats and non-empirical based literature, 39 articles remained. These articles were retrieved and evaluated based on the scoring of 2 independent raters using "The Quality of Study Rating Form"[1]. Articles that received a rating of at least 60 out of 100 points were selected for inclusion in this statement. Any article that scored between 55 and 65 points was scored again by a second rater to confirm inclusion or exclusion. Finally, twenty-six articles met the selection criteria (See Table 2 for a complete list of citations).

Since evidence-based practice represents an integration of the best available research along with clinical experience[1], this statement was reviewed by certified child life specialists across North America in order to ensure clinical applicability. In addition, evidence-based practice acknowledges patient preferences and needs when determining the most appropriate clinical interventions for the child and family.

2

Child Life Assessment: Why is it important?

Children's negative responses to hospitalization and medical procedures are well documented in the literature[2-6]. In an effort to reduce the negative impact of hospitalization on pediatric patients, child life specialists must determine whether a child is at risk for experiencing negative psychological sequelae. Given that the quality and intensity of a child's reaction to hospitalization can be influenced by many variables, child life specialists must consider the most significant variables[7, 8] when conducting assessments. Without an understanding of these variables, accurate assessments of hospitalized children are not possible and the ability to engage in evidence-based practice is thwarted.

How Studies Identify Factors Associated with Coping

Research in this area is complex, predominantly because several variables can be associated with children's ability to cope with hospitalization. For the most part, this research is quantitative and correlational in design. These studies typically attempt to link results obtained through self-report scales completed by children and their parents with behavioral outcomes. It must be noted, however, that correlational designs do not allow conclusions to be drawn with respect to causality. Despite the shortcomings of correlational designs, the findings reviewed here identify key issues associated with how children cope with hospitalization. From the studies reviewed in this statement, four categories of variables emerged:

1) Child variables
2) Family variables
3) Illness variables
4) Medical experiences

Child Variables

Temperament

Temperament can be defined as an individual's consistent and stable pattern of behavior or reaction, one that persists across time, activity, and context. Generally, an individual's temperament consists of nine dimensions including activity level, adaptability, threshold of responsiveness, mood, intensity of reaction, distractibility, attention span and persistence, and predictability[9]. Two studies investigated the relationship between a child's temperament and his or her response to hospitalization. Children who responded best to hospitalization tended to be more positive in mood, more predictable, easier to distract, more approachable and adaptable while being less reactive to stimuli[9, 10]. In addition, McClowry found that temperament accounts

3

for as much as 50% of the variance in children's behavioral responses prior to and up to one month after hospitalization[9].

The level of anxiety exhibited by a child in hospital can reflect his or her underlying temperament and associated responses to stressful situations. In addition, distinctions need to be made between the different types of anxiety. For instance, *trait anxiety*, which refers to the stable and relatively constant tendency to be anxious, has a significant influence on the quality of a child's reaction to hospitalization[11-13]. Children with higher trait anxiety are significantly more likely to perceive their coping as ineffective and appraise hospitalization as a stressful experience than are children with lower trait anxiety[11, 12]. Trait anxiety has also been found to positively correlate with a child's self-reported fear, indicating that highly anxious children require additional support in order to cope effectively with stressful events[13]. In addition to trait anxiety, *state anxiety* refers to anxiety created as a result of a specific experience. Tiedeman and Clatworthy found that this form of anxiety dissipates from the time of admission to discharge for hospitalized children between the ages of 5 and 11[14].

In the event that a child life specialist is presented with an anxious child, discussions with the child and family can help determine whether the child is exhibiting a form of trait or state anxiety. For example, if the child is normally anxious in other areas of his or her life, this may be indicative of a more pervasive form of anxiety. In this case, child life interventions supplemented by a referral to psychiatry may be necessary in order to rule out an underlying anxiety disorder.

Coping Style

Coping is the process used to alter, manage, or tolerate a stressful situation[15]. An individual's preferred style of coping is a combination of his or her temperament as well as an appraisal of the stressful situation. Researchers have typically divided the coping strategies children use into two categories: avoidant and vigilant[16, 17]. Avoidant coping occurs when children restrict their thoughts about an upcoming event, deny their worries, and detach from a stressful stimulus. Vigilant coping strategies consist of seeking out detailed information and alertness to a stressful stimulus. LaMontagne et al., found that vigilant coping was associated with a timely return to normal activities over the course of recovery[16]. In a related study, LaMontagne et al., classified children based on how they focused on aspects of impending surgery. Children who focused their attention on concrete aspects of the experience (i.e., details about recovery) tended to use vigilant coping and were able to return to their usual activities sooner. Children who had less information about the procedure (provided few descriptions of the experience, tended to avoid information) had the least favorable outcome on the "activities" subscale of the Youth Self-Report and Profile which assesses the child's usual activities (i.e.,

4

sports, chores, etc.)[17]. Similarly, Knight et al., found that children who sought information about their upcoming procedure exhibited less physiological and affective distress than children who denied the experience or avoided information[18].

However, other studies suggest that the relationship between coping style and outcomes is more complex[16, 19]. Lowery Thompson found that children who used either information-seeking (vigilant) *or* information-limiting (avoidant) coping behaviors were less anxious than children using a combined approach[19]. Furthermore, different strategies can be associated with favorable outcomes at different time periods; while avoidant strategies were found to be more effective in reducing stress initially after surgery, children using a vigilant approach reported better long-term recovery[16].

In one study, children's baseline behavior was assessed as a predictor for how a child might behave during and after hospitalization. For instance, if a child is more likely to exhibit internalizing behaviors (i.e. anxiety, depression) prior to hospitalization, this coping style can consistently predict later internalizing behaviors following hospitalization. The same was found true for externalizing behaviors such as aggression and hyperactivity[20].

Although the findings reveal complexities, children's coping styles appear to predict psychological outcomes related to hospitalization. For the most part, avoidant characteristics appear to be less effective at ameliorating stressors associated with hospitalization. Therefore, a child's coping style as shown by his or her willingness to seek and accept information can predict the degree of psychological risk.

Age

Several studies included in this review examined the relationship between a child's chronological age and his or her likelihood of experiencing negative behavior and/or psychological sequelae in response to hospitalization[13, 14, 21-24]. It should be noted that these studies did not make distinctions between chronological age and developmental levels. Despite the fact that older children (latency age) are assumed to cope better with hospitalization than younger children, the literature indicates that the relationship is more complex. For example, some studies found no link between a child's age and his or her response to hospitalization, post-behavioral upset, anxiety or fear[19, 25]. Conversely, some researchers found that younger children were more likely to be anxious and fearful compared to older children[14-16, 20-24, 26]. Younger children were also less likely to feel in control of their health as measured by the Children's Health Locus of Control Scale[22].

The impact of age on children's coping strategies is also unclear. Assessed by the Preoperative Mode of Coping Interview, two studies cited contradictory findings: Lowery

5

Thompson found that age is not related to children's coping behavior while LaMontagne et al., discovered that older children are more likely to use effective coping strategies[16, 19]. Given these discrepant findings, it cannot be assumed that the age of the child will accurately predict the degree of upset experienced by a hospitalized child. Hence, it is critically important to examine other variables in addition to age when making assessments regarding coping.

Gender

Many studies in this review examined the effects of gender on a child's response to hospitalization[11-14, 19, 20, 22, 23, 25-28]. However, the findings from these studies are inconclusive. Tiedeman and Clatworthy found that boys tended to be more anxious than girls at admission, discharge and post-discharge, while other studies found that girls were more anxious than boys[20, 22, 25, 27] and finally some concluded that gender was unrelated to anxiety or the expression of fear[11-13, 19]. A number of studies also revealed that gender differences are not evident in behavioral upset[23], focus of attention[17], coping strategies and perception of its effectiveness[11] and the type of events children appraised as stressful during hospitalization[12].

Family Variables

Parental Anxiety and Distress

Of all the family variables, parental anxiety is most strongly correlated with children's adverse responses during hospitalization[10, 15, 16, 20, 21, 24, 26, 29]. Maternal anxiety not only predicts children's emotional distress[10, 15, 16, 20, 24, 29], but also correlates positively with children's distress during invasive procedures[21, 26]. In one study, high levels of maternal state anxiety at first contact (6-16 hours following the child's admission to the intensive care unit) was found to significantly increase a child's likelihood to engage in negative behavioral responses such as hyperactivity and aggression[20]. Maternal anxiety also mediates the positive effect of an intervention on hospitalized children's post-hospital behavior, suggesting that it may be beneficial to provide support to highly-anxious mothers in order to enhance the psychosocial outcomes of hospitalized children[30].

Only one study found that at the time of admission to the hospital, parental anxiety did not significantly affect child's anxiety[14]. However, there was a significant relationship between parental anxiety and children's anxiety following hospitalization. These inconsistent findings were partially explained by the fact that different questionnaires were used at various times during hospitalization.

Family Characteristics

6

Three studies provided an in-depth examination of family characteristics associated with post-hospitalization outcomes[10, 20, 23]. The main variables included the marital status of a child's parents[20], family size, and family composition[10, 23]. One study by Small & Melnyk (2006) found that marital status significantly predicted a child's likelihood of displaying internalizing (focused inward, i.e. anxiety, depression) or externalizing (focused outward, i.e. aggression, hyperactivity) behaviors post-hospitalization[20]. For example, mothers who had been married more than once had children who demonstrated more internalizing behaviors three months post-hospitalization than children whose mothers had not been married or were married for the first time. Additionally, mothers' anxiety and level of involvement to the emotional needs of the child were primary predictors of internalizing and externalizing behaviors, as well as post-hospitalization anxiety. However, family size and composition were found to be unrelated to a child's post-hospital adjustment [10, 20, 23].

Socioeconomic Status

Studies have investigated the relationship between a family's socioeconomic status (SES) and a child's response to hospitalization[10, 13, 20, 22, 23]. While two studies found no association between SES and children's responses to hospitalization[10, 23],[20], Hart & Bossert found that children with higher trait anxiety from families with a lower yearly income reported a higher amount of fear[13]. In terms of maternal education, Rennick et al., reported that children with mothers who had higher education were more likely to feel in control of their health[22].

Parental Presence and Involvement

Studies have also sought to determine the extent to which a parent's presence is associated with how a child responds to hospitalization. In a pediatric emergency care study, 96 children were administered a venipuncture[31]. The children were randomly assigned to two groups; one in which a parent was present, and another in which a parent was absent. Both parents and children exhibited less distress when a parent was present during the procedure. In contrast, another study randomly assigned 20 children to either a condition with mother present during an injection and another condition where the mother was absent[32]. Children's behavior during and after the injection was rated as significantly more negative for the children in the mother-present condition. The authors concluded that children may feel more comfortable protesting during a procedure when a parent is present.

The level of parental involvement in the care of hospitalized children can exert significant influence on a child's ability to cope with medical experiences[10, 20, 24, 30]. In one controlled study by Mazurek Melnyk and Feinstein, researchers found that when parents received information regarding common child behaviors during hospitalization, their participation in the care of their

7

child increased[30]. In turn, these children experienced less negative behaviors following hospitalization. To measure the level of maternal involvement in care, the Index of Parent Participation was used (IPP; Melynk, Alpert-Gillis, Hensel, Cable-Beiling & Rubenstein, 1997)[33]. The scale consists of a 36-item checklist of self-reported parenting behaviors during childhood hospitalization. Examples of these behaviors included playing, bathing, feeding and explaining medical procedures to the child. The authors yielded scores which reflected low, moderate and high levels of involvement. The study found that moderate parental involvement resulted in positive outcomes for hospitalized children while excessive or limited parental involvement was shown to result in negative outcomes. For instance, children with highly involved parents exhibited worse post-hospital adjustment, more internalized coping such as anxiety and depression[24], and more behavioral disturbance than children with less involved parents[10, 20, 24].

Illness Variables

Chronic vs. Acute Illness

Few studies have investigated whether children with chronic or acute conditions experience hospitalization differently. In one study, the degree of children's fears was not associated with whether they had chronic or acute illnesses[13]. However, in another study, acutely ill children were more likely to perceive their coping as effective than were chronically ill children[11]. Bossert compared chronically ill and acutely ill children on their perceptions of what is stressful. Chronically ill children identified more intrusive events and acutely ill children identified more physical symptoms as stressful[12]. In regards to post-hospital behavior, children from intensive care were compared with those from a general medical ward. Scores on post-hospital behavior scales revealed similar findings for the two samples[34].

Length of Hospitalization

In two studies, the length of hospitalization was examined in regards to children's adjustment to hospitalization[14, 22]. While this variable appeared to have minimal effects on children's responses to hospitalization in one study[22], another study found that shorter hospital stays were associated with higher levels of anxiety by children at discharge[14].

Medical Experiences

Exposure to Invasive Procedures

Studies reveal that the number of invasive procedures experienced by a child is positively associated with the level of stress, anxiety and fear experienced during and following hospitalization[22, 25, 28, 29]. In particular, two studies found that the number of invasive procedures was a strong predictor of children's psychological distress, manifested in symptoms of

8

depression, anxiety, fear and post-traumatic stress[25, 28]. Rennick et al., found that children subjected to a higher number of invasive procedures tended to have more intrusive thoughts and avoidance behaviors. These findings were particularly noteworthy for younger, more severely ill children who had endured many invasive procedures[22]. Rennick et al., replicated these findings and found that children between the ages of 6 to 17 years who were exposed to high numbers of invasive procedures experienced the most psychological sequelae post discharge[28]. Only one study did not find an association between the number of medical procedures and children's depressive or anxious symptoms. The authors hypothesize that participants in their study had experienced frequent hospitalizations and may have learned effective coping strategies[15].

Previous Hospitalizations

The research on whether previous hospitalization has an effect on a child's ability to cope with hospitalization is inconclusive. Some research found that previous hospitalizations are not related to the level of anxiety or coping experienced by the child[19, 25] while in a study by Tiedeman and Clatworthy, children with no previous hospital experience were more anxious than those who had been in hospital before, alluding to the potential benefits of being familiar with the hospital setting[14]. Support for these findings can be found in Wells and Schwebel where children with fewer previous surgeries exhibited greater disturbance and anxiety[24].

Gaps in the Literature

Since studies report mixed findings on a variety of variables (i.e. age, previous hospitalizations), additional research using randomized designs with cross-sectional samples could reveal the degree to which particular variables impact on children of various ages. For instance, there is a lack of studies that compare children of different ages with a variety of diagnoses or chronic conditions. Current research has also made no distinctions between chronological age and the developmental levels of the participants. This issue may have bearing on research findings given that children sampled from pediatric settings are more likely to have a range of developmental delays which can affect their ability to cope. In addition, future research should address whether particular diagnoses and associated treatment plans place children at greater risk for negative psychological outcomes. Taken together, this information has implications for determining appropriate staff to patient ratios in specific medical areas where child life may be needed most.

According to Rodriguez and Boggs, the evaluation of emotional distress in pediatric settings is further complicated by the scarcity of measures designed specifically for the *assessment of children who are hospitalized*[23]. Given that a parent's anxiety is strongly

9

correlated with a child's anxiety, additional measures which address a range of family variables are also needed. Finally, the literature lacks relevant discourse on issues related to culture (i.e. values, beliefs), diversity and family background.

Conclusions

A systematic review of the best available research revealed key variables to be considered in a child life assessment. In particular, the child's temperament, and the level of child and parental anxiety (state or trait) are very significant factors. Small and Melnyk underscore the importance of baseline knowledge concerning a child's usual behavior patterns, citing that this information can identify patients most in need of psychosocial interventions during and following hospitalization[20]. Therefore, an initial assessment of the child's temperament is an important place to start in addition to determining parental stress levels. An assessment of these key variables will help determine whether the child is experiencing state or trait anxiety. Indeed, highly anxious children may require more emotional support in order to deal with stressful events and this may be particularly significant for children who have experienced many invasive medical procedures. Finally, the research tells us that we cannot assume a child will cope poorly solely because he or she is young without considering other important variables.

The research in this area presents a complicated array of issues for child life consideration. For child life specialists who observe parents exhibiting or reporting high stress levels, collaborating with other health care professionals such as social work can make a significant difference in patient and family outcomes. Although child life specialists play an important role in children's adaptation to hospitalization, evidence-based practice models support inter-professional collaboration as a means of strategically addressing complex issues associated with how children and their parents cope with medical challenges[35-41].

References

1. Gibbs L. Quality of Study Rating Form: An Instrument for Synthesizing Evaluation Studies. *Journal of Social Work Education.* 1989;25(1):67.

2. Vernon DT, Schulman JL, Foley JM. Changes in children's behavior after hospitalization. *American Journal of Diseases of Children.* 1966;111:581-593.

3. Bowlby J, Robertson J, Rosenbluth D. A two-year-old goes to the hospital. *Psychoanalytic Study of the Child.* 1952;7:82-94.

4. Fletcher B. Psychological upset in posthospitalized children: A review of the literature. *Maternal-Child Nursing Journal.* 1981;10:185-195.

5. Vernon DT, Foley JM, Sipowicz RR, Schulman JL. *The psychological responses of children to hospitalization and illness.* Springfield, Ill: Charles C. Thomas; 1965.

6. Thompson R, Stanford, G. *Child Life in Hospitals: Theory and Practice.* Springfield, IL: Charles C. Thomas; 1981.

7. Melamed BG, Dearborn M, Hermecz DA. Necessary considerations for surgery preparation: Age and previous experience. *Psychosomatic Medicine.* 1983;45(6):517-525.

8. Lynch M. Preparing children for day surgery. *Children's Health Care.* 1994;23(2):75-85.

9. McClowry SG. The relationship of temperament to pre- and posthospitalization behavioral responses of school-age children. *Nursing Research.* 1990;39(1):30-35.

10. Carson DK, Council JR, Gravley JE. Temperament and family characteristics as predictors of children's reactions to hospitalization. *Developmental and Behavioral Pediatrics.* 1991;12(3):141-147.

11. Bossert E. Factors influencing the coping of hospitalized school-age children. *Journal of Pediatric Nursing.* 1994;9(5):299-306.

12. Bossert E. Stress appraisals of hospitalized school-age children. *Children's Health Care.* 1994;23(1):33-49.

13. Hart D, Bossert E. Self-reported fears of hospitalized school-age children. *Journal of Pediatric Nursing.* 1994;9(2):83-90.

14. Tiedeman ME, Clatworthy S. Anxiety responses of 5- to 11-year-old children during and after hospitalization. *Journal of Pediatric Nursing.* 1990;5(5):334-343.

15. Mabe PA, Treiber FA, Riley WT. Examining emotional distress during pediatric hospitalization for school-aged children. *Children's Health Care.* 1991;20(3):162-169.

16. LaMontagne LL, Hepworth JT, Johnson BD, Cohen F. Children's preoperative coping and its effects on postoperative anxiety and return to normal activity. *Nursing Research.* 1996;45(3):141-147.

17. LaMontagne LL, Johnson JE, Hepworth JT, Johnson BD. Attention, coping, and activity in children undergoing orthopaedic surgery. *Research in Nursing & Health.* 1997;20:487-494.

18. Knight RB, Atkins A, Eagle CJ, et al. Psychological stress, ego defenses, and cortisol production in children hospitalized for elective surgery. *Psychosomatic Medicine.* 1979;41(1):40-49.

19. Lowery Thompson M. Information-seeking coping and anxiety in school-age children anticipating surgery. *Children's Health Care.* 1994;23(2):87-97.

20. Small L, Melnyk BM. Early predictors of post-hospital adjustment problems in critically ill young children. *Research in Nursing & Health.* 2006;29:622-635.

21. Dahlquist LM, Power TG, Cox CN, Fernbach DJ. Parenting and child distress during cancer procedures: A multidimensional assessment. *Children's Health Care.* 1994;23(3):149-166.

22. Rennick JE, Johnston CC, Dougherty G, Platt R, Ritchie JA. Children's psychological responses after critical illness and exposure to invasive technology. *Developmental and Behavioral Pediatrics.* 2002;23(3):133-144.

23. Rodriguez CM, Boggs SR. Behavioral upset in medical patients - Revised: Evaluation of a parent report measure of distress for pediatric populations. *Journal of Pediatric Psychology.* 1994;19(3):319-324.

24. Wells RD, Schwebel AI. Chronically ill children and their mothers: Predictors of resilience and vulnerability to hospitalization and surgical stress. *Developmental and Behavioral Pediatrics.* 1987;8(2):83-89.

25. Saylor CF, Pallmeyer TP, Finch AJ, Eason L, Trieber F, Folger C. Predictors of psychological distress in hospitalized pediatric patients. *Journal of the American Academy of Child and Adolescent Psychiatry.* 1987;26(2):232-236.

26. Jacobsen PB, Manne SL, Gorfinkle K, Schorr O, Rapkin B, Redd WH. Analysis of child and parent behavior during painful medical procedures. *Health Psychology.* 1990;9(5):559-576.

27. LaMontagne LL, Wells N, Hepworth JT, Johnson BD, Manes R. Parent coping and child distress behaviors during invasive procedures for childhood cancer. *Journal of Pediatric Oncology Nursing.* 1999;16(1):3-12.

28. Rennick JE, Morin I, Kim D, Johnston CC, Dougherty G, Platt R. Identifying children at high risk for psychological sequelae after pediatric intensive care unit hospitalization. *Pediatric Critical Care Medicine.* 2004;5(4):358-363.

29. Fosson A, Martin J, Haley J. Anxiety among hospitalized latency-age children. *Developmental and Behavioral Pediatrics.* 1990;11(6):324-327.

30. Mazurek Melnyk BM, Feinstein NF. Mediating functions of maternal anxiety and participation in care on young children's posthospital adjustment. *Research in Nursing & Health.* 2001;24:18-26.

31. Wolfram RW, Turner ED, Philput C. Effects of parental presence during young children's venipuncture. *Pediatric Emergency Care.* 1997;3(5):325-328.

32. Shaw EG, Routh DK. Effect of mother presence on children's reaction to aversive procedures. *Journal of Pediatric Psychology.* 1982;7(1):33-42.

33. Melnyk BM, Alpert-Gillis, LJ, Hensel, PB, Cable- Beiling, RC, & Rubenstein, JS. Helping mothers cope with a critically ill child: A pilot test of the COPE intervention. *Research in Nursing & Health.* 1997;20:3-14.

34. Youngblut JM, Shiao S-YP. Child and family reactions during and after pediatric ICU hospitalization: A pilot study. *Heart and Lung.* 1993;22(1):46-54.

35. Aston J, Shi E, Bullot H, Galway R, Crisp J. Qualitative evaluation of regular morning meetings aimed at improving interdisciplinary communication and patient outcomes. *International Journal of Nursing Practice.* 2005;11(5):206-213.

36. Baggs JG, Ryan SA, Phelps CE, Richeson JF, Johnson JE. The association between interdisciplinary collaboration and patient outcomes in a medical intensive care unit. *Heart & Lung.* 1992;21(1):18-24.

37. Knaus WA, Draper EA, Wagner DP, Zimmerman JE. An evaluation of outcome from intensive care in major medical centers. *Annals of Internal Medicine.* 1986;104(3):410-418.

38. Larson E. The impact of physician-nurse interaction on patient care. *Holistic Nursing Practice.* 1999;13(2):38-46.

39. Mitchell PH, Armstrong S, Simpson TF, Lentz M. American Association of Critical-Care Nurses Demonstration Project: profile of excellence in critical care nursing. *Heart & Lung.* 1989;18(3):219-237.

40. Baggs JG, Schmitt MH, Mushlin AI, et al. Association between nurse-physician collaboration and patient outcomes in three intensive care units. *Critical Care Medicine.* 1999;27(9):1991-1998.

41. Zimmerman JE, Shortell SM, Rousseau DM, et al. Improving intensive care: observations based on organizational case studies in nine intensive care units: a prospective, multicenter study. *Critical Care Medicine.* 1993;21(10):1443-1451.

Appendix

Table 1. List of keywords used to conduct literature search
Three databases were used to generate literature searches. A variety of search words were used to conduct literature searches with the assistance of a medical librarian.

MEDLINE

Category	Search Words
Coping	Psychological adaptation, adjustment, stress, psychological stress, social adjustment
Hospitalized Children	Inpatient (limited to all children), hospitalized child, hospitalized adolescent

PsycINFO

Category	Search Words
Coping	Coping behavior, adjustment, emotional adjustment, social adjustment
Hospitalized Children	Hospitalized patients (limited to childhood and adolescence)

CINAHL

Category	Search Words
Coping	Child adaptation to hospitalization, psychological adaptation, social adjustment
Hospitalized Children	Hospitalized infant, hospitalized children, hospitalized adolescent, inpatients (age limited to 0-18 years)

Table 2. Final selection of studies included in this review
Twenty-six articles were evaluated using "The Quality of Study Rating Form" (Gibbs, 1989). Articles that scored between 60 and 100 points were selected for inclusion in this statement.

Bossert E. Factors influencing the coping of hospitalized school-age children. *Journal of Pediatric Nursing.* 1994;9(5):299-306.

Bossert E. Stress appraisals of hospitalized school-age children. *Children's Health Care.* 1994;23(1):33-49.

Carson DK, Council JR, Gravley JE. Temperament and family characteristics as predictors of children's reactions to hospitalization. *Developmental and Behavioral Pediatrics.* 1991;12(3):141-147.

Dahlquist LM, Power TG, Cox CN, Fernbach DJ. Parenting and child distress during cancer procedures: A multidimensional assessment. *Children's Health Care.* 1994;23(3):149-166.

Fosson A, Martin J, Haley J. Anxiety among hospitalized latency-age children. *Developmental and behavioral pediatrics.* 1990;11(6):324-327.

Hart D, Bossert E. Self-reported fears of hospitalized school-age children. *Journal of Pediatric Nursing.* 1994;9(2):83-90.

Jacobsen PB, Manne SL, Gorfinkle K, Schorr O, Rapkin B, Redd WH. Analysis of child and parent behavior during painful medical procedures. *Health Psychology.* 1990;9(5):559-576.

Knight RB, Atkins A, Eagle CJ, et al. Psychological stress, ego defenses, and cortisol production in children hospitalized for elective surgery. *Psychosomatic Medicine.* 1979;41(1):40-49.

LaMontagne LL, Hepworth JT, Johnson BD, Cohen F. Children's preoperative coping and its effects on postoperative anxiety and return to normal activity. *Nursing Research.* 1996;45(3):141-147.

LaMontagne LL, Johnson JE, Hepworth JT, Johnson BD. Attention, coping, and activity in children undergoing orthopaedic surgery. *Research in Nursing & Health.* 1997;20:487-494.

LaMontagne LL, Wells N, Hepworth JT, Johnson BD, Manes R. Parent coping and child distress behaviors during invasive procedures for childhood cancer. *Journal of Pediatric Oncology Nursing.* 1999;16(1):3-12.

Lowery Thompson M. Information-seeking coping and anxiety in school-age children anticipating surgery. *Children's Health Care.* 1994;23(2):87-97.

Mabe PA, Treiber FA, Riley WT. Examining emotional distress during pediatric hospitalization for school-aged children. *Children's Health Care.*1991;20(3):162-169.

McClowry SG. The relationship of temperament to pre- and post-hospitalization behavioral responses of school-age children. *Nursing Research.* 1990;39(1):30-35.

15

Mazurek Melnyk B, Feinstein NF. Mediating functions of maternal anxiety and participation in care on young children's post-hospital adjustment. *Research in Nursing & Health.* 2001;24:18-26.

Melnyk, BM, Alpert-Gillis, LJ, Hensel, PB, Cable-Beiling, R.C., & Rubenstein, J.S. (1997). Helping mothers cope with a critically ill child: A pilot test of the COPE intervention. *Research in Nursing & Health*, 20, 3–14.

Rennick JE, Johnston CC, Dougherty G, Platt R, Ritchie JA. Children's psychological responses after critical illness and exposure to invasive technology. *Developmental and Behavioral Pediatrics.* 2002;23(3):133-144.

Rennick JE, Morin I, Kim D, Johnston CC, Dougherty G, Platt R. Identifying children at high risk for psychological sequelae after pediatric intensive care unit hospitalization. *Pediatric Critical Care Medicine.* 2004;5(4):358-363.

Rodriguez CM, Boggs SR. Behavioral upset in medical patients - Revised: Evaluation of a parent report measure of distress for pediatric populations. *Journal of Pediatric Psychology.* 1994;19(3):319-324.

Saylor CF, Pallmeyer TP, Finch AJ, Eason L, Trieber F, Folger C. Predictors of psychological distress in hospitalized pediatric patients. *Journal of the American Academy of Child and Adolescent Psychiatry.* 1987;26(2):232-236.

Shaw EG, Routh DK. Effect of mother presence on children's reaction to aversive procedures. *Journal of Pediatric Psychology.* 1982;7(1):33-42.

Small L, Melnyk BM. Early predictors of post-hospital adjustment problems in critically ill young children. *Research in Nursing & Health.* 2006;29:622-635.

Tiedeman ME, Clatworthy S. Anxiety responses of 5- to 11-year-old children during and after hospitalization. *Journal of Pediatric Nursing.* 1990;5(5):334-343.

Wells RD, Schwebel AI. Chronically ill children and their mothers: Predictors of resilience and vulnerability to hospitalization and surgical stress. *Developmental and Behavioral Pediatrics.* 1987;8(2):83-89.

Wolfram RW, Turner ED, Philput C. Effects of parental presence during young children's venipuncture. *Pediatric Emergency Care.* 1997;3(5):325-328.

Youngblut JM, Shiao S-YP. Child and family reactions during and after pediatric ICU hospitalization: A pilot study. *Heart and Lung.* 1993;22(1):46-54.

16

Child Life Council Evidence-Based Practice Statement

Preparing Children and Adolescents for Medical Procedures

Submitted by:

Donna Koller, PhD

Academic and Clinical Specialist in Child Life

Hospital for Sick Children

Toronto, Ontario, Canada

Approved by the Child Life Council Executive Board November 2007

Rebecca Mador and Wendy Lee, research assistants at the Hospital for Sick Children, are gratefully acknowledged for their contributions in the preparation of this statement.

1

Preparing Children and Adolescents for Medical Procedures
Preamble

The purpose of this statement is to outline the key components of effective psychological preparation and, by using the best empirical evidence currently available, to validate the methods employed by child life specialists.

This statement is based on an exhaustive search of the literature, which was conducted on i) PsycINFO, which records the literature from psychology and related disciplines such as medicine, psychiatry, nursing, sociology, and education; ii) MEDLINE, which focuses on biomedical literature; and, iii) CINAHL, the Cumulative Index to Nursing & Allied Health Literature, which covers literature relating to nursing and allied health professions. A variety of keywords and combinations such as "preparation"; "fear"; "anxiety", "pain"; "pediatrics" and "medical procedures" were used to conduct the search, which was completed in August 2006 with the assistance of a medical librarian. Searches revealed approximately 350 articles related to pediatric preparation; however, after the results were sorted to exclude repeats and non-empirical based literature, 40 articles remained. These articles were retrieved and evaluated based on the scoring of 2 independent raters using "The Quality of Study Rating Form"[1]. Those articles that received a rating of at least 60 out of 100 points were selected for inclusion in this statement. Any article that scored between 55 and 65 points was re-scored by a second rater to confirm inclusion or exclusion. Finally, 30 articles met the selection criteria. Only 3 of these selected studies specifically evaluated preparation performed by child life specialists[2-4].

Since evidence-based practice represents an integration of both clinical experience[1] and the best available research[5, 6], this statement was also reviewed by certified child life specialists across North America in order to ensure clinical applicability. In addition, evidence-based practice acknowledges patient preferences and needs when determining the most appropriate clinical applications for the child and family.

Why Prepare?

The primary goal of preparation is to reduce the fear and anxiety experienced by a child who is undergoing a medical procedure and to promote his or her long-term coping and adjustment to future health care challenges[7-10]. Heightened feelings of stress and anxiety, eating and sleeping disturbances, as well as separation fears are commonly found in children and adolescents undergoing even minor medical procedures[8, 10-12]. The long-term implications of a negative medical experience can be profound; post-traumatic stress, increased fears, and decreased cooperative behavior have been documented among pediatric patients who have not been effectively prepared for a medical experience[9, 13, 14]. Participation in a preparation program has been shown to reduce significantly the negative psychological sequelae experienced by children both immediately before and after the procedure and for up to a month later[9, 14-16]. In this review, 29 of the 30 studies concluded that children who were prepared for surgery experienced fewer negative symptoms than did children in control groups who did not receive preparation[20].

How Studies Evaluate the Effectiveness of Preparation

The majority of research on preparation is quantitative and experimental in design. These studies use anxiety or behavioral manifestation scales to assess the quality and degree of a child's coping. For example, less anxiety and fewer negative behaviors reflect increased coping. Of the 30 studies included in this statement, the most commonly used outcome measures were: a) The Observation Scale of Behavioral Distress revised (OSBD-r)[17], which records behavior over time from the 'anticipation-of-procedure' to the 'post-procedure' phase; b) The Manifest Upset Scale and Cooperation Scale[14], which are two five-point scales that rate the child's degree of negative emotional arousal and behavioral upset; c) The Post-Hospital Behavior Questionnaire[18], which asks parents to rank their child's behavior after discharge from the hospital; and d) the State-Trait Anxiety Inventory for Children (STAI-C)[19], which compares the child's dispositional anxiety with the anxiety he or she is currently experiencing.

Approaches to Pediatric Preparation

Although preparation programs are standard practice in many pediatric hospitals[14], the variability in the approaches and outcomes of these programs is substantial. The literature reveals that preparation programs have included role rehearsals with dolls[4, 20, 23-25], puppet shows[15, 23, 26], the teaching of coping and relaxation skills[27, 28], orientation tours of the operating room[20, 24], as well as educational videos[9, 29],

3

books[16, 30], and pamphlets[25, 31]. Some programs focus exclusively on preparing the child[2, 9, 10, 22, 32-34] while other programs attempt to educate and support the parents[30, 35-37] and siblings as well[12]. Despite variation in approaches, the literature reveals three common elements that underlie effective preparation and result in improved psychosocial outcomes for children and adolescent patients.

Key Elements of Effective Preparation for Medical Procedures

A child's ability to cope with a medical procedure and the quality and intensity of his or her reaction are influenced by many variables[10, 22]. Such variables include the child's age and developmental level, personality, ability to cope with new situations, prior health care experiences and previous encounters with medical professionals, as well as his or her diagnosis and the complexity/invasiveness of the upcoming procedure[3, 10, 22, 38]. Similarly, family variables such as the family's composition and level of parental anxiety can also influence a child's response[3, 38].

Regardless of the medical procedure for which a child is being prepared, the key elements of effective preparation are: (1) the provision of developmentally appropriate information; (2) the encouragement of emotional expression; and, (3) the formation of a trusting relationship with a health care professional[39, 40]. These three elements were proposed previously by Vernon et al. in 1965 following a review of the literature at the time[40]. Three decades later, in a review of 400 studies and a meta-analysis of a final sample of 22, O'Connor-Von[39] substantiated these three components as the essential elements of effective preparation for pediatric patients. These three elements were also evident in the articles reviewed here.

1. Provision of Information

Of the 30 articles reviewed in this statement, all described information dissemination as an integral part of the preparation program. Providing accurate medical information to children lessens negative behavior and promotes faster recovery post-operatively[9, 16, 21, 34] while also attenuating fear and anxiety[7-9, 26]. Although there are a variety of ways in which child life specialists can provide developmentally appropriate information to children; the emphasis should be on providing clear and accurate messages[14]. In addition, information about a medical procedure should be as specific as possible as this can lead to a greater reduction in anxiety than when children receive only standard or more generalized forms of information[7, 14, 28].

4

While it is evident that information is a necessary and important component of preparation, the methods should vary with the child's age and developmental level[10]. Information should include both *what* will happen during the upcoming medical procedure as well as *why* it will happen[41]. For example, Campbell et al.[41] found that providing children with the reasons for the medical procedure as well as the sequence of events significantly reduced their anxiety when compared with control groups who did not receive this information. In addition, explanations should include sensations that the child can expect to experience such as the sights, sounds, smells and feelings[10, 14]. Of the published studies that specifically reported providing procedural *and* sensory information to children in the experimental group, all reported that these children demonstrated less emotional distress than children in control groups[10, 14, 16].

As part of information sharing, coping techniques aimed at ameliorating fears and anxiety should be offered[21]. For example, Campbell et al.[41] found that when a preparation program included information regarding coping techniques, behavioral outcomes were more positive for children undergoing surgery. In another study, Peterson and Shigetomi[35] compared the effectiveness of providing children ages 2 to 10 years old with information only, coping techniques, filmed modeling or coping plus filmed modeling. Children who were provided with coping plus modeling techniques were more calm and cooperative than children in the other groups. In addition, coping techniques introduced to a child should vary depending on the procedure, the child's developmental level and his or her preferred coping style[2]. Effective coping techniques have been found to include visual and auditory distraction, tactile stimulation, counting and singing, and verbal interaction[2]. Six of the 30 studies were found to include information regarding coping as part of their preparation programs and all reported significant positive outcomes[2, 27, 28, 35, 37, 41].

2. Opportunities for Emotional Expression

During the course of preparation, it is essential that potential stressors are anticipated and misconceptions and fears are addressed[3, 42]. This requires the child life specialist to pay careful attention to a variety of cues such as facial expressions and other forms of non-verbal communication. Fegley[33] compared two groups of children, one that received standard information about a radiological procedure and another in which children were encouraged to ask questions and express feelings about the procedure. Findings indicated that children who asked questions and expressed

5

concerns were less distressed and spent significantly less time seeking information during the procedure.

3. Establishing Trust with Members of the Pediatric Health Care Team

Preparation programs can provide the context in which children can develop trusting relationships with their health care team[21]. Through the provision of accurate information, the teaching of coping techniques, and the encouragement of emotional expression, the child life specialist is poised to establish a supportive and trusting relationship with the child[2]. In an evaluation of child life intervention in the emergency department, Stevenson et al.[2] noted that the child life specialist played an integral role in establishment of trust with the child. Key strategies for building rapport included asking the child questions about topics such as age, grade in school, pets, or the number of siblings. In another study, Wolfer and Visintainer[14] randomly assigned children to one of five experimental groups or a control group. The experimental groups consisted of combinations of home preparation with different types of in-hospital preparation which included supportive care. Supportive care was defined as the nurse making a special effort to establish a trusting and supportive relationship with the child and parent. Children and families who received any form of preparation and supportive care expressed significantly greater satisfaction with their hospital experience when compared with children and families in other groups.

Research Gaps and Confounding Issues

Over the past 30 years, our knowledge of the substantive issues associated with effective preparation has improved. However, this review reveals several existing gaps and confounding issues. For example, critical questions remain regarding how best to prepare children of different developmental levels[39, 40]. Much of the literature focuses on the psychological preparation of preschool and early school age children. This is most likely because this group is more at risk for misunderstanding medical explanations. As such, less is known about the effectiveness of preparation with toddlers and adolescents.

A related developmental issue concerns the notion of timing. In only one study, the timing of the preparation program relative to the day of surgery was identified as a significant variable in that preparation was not uniformly effective for all children[20]. For example, only children who were 6 years or older and who received the preparation at least five days prior to surgery benefited from the intervention[20]. Preparation had a negative effect on young children with a history of previous hospitalization, suggesting that these children require specialized methods for preparation and alternate timing [21, 22].

Given that many pediatric facilities offer group preparation with two or more children at the same time, it is essential that this approach be properly evaluated. Only one study in this review addressed group preparation[43]. McGrath prepared children 3-12 years old for surgery in small groups and found that children who were prepared in groups experienced significantly less anxiety and more satisfaction with their surgical experience than children who were prepared individually. Currently, limited research on group preparation inhibits the development of evidence-based practice in this area.

Some studies offer poor descriptions of the programs under evaluation and do not adequately control for key variables such as age, gender, prior hospital experience, and personality variables such as anxiety proneness[39]. As clinical experiences have shown, standard preparation programs are not beneficial for all children[21] particularly in the case of children who exhibit heightened levels of anxiety during and after preparation for medical procedures. Unfortunately, minimal research has investigated the impact of personality traits and associated coping styles on the effectiveness of preparation. Future research should begin to ascertain which children and adolescents are least likely to benefit from standard forms of preparation. These types of research initiatives can begin to address alternate forms of psychosocial support for this population leading to enhanced levels of evidence-based practice.

A myriad of approaches to preparation exist and are used by a variety of health care professionals across pediatric settings. In some settings, children are prepared by child life specialists, while in others, nurses may be involved. For this reason, methods of preparation can vary tremendously depending on the experience, philosophy and educational training of the professional. Since there are only a few studies that directly address preparation by child life specialists, it is imperative that research evolves to include impartial evaluations of various approaches across disciplines.

Finally, current research methods in this area are predominantly quantitative and few studies include participants from various cultural backgrounds. The processes involved in preparation are complex; consisting of several known and possibly unknown variables. Additional research from within a qualitative paradigm can more adequately explore complex processes associated with pediatric preparation. Accessing the views and perspectives of children, adolescents, and their parents could assist in supporting a family-centered care model which can better acknowledge cultural differences.

7

Summary

An extensive review of the literature revealed that most children prepared for medical procedures experience significantly lower levels of fear and anxiety as compared to children who are not prepared. Preparation also promotes long term coping and adjustment to future medical challenges. Key elements of effective preparation include the provision of clear and accurate information about the medical procedure and potential coping strategies, the encouragement of emotional expression and the establishment of trust with a health care professional. Despite a greater understanding of how to prepare children for medical procedures, research gaps and confounding issues exist. In particular, studies must begin to address which methods of preparation are most effective for specific developmental levels, personality traits and cultural backgrounds. Studies should also explore how best to encourage emotional expression from children during the course of preparation. Since a variety of approaches are being used by different disciplines, research on pediatric preparation must evaluate which forms constitute the best outcomes for children and families. These studies should include both quantitative and qualitative methodologies in order to provide a comprehensive examination of current practices which can inform child life clinical practice and policy development across pediatric health care settings.

References

1. Gibbs LE. Quality of Study Rating Form: An Instrument for Synthesizing Evaluation Studies. *Journal of Social Work Education.* 1989;25(1):67.
2. Stevenson MD, Bivins CM, O'Brien K, Gonzalez del Rey JA. Child Life intervention during angiocatheter insertion in the pediatric emergency department. *Pediatric Emergency Care.* 2005;21(11):712-718.
3. Brewer S, Gleditsch SL, Syblik D, Tietjens ME, Vacik HW. Pediatric anxiety: Child Life intervention in day surgery. *Journal of Pediatric Nursing.* 2006;21(1):13-22.
4. Schwartz BH, Albino JE, Tedesco LA. Effects of psychological preparation on children hospitalized for dental operations. *Journal of Pediatrics.* 1983;102(4):634-638.
5. Child Life Council, Committee on Hospital Care. Child Life Services. *Pediatrics.* 2006;118(4):1757-1763.
6. Institute of Medicine. *Crossing the quality chasm: A new health system for the 21st century.* Washington: DC: National Academy Press; 2001.
7. Edwinson M, Arnbjornsson E, Ekman R. Psychologic preparation program for children undergoing acute appendectomy. *Pediatrics.* 1988;82(1):30-36.
8. Roberts MC, Wurtele SK, Boone RR, Ginther LJ, Elkins PD. Reduction of medical fears by use of modeling: A preventive application in a general population of children. *Journal of Pediatric Psychology.* 1981;6(3):293-301.
9. Melamed BG, Siegel LJ. Reduction of anxiety in children facing hospitalization and surgery by use of filmed modeling. *Journal of Consulting & Clinical Psychology.* 1975;43(4):511-521.
10. Lynch M. Preparing children for day surgery. *Children's Health Care.* 1994;23(2):75-85.
11. Tiedeman ME, Clatworthy S. Anxiety responses of 5- to 11-year-old children during and after hospitalization. *Journal of Pediatric Nursing.* 1990;5(5):334-343.
12. Skipper JK, Leonard RC. Children, stress, and hospitalization: A field experiment. *Journal of Health and Social Behaviour.* 1968;9(4):275-287.
13. Cassell S, Paul MH. The role of puppet therapy on the emotional responses of children hospitalized for cardiac catheterization. *Journal of Pediatrics.* 1967;71(2):233-239.
14. Wolfer JA, Visintainer MA. Prehospital psychological preparation for tonsillectomy patients: Effects on children's and parents' adjustment. *Pediatrics.* 1979;64(5):646-655.
15. Zahr LK. Therapeutic play for hospitalized preschoolers in Lebanon. *Pediatric Nursing.* 1998;23(5):449-454.
16. Margolis JO, Ginsberg B, Dear GdL, Ross AK, Goral JE, Bailey AG. Paediatric preoperative teaching: Effects at induction and postoperatively. *Paediatric Anaesthesia.* 1998;8:17-23.
17. Elliott CH JS, Woody P. An observation scale for measuring children's distress during medical procedures. *Journal of Pediatric Psychology.* 1987;12:543-551.
18. Vernon DTA, Schulman JL, Foley JM. Changes in children's behavior after hospitalization. *American Journal of Diseases of Children.* 1966;111:581-593.
19. Speilberger CD. *Manual for the State-Trait Anxiety Inventory for Children.* Palo Alto, CA: Consulting Psychologists Press; 1973.
20. Kain ZN, Mayes LC, Caramico LA. Preoperative preparation in children: A cross-sectional study. *Journal of Clinical Anesthesia.* 1996;8:508-514.

9

21. Melamed BG, Ridley-Johnson R. Psychological preparation of families for hospitalization. *Journal of Developmental & Behavioral Pediatrics.* 1988;9(2):96-102.

22. Melamed BG, Dearborn M, Hermecz DA. Necessary considerations for surgery preparation: Age and previous experience. *Psychosomatic Medicine.* 1983;45(6):517-525.

23. Cassell S. Effect of brief puppet therapy upon the emotional responses of children undergoing cardiac catheterization. *Journal of Consulting Psychology.* 1965;29(1):1-8.

24. Hatava P, Olsson GL, Lagerkranser M. Preoperative psychological preparation for children undergoing ENT operations: A comparison of two methods. *Paediatric Anaesthesia.* 2000;10:477-486.

25. Kain ZN, Caramico LA, Mayes LC, Genevro JL, Bornstein MH, Hofstadter MB. Properative preparation programs in children: A comparative examination. *Anesthesia & Analgesia.* 1998;87(6):1249-1255.

26. Schulz JB, Raschke D, Dedrick C, Thompson M. The effects of a preoperational puppet show on anxiety levels of hospitalized children. *Child Health Care.* 1981;9(4):118-121.

27. LaMontagne L, Hepworth JT, Salisbury MH, Cohen F. Effects of coping instruction in reducing young adolescents' pain after major spinal surgery. *Orthopaedic Nursing.* 2003;22(6):398-403.

28. LaMontagne LL, Hepworth JT, Cohen F, Salisbury MH. Cognitive-Behavioral intervention effects on adolescents' anxiety and pain following spinal fusion surgery. *Nursing Research.* 2003;52(3):183-190.

29. Durst LM. Preoperative teaching videotape: The effect on children's behavior. *AORN Journal.* 1990;52(3):576-584.

30. Felder-Puig R, Maksys A, Noestlinger C, et al. Using a children's book to prepare children and parents for elective ENT surgery: Results of a randomized clinical trial. *International Journal of Pediatric Otorhinolaryngology.* 2003;67:35-41.

31. Naylor D, Coates TJ, Kan J. Reducing distress in pediatric cardiac catheterization. *American Journal of Diseases of Children.* 1984;138:726-729.

32. Fassler D. Reducing preoperative anxiety in children: Information versus emotional support. *Patient Counselling and Health Education.* 1980;2(3):130-134.

33. Fegley BJ. Preparing children for radiologic procedures: Contingent versus noncontingent instruction. *Research in Nursing & Health.* 1988;11:3-9.

34. Ferguson BF. Preparing young children for hospitalization: A comparison of two methods. *Pediatrics.* 1979;64(5):656-664.

35. Peterson L, Shigetomi C. The use of coping techniques to minimize anxiety in hospitalized children. *Behavior Therapy.* 1981;12:1-14.

36. Pinto RP, Hollandsworth JG, Jr. Using videotape modeling to prepare children psychologically for surgery: Influence of parents and costs versus benefits of providing preparation services. *Health Psychology.* 1989;8(1):79-95.

37. Zastowny TR, Kirschenbaum DS, Meng AL. Coping skills training for children: Effects on distress before, during, and after hospitalization for surgery. *Health Psychology.* 1986;5(3):231-247.

38. Tideman ME, Clatworthy S. Anxiety Responses of 5- to 11-Year-Old Children During and After Hospitalization. *Journal of Pediatric Nursing.* 1990;5(5):334-343.

39. O'Connor-Von S. Preparing children for surgery: An integrative research review. *AORN Journal.* 2000;71(2):334-343.

10

40. Vernon DTA, Foley JM, Sipowicz RR, Schulman JL. *The psychological responses of children to hospitalization and illness*. Springfield, Ill: Charles C. Thomas; 1965.

41. Campbell LA, Kirkpatrick SE, Berry CC, Lamberti JJ. Preparing children with congenital heart disease for cardiac surgery. *Journal of Pediatric Psychology*. 1995;20(3):313-328.

42. Kratz A. Preoperative education: Preparing patients for a positive experience. *Journal of Post Anesthesia Nursing*. 1993;8(4):270-275.

43. McGrath MM. Group preparation of pediatric surgical patients. *Image*. 1979;11(2):52-62.

Table 1. Final selection of studies included in this review

- Kain ZN, Mayes LC, Caramico LA. Preoperative preparation in children: A cross-sectional study. *Journal of Clinical Anesthesia.* 1996;8:508-514.

- Fegley BJ. Preparing children for radiologic procedures: Contingent versus noncontingent instruction. *Research in Nursing & Health.* 1988;11:3-9.

- McGrath MM. Group preparation of pediatric surgical patients. *Image.* 1979;11(2):52-62.

- Melamed BG, Siegel LJ. Reduction of anxiety in children facing hospitalization and surgery by use of filmed modeling. *Journal of Consulting & Clinical Psychology.* 1975;43(4):511-521.

- Brewer S, Gleditsch SL, Syblik D, Tietjens ME, Vacik HW. Pediatric anxiety: Child Life intervention in day surgery. *Journal of Pediatric Nursing.* 2006;21(1):13-22.

- Margolis JO, Ginsberg B, Dear GdL, Ross AK, Goral JE, Bailey AG. Paediatric preoperative teaching: Effects at induction and postoperatively. *Paediatric Anaesthesia.* 1998;8:17-23.

- Lynch M. Preparing children for day surgery. *Children's Health Care.* 1994;23(2):75-85.

- Felder-Puig R, Maksys A, Noestlinger C, et al. Using a children's book to prepare children and parents for elective ENT surgery: Results of a randomized clinical trial. *International Journal of Pediatric Otorhinolaryngology.* 2003;67:35-4.

- Schulz JB, Raschke D, Dedrick C, Thompson M. The effects of a preoperational puppet show on anxiety levels of hospitalized children. *Child Health Care.* 1981;9(4):118-121.

- Roberts MC, Wurtele SK, Boone RR, Ginther LJ, Elkins PD. Reduction of medical fears by use of modeling: A preventive application in a general population of children. *Journal of Pediatric Psychology.* 1981;6(3):293-301.

- Edwinson M, Arnbjornsson E, Ekman R. Psychologic preparation program for children undergoing acute appendectomy. *Pediatrics.* 1988;82(1):30-36.

- Ferguson BF. Preparing young children for hospitalization: A comparison of two methods. *Pediatrics.* 1979;64(5):656-664.

- Wolfer JA, Visintainer MA. Prehospital psychological preparation for tonsillectomy patients: Effects on children's and parents' adjustment. *Pediatrics.* 1979;64(5):646-655.

- Skipper JK, Leonard RC. Children, stress, and hospitalization: A field experiment. *Journal of Health and Social Behaviour.* 1968;9(4):275-287.

- Cassell S, Paul MH. The role of puppet therapy on the emotional responses of children hospitalized for cardiac catheterization. *Journal of Pediatrics.* 1967;71(2):233-239.

- Zahr LK. Therapeutic play for hospitalized preschoolers in Lebanon. *Pediatric Nursing.* 1998;23(5):449-454.

- Pinto RP, Hollandsworth JG, Jr. Using videotape modeling to prepare children psychologically for surgery: Influence of parents and costs versus benefits of providing preparation services. *Health Psychology.* 1989;8(1):79-95.

- Melamed BG, Dearborn M, Hermecz DA. Necessary considerations for surgery preparation: Age and previous experience. *Psychosomatic Medicine.* 1983;45(6):517-525.

- Tiedeman ME, Clatworthy S. Anxiety Responses of 5- to 11-Year-Old Children During and After Hospitalization. *Journal of Pediatric Nursing.* 1990;5(5):334-343.

- Naylor D, Coates TJ, Kan J. Reducing distress in pediatric cardiac catheterization. *American Journal of Diseases of Children.* 1984;138:726-729.

- Zastowny TR, Kirschenbaum DS, Meng AL. Coping skills training for children: Effects on distress before, during, and after hospitalization for surgery. *Health Psychology.* 1986;5(3):231-247.

- Peterson L, Shigetomi C. The use of coping techniques to minimize anxiety in hospitalized children. *Behavior Therapy.* 1981;12:1-14.

- LaMontagne LL, Hepworth JT, Cohen F, Salisbury MH. Cognitive-Behavioral intervention effects on adolescents' anxiety and pain following spinal fusion surgery. *Nursing Research.* 2003;52(3):183-190.

- LaMontagne L, Hepworth JT, Salisbury MH, Cohen F. Effects of coping instruction in reducing young adolescents' pain after major spinal surgery. *Orthopaedic Nursing.* 2003;22(6):398-403.

- Stevenson MD, Bivins CM, O'Brien K, Gonzalez del Rey JA. Child Life intervention during angiocatheter insertion in the pediatric emergency department. *Pediatric Emergency Care.* 2005;21(11):712-718.

- Fassler D. Reducing preoperative anxiety in children: Information versus emotional support. *Patient Counselling and Health Education.* 1980;2(3):130-134.

- Hatava P, Olsson GL, Lagerkranser M. Preoperative psychological preparation for children undergoing ENT operations: A comparison of two methods. *Paediatric Anaesthesia.* 2000;10:477-486.

- Schwartz BH, Albino JE, Tedesco LA. Effects of psychological preparation on children hospitalized for dental operations. *Journal of Pediatrics.* 1983;102(4):634-638.

- Campbell LA, Kirkpatrick SE, Berry CC, Lamberti JJ. Preparing children with congenital heart disease for cardiac surgery. *Journal of Pediatric Psychology.* 1995;20(3):313-328.

13

Module 4:
Therapeutic Interventions

Visions: Present and Future

In one situation the medical student helped with the necessary therapy for a seven-year-old with cystic fibrosis. As he was tucking him into bed and listening to his nightly prayers, the child included the following, "... and bless Mommy and Daddy and help Jack [the medical student] with his test tomorrow." The medical problems were forgotten; and this made a real impact on the student. (Widrick, Whaley, DiVenere, Vecchione, Swartz, & Stiffler, 1991, p. 97)

Summary: A Journey with Families

In the past chapters, professionals have accompanied parents and children as they find their way through complex, ever-unfolding paths—the unexpected peaks and valleys of life with a serious chronic illness and/or disability. Parents at various points along this journey of change and hope have discussed their fears, joys, sorrows, needs, and triumphs. Throughout the child's experience, professionals will be called upon to travel with parents; to join parents in creating mutual goals; to offer support; to alleviate isolation; and to remove roadblocks to good care. The mother of Michael, a little boy whose first 80 days of life were spent in the NICU, speaks to both caregivers and parents:

We need you [health care professionals] on our side. In these days of mass production medicine, people often feel alone and helpless. It is exhausting, heartrending work to be the parent of a child with cerebral palsy, or mental retardation, or genetic abnormalities, or asthma, or any type of chronic medical problem.

But we parents must also recognize that it is not easy to be in your shoes; it is hard to be a health professional who works with such children and their families. It is difficult to remain human in sometimes inhuman circumstances. But please, don't distance yourselves from the bodily and psychic pain suffered by babies and their parents. Honesty, patience, humility, and kindness on both sides will help move us from anguish to healing action. (Ronnie Londner, IVH Parents, 1991)

How can professionals be of greatest assistance to parents? How can professionals help parents as they chart new territory in the care of their children and navigate complex health systems? Although the road from diagnosis through ongoing care is unique for each child and family and is constantly changing, the common landmarks of good care emerge:

- the importance of values in caring for children who are not perfect
- respect for each family's unique needs and strengths
- the healing power of *listening* to parents
- equality in the decision-making process
- partnership.

Parents as Resources for Student Professionals

Parents are sharing their insights and hard-won expertise as consultants to state agencies, as members of hospital boards, and as parent consultants/advocates on hospital wards and in clinics (Damrosch, Lenz, & Perry, 1985; Pitel, Pitel, Richards, Benson, Prince, & Forman, 1985; Diffine & Stanton, 1989). In order to reap the full benefits of a growing awareness of the pivotal role of the family in the comprehensive care of children, students need parents to participate in their earliest clinical training and professional experiences. Writing in the *Physician Education Forum Report*, a physician describes the power of the parent consultant role in changing perspectives—broadening his awareness and, thus, the awareness of his students:

One day our parent consultant stopped a physician in the hall to tell him that a family had been waiting awhile to see him; I might as well tell you that the physician was me. It was in the middle of clinic, and I was teaching a resident; we were reviewing a chart.

I told the parent consultant that, although I understood that the family had been waiting, we were a teaching hospital and that there were many benefits to patients and families from being in a teaching hospital. I said I would go to the family as quickly as I could, but that it was my responsibility to teach the resident. You can imagine the spiel that I made.

The next day, the parent consultant came to see me. She asked me, "What is it that you are teaching these students? You are

teaching them that people can wait."

That was not what I wanted to be teaching them. I decided no more of this! We teach after people go home. I tell our students and residents to shadow me. If I can teach them a few points, that's one thing, but people do not wait. I want them to learn that in our clinic. [This] experience provided an insight that turned our program around. (Edwin Forman, 1990, pp. 28-29)

It is hoped that "model programs," burgeoning opportunities for students and parents, will encourage a new educational agenda: the integration and full participation of parents in clinical teaching (Guralnick, Richardson, & Heiser, 1982; Shonkoff, 1983; Desguin, 1986; Healy & Lewis-Beck, 1987; Poyadue, 1988; Sharp & Lorch, 1988; Physician Education Forum Report, 1990; Widrick, Whaley, DiVenere, Vecchione, Swartz, & Stiffler, 1991). A mother speaks of her role in the continuing education of occupational therapists:

I was a bit intimidated by the term "parent faculty." Although I had worked with professionals in a variety of settings, now I was being asked to actually "teach" occupational therapists about being a parent of a child with special needs....

In attending many multi-disciplinary meetings, I have observed that parents often group together, perhaps seeking strength, reassurance, and comfort. At the project's "trial run" weekend . . . we were separated in small groups so that each parent had the opportunity to interact with several O.T.'s. As the weekend progressed, I found that my input was asked for and listened to, even though my experience with occupational therapy (OT) was very limited. I had a unique perspective that the others in my group did not have—I had lived for 18 years with a child *who* has special needs. . . (Betsy Trombino, member of the new AOTA training program for occupational therapists working with infants and toddlers, *ACCH Network*, Vol. 7, No. 1, Winter, 1989)

Parents stress that from the moment of birth they are accumulating experiences, learning from their children, and developing new ways of understanding family life. The road traveled by parents of children with special needs is long and complex; change and accommodation are constant features of parents' journeys. For example, newly-informed parents appreciate the support of meeting veteran parents but may not fully believe they will ever achieve the equilibrium they see the experienced parents displaying.

Young professionals will work with parents at various places along the path. Of crucial importance is respect for each parent's experience and perspective. Laura's mother explains:

Experiences with our children may be "felt" differently (a) when they occur, (b) a little later, and then (c) much later—"in retrospect." Students gain from seeing parents at all stages along the journey. . . .

Although the following comments and suggestions address the needs of medical students and young physicians, they also apply to health care professionals of many disciplines A mother offers *A Few Words to Young Professionals* (Sherelyn Campbell):

• **Invite experienced parents to speak to medical students both in classroom and informal settings.** A personal encounter with a family living with hemophilia or cystic fibrosis gives perspective and depth to textbook/lecture learning and will enhance clinical experience.

• **Include parents as discussion leaders, panelists, and guest speakers when planning seminars for health professionals.** They are an untapped resource, and most would welcome the opportunity to share their hard-earned wisdom.

• **Allow medical students ample opportunities for role-playing.** Possible assignments could include: negotiating a dispute between parents and house staff over a particular procedure; giving bad news to a family waiting near the operating room; talking with a distraught mother who is transferring her anxieties to her sick child, etc. Role-playing can involve experienced parents playing "devil's advocate" or doctors exchanging roles with parents.

• **Encourage "home residencies" for medical students, interns and/or residents.** A week spent with a family coping with a chronic illness or disability gives doctors a realistic look at the therapies, medication schedules, and activity limitations they will be prescribing. It also gives the doctor a chance to view the impact an illness has on the rest of the family.

• **Let young professionals help to staff respite care facilities as part of their training.** The term "on call" takes on a whole new meaning when you have 24 hour a day / 7 day a week responsibility for someone.

When Families and Students Share Experiences

Initial steps in creating such learning situations—sharing a meal with a family; spending an afternoon in the home of a family—may deeply affect student attitudes and perspectives. A medical student describes his reactions to such an experience—his coming to know Paul, a 25-year-old man with Down syndrome, and Paul's family:

To interview a family with a son who has a mental handicap was challenging for me, not only because of my lack of knowledge, but also because I would have to go into a home and interview a family I did not know. It was my first real contact with someone who might be a patient. Compounding these two anxieties was my apprehension of having contact with an individual with a mental handicap. My past experience with people with a mental handicap was very limited. Questions came to my mind: "How will I react?" "Will I be comfortable?" "What will he look like?" "Will I be able to talk to him?" "Will he talk to me?" "Can he talk?" I was totally unaware of what I was getting into. I did not know enough to have an opinion but, as in most unknown situations, I was afraid to face it. . . .

Paul's mother, Jane, is a warm person, and she made me very comfortable. I felt progressively more comfortable asking her questions about most aspects of her family life, but when it came to asking questions about Paul, I couldn't. The words would not come out of my mouth. She kept reassuring me that any questions I asked she surely had heard before. The fact that Paul was present right beside me made it even harder. I didn't want to say anything to upset or downgrade him.

Paul's father was quieter. . .but from his remarks I learned that as much as possible, he treated Paul as he treated his other son. . .

I was dismayed by the attitudes toward Paul taken by aunts and uncles, friends, professionals and his community. Upon learning that Paul indeed had a mental handicap, all of the family no longer felt it essential to visit. Paul was no longer the cute baby he once was, but rather an oddball who should be ignored. . .Paul and his family were completely shut off emotionally from the rest of the family.

This situation repeated itself with most of their friends. Even people whom the family had known for long periods of time would no longer visit. Within the first few minutes, the family always knew who would accept him and who wouldn't. . .

. . .There is no doubt that Paul's development relied on his mother's push to get things done. Because of the lack of support available, it took special parents to raise Paul.

The most staggering information gained from the interview was the attitude taken by the medical profession. They were shocking. There was often a coldness towards the family. The family learned over the telephone that their son had Down Syndrome. The family needs to be comforted and the doctor should be available to help. The doctor's opinion was categorical. He believed that people with a mental handicap are unfit to make decisions and should be treated as children.

Paul was to have an operation when he was old enough to sign the consent form but the doctor asked his mother to sign. She would not sign it and forced the doctor to let Paul sign.

Neglect was also a major problem, as shown by both his dentist and doctor. After having his wisdom teeth out, Paul had an adverse reaction and regurgitated all over himself. Although she was told he would be cleaned up, his mother found nothing had been done when she came back the next day. . . .

The trouble a family must go through to get proper care for their son or daughter is excessive. There is no reason why one individual should be treated better than another. Of course, these attitudes are not held by all professionals and may be due to an uneasiness, anxiety and inadequate training in medical schools

. . .

When asked by Paul's mother what I had learned from the interview, I replied, "Everything." Of course, my new knowledge was far from everything, but I had learned so much. Attitudes held by many are due to ignorance, and this leads to improper treatment of people with a mental handicap. . . .

The knowledge and understanding about people with a mental handicap that I have gained from this experience will remain with me for the rest of my life. It has given me the opportunity to challenge my attitudes about mental handicaps. Finally, my promise to the family was to make my colleagues aware that individuals with a mental handicap are people too and should be treated as such.

In relating my experience to my classmates, I was not surprised to find that they were as ignorant as I had been. The group discussions centred around the immediate family strengths, the abandonment of the extended family and friends, as well as our

attitudes as physicians. It was pointed out to me that my discussion centred mainly around Paul's mother. I believed that my lack of interaction with Paul was related to my inexperience but also to my self-consciousness and fear of offending him. I also understood that in this way I was not treating him like an adult.

The group was appalled at the treatment given to people with a mental handicap and couldn't believe something like this was actually happening in Canada. Everyone agreed they learned a great deal and that their minds opened up to a totally unfamiliar aspect of medicine. They learned enough that they hoped their treatment of people with a mental handicap would be far better than that given to Paul. (Yves Talbot and Richard Shaul, 1987, pp. 7-9)

How will this new vision and enhanced point of view be reinforced, even rewarded, as students begin to provide care for patients and families? Will such positive goals fade under the pressures and constraints of demanding training programs that emphasize technical knowledge at the expense of "care"?

Techniques to comfort children during stressful procedures

Barbara Kurfis Stephens, Mary E. Barkey, and Howard R. Hall

Barbara Kurfis Stephens MAN, CRRN, is a Clinical Nurse Specialist at Health Hill Hospital for Children in Cleveland OH (USA); Mary E Barkey MA, CCLS, is a Child Life Clinical Specialist and Howard R. Hall, PhD, PsyD* is in the Division of Behavioral Pediatrics, both at Rainbow Babies and Children's Hospital in Cleveland, OH (USA).

Abstract: Medical procedures can be unpleasant experiences for children, their parents, and health care providers. We present this model of working with children having invasive procedures with the aim of helping to increase the comfort of infants and children and also parents and medical staff. The model has five parts: (1) Preparing the child and parent for the procedure and for their role during the procedure; (2) inviting the parent/caregiver to be present; (3) utilizing the treatment room for stressful procedures; (4) positioning the child in a comforting manner; and (5) maintaining a calm, positive atmosphere.

Introduction

Some of the most distressing aspects of a disease or hospitalization for many children as well as for their parents and their health care providers are invasive medical procedures. These range from venipunctures to spinal taps to the placement of nasogastric tubes (Agency for Health Care Policy and Research 1992). Anxiety surrounding being hurt has been identified as one of the greatest fears of children (Slaw et al. 1986). Parents also cite invasive procedures as traumatic events (Jay & Elliot 1990). A child's memories of such procedures can remain upsetting for many years (Davies et al. 1972; Stuber et al. 1996).

The previous standard manner of conducting such procedures at Rainbow Babies and Children's Hospital (in Cleveland, OH), can perhaps be taken as representative. The child was taken into the treatment room while the parents huddled outside the door. Often the child was not prepared in any way for the procedure other than being told the type of procedure to be performed–

"You need an i.v.," for example, or "We are going to put a tube into your nose." The child was forced to lie supine on a table with staff members pinning the child down. The number of staff were increased until the child was sufficiently immobilized to perform the procedure, at times requiring 4 to 5 adults. A similar pediatric approach was followed in seven hospitals in four states in which the first author has been employed. Such an approach is not only stressful to the child but also to staff and to parents who in particular often feel helpless and distressed not knowing how to comfort their children during painful and anxiety-related procedures (Kuttner 1989).

There is a general consensus that a crucial obligation of health care professionals, particularly those treating children, is the management of pain and the relief of suffering (Agency for Health Care Policy and Research 1992). As a

*This research was supported in part by NIDA Grant #DA07957.

---

result, there has been a growing interest in nonpharmacological approaches to pain management in children for invasive procedures (Campos 1994; French et al. 1994; Kuttner 1989; Olness & Kohen 1996; Wall 1991). These approaches have been characterized either as kinesthetic methods, such as rocking, distraction, blowing bubbles, and reading pop-up books; or as imaginal methods, employing hypnotherapy approaches (Kuttner 1989). Despite these interventions, no prescriptions for managing pain in children have developed, and there remains a need for providing better ways of managing pain, particularly in the younger child (Agency for Health Care Policy and Research 1992). This concern has led the authors to the development, starting around 1985, of a five-part model using kinesthetic, nonpharmacological means to comfort children under five years of age during invasive medical procedures. We present this model here.

We note that tools measuring stress and pain in children under five, our target population, were just beginning to appear in publication in the late 1980s. Observations of nonverbal responses and autonomic measurements in preverbal children were documented (Craig et al. 1984; Owens 1984; Hahn & McLone 1984), but elements of subjective judgment exist in each study. Tools that objectively measure stress and pain in the preverbal child continue to be developed, studied, and revised (Fuller & Conner 1995). The assessment of our five-part model using such tools remains to be done.

1. Preparing the child and parent

To prepare for invasive procedures, parents and children need information about a procedure's importance to the health or diagnosis of the child – simply, why we need to do it. They also need to know what to expect during the procedure and what their differing individual roles will be. For children, the information should be developmentally appropriate and timed to meet the individual child's needs and preferences (Agency for Health Care Policy and Research 1992).

Parents and children may have had previous experiences with invasive procedures that will influence their responses (Dahlquist et al. 1986). Thus, an important part of medical data collection is information about the child's past experience with painful procedures and pain control approaches (Agency for Health Care Policy and Research 1992). By exploring these past experiences, we can identify, if necessary, additional interventions to support the child's coping skills (Melamed & Siegel 1975).

Fear, anxiety, and tension can heighten the response to pain in a child no less than in adults (Ross & Ross 1984, Frankel 1964). Uncertainty about any aspect of the elements involved in an invasive procedure can limit the child's ability to develop any effective control and thereby increase feelings of helplessness and stress (Lazarus & Folkman 1984). At times, hospital staff omit basic information that the child and his or her parents need to understand the procedure. For example, a $3\frac{1}{2}$-year-old began screaming to put the cream back on when the topical anesthetic cream *EMLA* was wiped off prior to needle insertion. The explanation of hospital staff during preparation omitted the fact that the cream would still work, even when it was removed. This additional information helped calm the child.

Child life specialists, who are especially trained to work with children, provide a valuable resource to the health care team in preparing parents and children for invasive procedures. These specialists are skilled in translating hospital jargon into ordinary language and in giving explanations at the developmental level of a child. We can report that we have seen children regress during stressful situations, so at times explanations may need to be adapted to a developmental level that is younger than a child's chronological age.

Many health care workers theoretically accept the benefits of verbal preparation for children and parents, but in practice they view it as a time-consuming event that imposes an extra burden on their tight schedules. With this in mind, we have developed simple, short explanations that can be completed in as brief a time as 3 to 5 minutes. (If more time is available, a lengthier preparation can occur.) The staff sets up for the procedure at the

108

same time that the family is being prepared, thus eliminating the perception of delay. Results show that time invested in preparation is easily redeemed in time saved during the procedure. The child is able to cooperate with the procedure, and the parents remain calm (Kachoyeanos & Friedhoff 1993).

The demeanor of the people preparing the child and performing the procedure must match the emotions the child is likely to be feeling. Invasive procedures are very serious for children, and a joking, laughing adult is seen as lacking understanding, empathy, and compassion (Ross & Ross 1982). Our responsibility is not to try to make the child smile or feel happy, but rather to offer information and reassurance and to plan.

Since it is not clear when a child begins to comprehend, we give explanations to children as young as one year. The following is an example of the approach we recommend to staff in preparing children 1–6 years old for a venipuncture procedure (entering a vein, usually to draw blood or provide medicine).

Eliminate distractions as much as possible. Sit facing the child and parent, and use a quiet, low, serious tone of voice. Act as if this is the most important thing you will do today, and that you have all day to do it. State that you have something important to discuss. At this point children often turn to cling to a parent or look worried, but usually they continue to give their attention to what is being said to them. Emphasize that the child will have one job, which in most procedures is to hold still. Repeat the job several times in such a way that the child will be certain that the job applies to the whole procedure.

Ask the child to look at the veins in an adult hand, and explain that the same blue lines are in the child's hand. A parent or staff member can point out the blue lines. Tell the child that you need to slip a tube into the little blue line, and explain the reason why – for example, because "your blood can help us find out why you are sick," or to "give you medicine in a way you cannot take at home." When mentioning medicine, link it, if possible, to treating a specific symptom in the child.

The next step is to give a demonstration that illustrates an intravenous insertion. Tell the child

to imagine that an index finger of an adult in the room is an intravenous tube. Move the finger toward the veins of the adult's other hand. If the child is calm and comfortable, the child's own hands can be used to demonstrate the procedure. Move the hand receiving the tube back and forth, to illustrate what will happen if the child moves the hand while the tube is being inserted. Ask if the child can see how moving the hand makes it very hard to get the tube in. Children as young as 2 or 3 years often nod their heads, "Yes." Next, illustrate how much easier the tube could slip in if the child's hand is held very still and does not wiggle. State what a big help it is when the hand holds still. Ask the child if she or he could help by holding still. Again, the child usually nods "Yes." Re-emphasize how helpful it is when the hand is very still, that this is the only thing the child needs to do. Assure the child that you will help the child hold still.

Now, this explanation omits some traditional statements in pediatric health care. In an attempt to be honest, for example, the traditional statement may include an adult assessment of how a procedure is likely to feel – in particular that it is going to hurt. But such an assessment focuses the child on the hurt. Some children, of course, will ask if a procedure will hurt. In this case, because procedures feel different for each child, one can honestly respond by saying that some children think it is uncomfortable and some children think it is okay – thus avoiding the word pain or hurt altogether. Then add, "We want to know how it feels for you." (The LaMaze method of childbirth follows a similar verbal approach, in using the term "contractions" for "labor pains.")

Another tradition in pediatrics is to say, "It's okay to cry." But do children (or adults) wait for permission before crying? When information is foreign (for example, involving an i.v. or drawing blood), children may remain somewhat confused after the explanations. If a statement is then included saying "It's okay to cry," the suggestion implies that what is about to happen will be so bad the child will want to cry, an understanding that again changes the focus for the child. If, during the procedure, a child does cry, you can respond by saying that you are sorry you have to do

109

something the child does not like. Then make positive statements praising the child for being a terrific helper at holding still. There is no limit to the amount of praise to give during a procedure.

Again, children and parents traditionally are not asked what would help them during a procedure. Or if they do propose ideas, their thoughts and observations usually do not seem helpful or acceptable to "experts" like us. Be willing to explore and incorporate such ideas in any and every way possible. Christine, a 4-year-old, demanded to stay in her stroller while a nasogastric tube was inserted into her nose. The authors (Stephens and Barkey) had never done the procedure this way before but realized that the child's position in the stroller was exactly what was needed. During the insertion, Christine's hands were held and stroked by her mother who had eye-to-eye contact with her daughter. Christine kicked her feet, but no one had to assist her in holding her head still as the tube was inserted. Planning a procedure with child and parent and soliciting their opinions not only conveys respect but also results in greater cooperation to achieve the goal (Jacobsen et al. 1990; Visintainer & Wolfer 1975).

Child and parent need to feel that they are integral to a team that is working together. Parents who are paid little attention and have less input, remain more anxious and, focusing on the procedure, tend to ignore their child, while parents who interact with their child during a procedure are calmer (Melamed & Siegel 1975; Peterson & Shigetomi 1981). Further, parents who are prepared for a procedure provide information about it to their own child and so reduce fears and uncertainty. When a child and/or parent does not initiate ideas, suggest some choices for them to make. For example, you could ask a child, "Who would you like to have with you?" or "Do you want to sit in a lap or on a chair?" Or "Is there a song you would like to sing?"

In addition to verbal preparation, the topical anesthetic cream of *EMLA*, mentioned earlier, is available to alleviate pain for procedures involving needles. *EMLA* is applied to intact skin 1 to 4 hours in advance of a procedure (Ehrenstrom-Reiz & Reiz 1982). Based on reports by verbal children,

studies support the effectiveness of the cream in preventing the sensation of pain (Taddio et al. 1994). However, we note that owing to the anxiety of a needle and of other stressors of a procedure, the effectiveness of *EMLA* alone may be difficult to assess (McGrath & McAlpine 1993). But when *EMLA* is used in tandem with this model, the infant or child is comforted and has the opportunity to experience the full benefit of the cream.

2. Inviting the parent/caregiver to be present

By 1 to 2 months infants recognize faces, and at 5 months, they express their fear of strangers through loud protest. Both Spock and Brazelton suggest keeping strangers at a distance until the infant has the opportunity to adjust (Brazelton 1992; Spock 1946). In the traditional hospital setting, however, parents are often separated from their children within minutes of a child's admission, and the child is whisked off to a procedure. Despite this general practice (or perhaps because of it) parents regularly express a desire to be present while their child is having a procedure (Bauchner et al. 1991, Bauchner et al. 1996). Studies show that the presence of parents does not have a negative impact on the performance of medical staff and that being with their child also results in less anxiety in the parents (Bauchner et al. 1991; Bauchner et al. 1996).

Children clearly want a parent to remain with them. In the early 1980s nearly 1000 children aged 5 to 12 years old were asked what would help them the most if they were in the worst pain. Ninety-nine percent said having a parent with them, even though the children did not expect the parents to be able to do anything to relieve the pain (Ross & Ross 1984).

Parents must receive encouragement and guidance from the staff to be able to continue in the role of parent while in the hospital. Partnerships should be encouraged between families and professionals to ensure family-centered care (Johnson et al. 1992). Parents must not merely be allowed to be present at a procedure, but must actively be *invited*.

It is our experience that with such a team approach, parents are also more likely to accept a failure in completing a procedure, without any negative judgments toward the staff. Prior to a venipuncture procedure, we have often heard parents say, "You get one try and that's it." We respond that we cannot promise that we will get it with one try, but we can promise to be kind, gentle, and take our time. We are not refused additional attempts when our behavior mirrors this statement.

Parents need a clearly defined role as part of a team (Zelter et al. 1990). The job for our parents is to accompany their child and to support and comfort him or her during the procedure. The parent should use techniques that are familiar to the child, those normally used when the child is upset. Frequently, both parents want to be present for the procedure. When both parents are present, a parent who is unsure of his or her role is tempted to assume the role of supervisor, which creates anxiety for all involved, including the "supervising" parent. This situation can be avoided by clearly defining a role for the second parent, such as comforting the other parent or providing distraction for the child.

Most parents instinctively use distraction techniques. Distraction can be simple, such as stroking, singing, or talking with the child. Visual and interactive distractions, such as pop-up books, suspension wands, puppets, water toys, bubbles, etc. are effective especially with children 3–6 years old (Kuttner 1991; Anderson et al. 1989). Children and their parents should choose which distractions to use. Guided imagery or self-hypnosis has been studied in children 5 years and older and, for these children, has proven extremely effective in coping with invasive procedures (Kuttner 1989; Olness & Gardner 1978). Younger children have not reached the stage of cognitive development that enables them to utilize this technique effectively.

Distraction toys should be used only in the treatment room. This ensures their availability for procedures and helps to maintain the child's interest in the toys' novelty. Incidentally, we refer to the distractors as "things" to use in the treatment room, on the presumption that when the word "toy" is affiliated with a stressful event, the association could cause confusion for the child. A negative name for the storage box holding the distractors, such as "hurt" or "pain" box, should also be avoided.

At times, a parent or family member is not available or is emotionally unable to remain with the child for a stressful procedure. We have learned from experience that some parents who doubt their ability to cope with the procedure are often able to participate and can effectively comfort their child when they have had a chance to express their fears, are prepared for the procedure, and receive support and encouragement from the staff. It is vital that during every stressful procedure someone is assigned the job of comforting the child. The Child Life Specialist is a valuable resource in preparing and supporting the family member who comforts the child, and, in the absence of a family member, is an excellent substitute in providing such comfort.

3. Utilizing the treatment room for stressful procedures

During hospitalization, respect for the privacy of the child's bedroom and the family's only personal space must be observed (Johnson et al. 1992). Ordinarily, staff enter the room unannounced, whenever they want, and in some cases perform stressful procedures in the child's bed. The child, thus, cannot discriminate if a health care giver is coming into the room for a safe or a stressful visit. Under such conditions of uncertainty, the child remains constantly vigilant and anxious. Yet we expect children to relax, rest, and heal in the very space that is not safe. Further, multiple-bed rooms and thin walls create additional anxiety as children experience sounds of distress from their wounded roommates.

The policy of using only the treatment room for procedures maintains the bed as a safe haven (Frederick 1991); it also preserves privacy, and moves the child's cries away from the other children. To a staff with limited time and little patience for delays, the time waiting for a child to be moved to the treatment room seems interminable. Initially, not moving the child could save time but at the ultimately greater expense of subsequent time to comfort a cautious child each time a caregiver enters the room.

Of course, clinical conditions, medical equipment, or hospital design may prevent moving the child. In these cases, a discriminating signal used whenever staff enter the room for a pending unpleasant event helps the child separate safe from stressful visits. The signal needs to be simple and to be used consistently – for example, carrying a particular stuffed animal, ringing a bell, wearing a distinctive hat.

If the child is old enough to understand what will occur, the choice of remaining in his or her bed, and not going to the treatment room for stressful procedures, should be honored. But one needs to be certain that the child is old enough to decide (and also that any roommates are protected from observing the procedure). One 7-year-old insisted on staying in her bed even though she had gone to the treatment room for all previous tests. But when the actual event occurred, she became very upset and unable to hold still. Because her bed had always been safe, she thought staying in bed would avoid the blood test.

There is the possibility that children will come to fear the treatment room. Staff have observed children crossing to opposite sides of the hallway or running past its door. Of course, they are not expected to like the treatment room. But when they leave the room, they are certain the stressful event is over.

4. Positioning the child in a comforting manner

The impetus for our model came from observing the behavior of children during invasive procedures. Four-year-old Boyd had been struggling for 45 minutes against 3 adults when one author (Stephens) responded to a request for more help. Stephens was told that even more people would be needed. Stephens asked Boyd if he could hold his arm still if he sat in her lap. He said yes. Stephens settled him into her lap into the

Fig. 1

straddling position shown in Figure 1. His arm was then secured flat onto the table. He did not move as the i.v. was inserted successfully with a single attempt.

The usual hospital practice is for staff to pin children down on the table, calling in reinforcements to prevent movement of "uncooperative" children. Boyd and many, many other children scream in panic and struggle fiercely as soon as they are placed in a supine position. Children with respiratory distress literally cannot breathe as this smothering hold is applied. Staff are often heard saying, "Why are you crying? We haven't done anything yet." The child's behavior is assumed to come from fear of the procedure. Years of pediatric tradition has missed the obvious: lying children down is frightening and results in a loss of control.

In describing the examination of a 1-year-old, Brazelton writes, "If I want to keep her happy through it [the examination], I ask a parent to hold her in the parent's lap" (Brazelton 1992). Parents often state that their child will do better sitting up, and when given the choice, the overwhelming majority of children emphatically choose sitting up over lying down. The authors of this article challenged each other to develop sitting positions that promoted comfort for the child as well as sufficient immobilization for success of the procedure. Our results have been dramatic. Parents hold their children in familiar positions of comfort. In these positions, children can cooperate and maintain a sense of control. They still cry, but they do not scream or frantically flail to escape. Children who are calm react with less intensity to negative stimulation than do children who are already upset for other reasons (Korner & Thoman 1972). Consequently, procedures require less time and fewer staff. The positions of comfort also lessen the chance that the procedure will fail (Figs 1–3).

We initiate sitting positions as soon as a child has achieved some trunk and head control, usually 3 to 5 months of age. Figures 1 and 2 show sitting positions that we use for venipuncture procedures. For maximum stability, the child's arm is positioned flat on a solid surface. If *EMLA* is not used, there is a reflex jerk when the needle touches the skin of an unsupported arm, and the site is likely to be lost. The arm of the parent may need to be over or under the child's shoulder, the height of the stool raised or lowered, or a bolster of linen placed under the child's arm to ensure a stable position. In all instances, it is essential that the position of the child and parent is secure before beginning.

In addition to the cooperation of the child, positions of comfort offer other advantages. These include:

- Greater immobility of the child's arm, since movement of the child in the parent's lap

Fig. 3

does not affect the movement of the child's arm held by a separate person.

- Minimal movement of the trunk, because when the legs are kicking, they swing back and forth from the knee.
- A large work area on an immobile table, because the child's movement does not move the table.
- Restriction by parents of the child's movement in a positive, comforting position.

Figure 2 demonstrates a staff member holding both the child and the arm. While skilled staff might be able to manage both jobs if the child is very cooperative, parents should not be asked to do this. Aside from the position's intrinsic difficulty, if the child moves, the burden of the procedure's success is inappropriately placed on the parent. In general, we recommend that one person hold the child and another person hold the arm.

Figure 3 shows the position of children whose straddle would not match the lap size of the holder. In this situation, if the child kicks, the body movement is more likely to make the arm move. Children 5 to 6 years old, especially boys, often choose this position or sitting on the stool alone with their parent next to them. A staff member holds the arm extended on the table.

Fig. 2

113

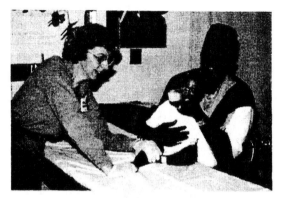

Fig. 4

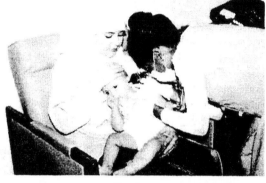

Fig. 6

Fig. 5

sitting up restricts leg movement enough so that one staff member is able to immobilize the legs. A similar position, with children sitting on the table or in their parent's lap, whichever is most comfortable and secure, is used when inserting a needle into a subcutaneous central venous port.

In Figure 7, the parent hugs the child who is sitting on the edge of the table. Only one person is needed to administer an injection. Bending the leg over the edge of the table interferes with the ability to contract the muscle. Injections into a relaxed muscle hurt less than injections into a tense muscle. The child's thigh is immobilized flat on

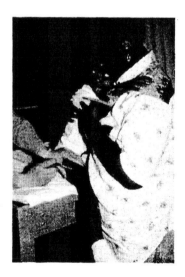

Fig. 7

Positions shown in Figures 4–6 can be used for examinations of the face and head, for obtaining specimens, and for placement of nasogastric tube. The parent's body supports the child's and allows maximal body contact. The position in Figure 4 is also used for phlebotomy procedures in the foot or for intramuscular injections in the thigh. In a supine position, leg movement from kicking is much greater and requires less effort. Merely

114

the table with one hand, and the injection is given with the other hand. The child can also sit in the parent's lap in a chest-to-chest position with the leg stabilized on the thigh of the parent as the injection is administered.

Many procedures require the child to be in a recumbent position; however, the child can continue to feel secure when maximum body contact is maintained with the parent. The parent lies on the table with the child lying on top of or nested next to the parent. For example, children must lie prone during allergy testing. Twisting or turning causes the allergens to run and could result in false results. A 1-year-old clung desperately as one author (Barkey) tried to lie her prone. When Barkey reclined with the child on her abdomen, the child relaxed and allowed the allergy testing to be completed. If the parent cannot lie next to the child, the parent should be positioned to maintain as much visual and tactile contact as possible. Parents are willing to sit under sterile drapes to maintain eye-to-eye contact with their child.

Figure 8 illustrates a position for urethral catheterization. The child's head rests in the lap of the staff member. The body of the staff member prevents the child from scooting toward the top of the table and away from the catheter. The same staff member separates the child's legs as the catheter is inserted. The parent should hold the child's hands in a midline position to enhance comfort and support organization (Als et al. 1989). The parent prevents the child from grabbing the catheter but does so in a positive manner, often stroking the hands while talking to the child.

Parents present for spinal taps can be positioned so their view of the needle entering the child's back is blocked (Fig. 9). If the child sits for the spinal tap, the parent can sit behind the staff member. The child's arms encircle the staff member, and the parent holds the child's hands.

Staff often prejudge parents, deciding that a certain procedure will be too upsetting for them. Spinal taps and bone marrow aspirations are two procedures that fall into this category. But staff should not make these a priori decisions for parents. We were told of an experience at one hospital in which a sedated child sat in the lap of his parent for a spinal tap. When the child was

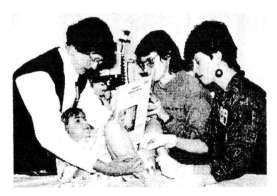

Fig. 8

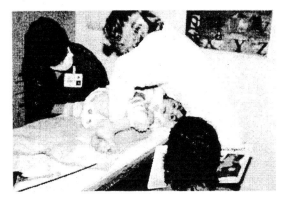

Fig. 9

moved to the table for a bone marrow aspiration, the child became agitated and upset. The doctor returned the child to the lap of the parent and performed the bone marrow aspiration on a relaxed child.

5. Maintaining a calm and positive atmosphere

Developing positive language and ego-supporting statements is integral to managing stressful procedures (Kuttner 1989). In our model, the child and parent are coached to hug each other. Hugging is one of the comforts of childhood that is not abandoned in adulthood and that benefits nearly everyone during stressful times. Hugging limits the child's movement, is a positive and comforting act, and offers a serendipitous advantage – that both arms stiffen in order to hug. Until about 5 to 7 years of age, the child is not coordinated enough to stiffen one arm and wiggle the other. Therefore, when hugging is encouraged, both arms stiffen. Because our only expectation of the child is to hold still, hugging assists them to be successful.

In addition to hugging, it is critical to focus on the desired behavior and to give positive reinforcement (Anderson et al. 1989). Because our only expectation of the child is to hold still, we take every opportunity to reinforce this. When the phlebotomist cleans the injection site, children generally hold still, and we use this opportunity to reinforce how terrific they are at holding still, complimenting them for doing exactly what they said they would do. Words like "terrific," "wonderful," "awesome," "super," "incredible," and "best" must be used abundantly. An overdose of praise is an error we should all make. Children gain a sense of achievement and pride as they are praised for being such wonderful helpers and holding so still.

The whole environment must be calm, with quiet, soothing voices (Zelter et al. 1990). Observe a conversation between two adults, one of whom has laryngitis. After a short time, both adults are whispering. In a quiet, calm environment, the adult who is yelling and commanding soon feels out of place and adjusts his or her voice to fit into the atmosphere. When voices escalate in volume, there is a greater level of excitement and anxiety. Negative, directive language soon follows. Hester and Ray (1987) interviewed 28 children ages 5 to 15. Behaviors the children identified as noncaring included "they ignored me," "shout at me," "get mad at me," "tell me to relax," "don't keep the noise down." The tone of voice is as important as the content when delivering a message.

When the procedure is completed, there should be continuing praise for the child to reinforce the accomplishments. A sticker or special band-aid should be used to help the child identify that the procedure is over and that escape from the treatment room is imminent. The sticker is not a reward, it is a signal of completion. Stickers should not be withheld for any reason. The parents also

appreciate recognition for their efforts, and need to hear that we think they did a good job too.

Participation in therapeutic medical play can be offered by a Child Life Specialist before and/or after a stressful procedure. Parents as well as children express their feelings through this activity. If a Child Life Specialist was not present at the procedure or does not know about it, the specialist needs to be informed about it. The Child Life Specialist can evaluate the response of the child and parent to the procedure and provide recommendations and assistance.

In conclusion, the management of pain during invasive procedures is particularly challenging for the patient who is a young child. The continued development and utilization of effective means of decreasing discomfort during invasive procedures is an important goal for health care professionals. In fact, pain management approaches have been recommended as part of a hospital's quality assurance procedures (Agency for Health Care Policy and Research 1992). With the availability of nonpharmacologic approaches to pain management such as positions of comfort, hospitals can develop and utilize effective standards of care for patients and families (Agency for Health Care Policy and Research 1992).

It should be pointed out that these comforting approaches can be applied not only to young children but also to adolescents who may regress during stressful procedures. One author (Hall) used a position of comfort introduced in this article with a 12-year-old sickle cell patient, who needed an intramuscular injection but was crying and anxious. Other possible recipients might include very irritable infants with neurodevelopmental disorders, perhaps because they have been drug exposed. The possible comforting effect of these positions of comfort for special populations needs further exploration.

Finally, much information can be gleaned from listening to our children and their parents, particularly before invasive procedures. Children often have very helpful suggestions for effective means of managing their pain and discomfort. Children have a right to receive care that offers the most comfort possible. We have an obligation to provide it.

REFERENCES

Agency for Health Care Policy and Research 1992. Acute pain management in infants, children and adolescents: operative and medical procedures. Maryland: Agency for Health Care Policy and Research.

Als H, Duffy FH, McAnultry GB, Badian N 1989. Continuity of neurobehavioral functioning in preterm and full-term newborns. In: Bornstein M, Krasnegar N (eds) Stability and continuity in mental development. New Jersey: Lawrence Fribaum: 5–28.

Anderson C, Zelter L, Fahurik D 1989. Procedural pain. In: Funk SM, Tornquist EM, Champagne MT, & Wiese RA (eds). Key aspects of comfort. New York: Springer Publishing: 435–459.

Bauchner H, Waring C, Vinci R 1991. Parental presence during procedure in an emergency room: results from 50 observations. Pediatrics 87(4): 544–548.

Bauchner H, Vinci R, Bak S, Pearson C, Corwin M 1996 Parents and procedures: A randomized controlled trial. Pediatrics 98(5): 861–867.

Brazelton TB 1992 Touchpoints, your child's emotional and behavioral development. New York: Addison–Wesley.

Campos RG 1994 Rocking and pacifiers: two comforting interventions for heelstick pain. Research in Nursing & Health 17(1): 321–331.

Craig KD, McMahon RJ, Morrison JD, Zashow C 1984 Developmental changes in infant pain expression during immunization injections. Social Science and Medicine 19: 1331–1337.

Dahlquist IM, Gil KM, Armstrong FD, DeLawyer DD, Green P, Wouri D 1986 Preparing children for medical examinations: the importance of previous medical experience. Health Psychology 5(3): 249–549.

Davies R, Butler N, Goldstein H 1972. Facts – why we must change our practice. From Birth to Seven: The Second Report of the National Child Development Study. London: National Children's Bureau.

Ehrenstrom-Reiz GM, Reiz S 1982 EMLA-Aeutetic mixture of local anesthetics for topical anaesthesia. Acta Anaesthesiol Scand 26: 596–598.

Frankel V 1964 Man's Search for Meaning. London: Hodder & Stoughton.

Frederick V 1991 Pediatric IV therapy: Soothing the patient. RN 54(12): 40–42.

French G, Painter EC, Coury DI 1994 Blowing away shot pain: A technique for pain management during immunization. Pediatrics 93(3): 384–388.

Fuller B, Conner D 1995 The effect of pain on infant behaviors. Clinical Nursing Research 43(3): 253–273.

Hahn Y, McLone D 1984 Pain in children with spinal cord tumors. Child's Brain 11: 36–46.

Hester N, Ray D 1987 Assessment of Watson's carative factors: a qualitative research study. Paper presented at the International Conference on Research and Maternal/Child Nursing. Montreal, Canada.

Jacobsen PB, Manne SL, Gorfinkle K, Schorr O, Rapkin B, Redd WH 1990 Analysis of child and parent behavior during painful medical procedures. Health Psychology 9(5): 559–576.

Jay S, Elliot C 1990 A stress inoculation program for parents whose children are undergoing painful medical procedures. Journal of Consulting and Clinical Psychology 58(6): 799–804.

Johnson B, Jeppson E, Redburn L 1992 Caring for Children and Families: Guidelines for Hospital. Bethesda, MD. Association for the Care of Children's Health.

Kachoyeanos MK, Friedhoff M 1993 Cognitive and behavioral strategies to reduce children's pain. MCN 18: 14–19.

Korner AF, Thoman E 1972 The relative efficacy of contact and vestibular proprioceptive stimulation in soothing neonates. Child Development 43: 443–453.

Kuttner L 1989 Management of young children's acute pain and anxiety during invasive medical procedures. Pediatrician 16: 39–44.

Kuttner L 1991 Helpful strategies in working with preschool children in pediatric practice. Pediatric Annals 20: 120–127.

Lazarus RS, Folkman S 1984 Stress Appraisal and Coping. New York: Springer Publishing.

McGrath PJ, McAlpine L 1993 Psychologic perspectives on pediatric pain. Journal of Pediatrics 122: 52–58.

Melamed BG, Siegel LJ 1975 Reduction of anxiety in children facing hospitalization and surgery by use of filmed modeling. Journal of Consulting and Clinical Psychology 43(4): 511–521.

Olness K, Gardner GG 1978 Some guidelines for uses of hypnotherapy in pediatrics. Pediatrics 62: 228–233.

Olness K, Kohen DP 1996 Hypnosis and Hypnotherapy With Children (3rd edn). New York: Guilford Press.

Owens ME 1984 Pain in infancy: conceptual and methodological issues. Pain 2: 213–230.

Peterson L, Shigetomi C 1981 The use of coping techniques to minimize anxiety in hospitalized children. Behavior Therapy 12: 1–14.

Ross DM, Ross SA 1982 A study of the pain experience in children. Final report Ref No. 1 ROIDH 13672-01. Bethesda, MD: National Institute of Child Health and Human Development.

Ross DM, Ross SA 1984 Childhood pain: the school-aged child's viewpoint. Pain 20: 179–191.

Slaw SN, Stephens IR, Holmes S 1986 Knowledge about medical instruments and reported anxiety in pediatric surgery patients. Children's Health Care 14: 134–141.

Spock B 1946 Baby and Child Care. New York: Pocket Books.

Stuber M, Christakis D, Houskamp B, Kazak A 1996 Post trauma symptoms in childhood leukemia survivors and their parents. Psychosomatics 37(3):254–256.

Taddio A, Nulman I, Goldbach M, Ipp M, Koren G 1994 Use of lidocaine–prilocaine cream for vaccination pain in infants. Journal of Pediatrics 124: 643–648.

117

Visintainer MA, Wolfer JA 1975 Psychological preparation for surgical pediatric patients: the effect on children's and parents' stress responses. Pediatrics 56(2): 187–202.

Wall V 1991 Developmental considerations in the use of hypnosis with children. In: Wester WC, O'Grady DJ (eds) Clinical Hypnosis With Children. New York: Brunner/Mazel: 3–18.

Zelter LK, Altman A, Cohen D, Lebaron S, Munuksela EL, Schechter NL 1990 Report of the subcommittee on the management of pain associated with procedure in children with cancer. Pediatrics 86(5): 826–831.

118

Child Life Council

Child Life Council Evidence-Based Practice Statement

Therapeutic Play in Pediatric Health Care: The Essence of Child Life Practice

Submitted by:

Donna Koller, PhD

Academic and Clinical Specialist in Child Life

Project Investigator, Research Institute

Hospital for Sick Children

Toronto, Ontario, Canada

Approved by the Child Life Council Executive Board April 2008

Rebecca Mador, research assistant at the Hospital for Sick Children, is gratefully acknowledged for her contributions in the preparation of this statement.

1

Therapeutic Play in Pediatric Health Care: The Essence of Child Life Practice
Preamble

The purpose of this statement is to present empirical findings regarding the value of play for children in the hospital and to assert that play constitutes an integral component of evidence-based practice in child life. This statement is based on a review of the best available research from the year 1960 to December 2006. The following search engines were used: i) PsycINFO, which records literature from psychology and related disciplines such as medicine, psychiatry, nursing, sociology, and education; ii) MEDLINE, which focuses on biomedical literature; and, iii) CINAHL, the Cumulative Index to Nursing & Allied Health Literature, which covers literature relating to nursing and allied health professions. A variety of keywords and combinations such as "therapeutic play," "hospitalized children," "recreation," and "pretend play" were used to conduct the search with the assistance of a medical librarian. (See Table 1 for a complete list of keywords used).

Searches revealed 62 articles pertaining to therapeutic play in pediatric settings. After the results were sorted to exclude repeats and non-empirical based literature, 41 articles remained, of which 26 were eliminated because their topics were beyond the scope of this review (e.g. pet therapy, music therapy, and video games). The remaining 15 articles were scored by one of two independent raters. For the quantitative studies, "The Quality of Study Rating Form"[1, 2] was used. Articles that received a rating of at least 60 out of 100 points were selected for inclusion. Any article that scored between 55 and 65 points was re-scored by a second rater to confirm inclusion or exclusion. For the qualitative studies, the Qualitative Study Quality Form[2] was used.

A total of 10 studies (nine quantitative and one qualitative) is included in this statement. Children involved in these studies ranged from 3 to 12 years of age and were hospitalized for a variety of reasons, including dental surgery, cardiac catheterization and tonsillectomies. Eight quantitative studies[3-10] used a randomized experimental design to examine the effects of therapeutic play, while one[11] provided a descriptive content analysis of interviews involving play. The single qualitative study examined the process of play when children engaged in expressive arts[12] (see Table 2 for a list of studies included in this review).

Since evidence-based practice represents an integration of both clinical experience[2] and the best available research[13], this statement was also reviewed by Certified Child Life Specialists across North America in order to ensure clinical

2

applicability. In addition, evidence-based practice acknowledges patient preferences and needs when determining the most appropriate clinical applications for a child and family.

The Value of Play

Children from all cultures play. Even in cultures where young children are expected to assume adult work responsibilities, anthropologists cite examples of how children manage to integrate play into their daily tasks[14]. This suggests that play is not only universal but essential to human development. Indeed, research has repeatedly shown that the benefits associated with play are profound and wide-ranging. Following a meta-analysis of 800 studies, Fisher concluded there was cogent evidence for the positive impact of play on children's developmental outcomes[15]. *Play was found to significantly promote cognitive and social aspects of development and these effects were magnified when adults participated in play with children.* Accordingly, childhood play is understood to be critical to children's development for multiple reasons, including the opportunity to communicate feelings, misunderstandings and concerns in their own language using both verbal and behavioral expression[9]. Since play teaches children how to handle the world and the social roles in it, play is the predominant context in which children interface with their environment.

What is Therapeutic Play?

Play can be broadly defined as any activity in which children spontaneously engage and find pleasurable[16]. For children in the hospital, specific forms of play can provide an effective venue for personal development and increased well-being. In particular, *therapeutic play* refers to specialized activities that are *developmentally supportive* and facilitate the emotional well-being of a pediatric patient.

The discourse on play acknowledges important distinctions between *therapeutic play* and *play therapy*. Although these terms are often used interchangeably, the focus of therapeutic play is on the promotion of continuing *'normal development'* while enabling children to respond more effectively to difficult situations such as medical experiences[17]. In contrast, *play therapy* addresses basic and persistent psychological issues associated with how a child may interact with his or her world. Therefore, *therapeutic play,* in a less structured way, focuses on the process of play as a mechanism for mastering developmental milestones and critical events such as hospitalization.

3

Since therapeutic play comprises activities that are dependent on the developmental needs of the child as well as the environment, it can take many forms[9]. For example, therapeutic play can be delivered through interactive puppet shows[10], creative or expressive arts[12], puppet and doll play[7], and other medically oriented play[3-6, 8, 9, 11]. It can be directive or non-directive in approach and may include re-enactments of medical situations to facilitate children's adaptation to hospitalization[3, 4, 16, 17].

Regardless of the form that therapeutic play takes, the child life specialist (CLS) ensures that the play is developmentally appropriate while using language that is understandable to the child[4, 5, 7]. During therapeutic play children are encouraged to ask questions to clarify misconceptions and express feelings related to their fears and concerns[3-9]. In this way, therapeutic play acts as a vehicle for eliciting information from children while also sharing information about what to expect from medical procedures and what sensations may be experienced[4].

Therapeutic play typically consists of at least one of the following types of activities: 1) the encouragement of emotional expression (e.g. re-enactment of experiences through doll play), 2) instructional play to educate children about medical experiences, and 3) physiologically enhancing play (e.g. blowing bubbles to improve breathing)[16]. The studies reviewed here predominantly address medically oriented play, including emotional expression and instructional play forms.

Research Espousing the Benefits of Therapeutic Play

Psychological and Behavioral Outcomes

Several studies have shown that therapeutic play is effective in decreasing anxiety and fears for children from the time of admission to immediately after surgery and to the time of discharge[4, 5, 8-10]. In one qualitative study, Wikstrom investigated how children in the hospital experienced expressive arts through the use of clay, paint and textile. The primary finding from this study was that the children spontaneously described themselves through their art by expressing emotions such as fear and powerlessness[12]. Thus, a defining feature of therapeutic play is its ability to elicit emotional expression leading to greater psychological well-being for a child in the hospital[4, 5]. Accordingly, in studies where children were offered therapeutic play, they exhibited greater cooperation during stressful procedures[4, 5] and were more willing to return to the hospital for further treatment[7].

4

In one study, Schwartz, Albino and Tedesco found that medically related therapeutic play was more effective than medically unrelated therapeutic play[4]. The authors examined the effects of preoperative preparation on stress reduction in 45 children aged 3 and 4 years. The children were randomly assigned into one of three groups: a control group, a medically unrelated play therapy group, and a medically related play therapy group. The medically related play included providing information to the child and parent and a role play that resembled actual medical procedures with hospital toys. Results from the study concluded that children in this group were more cooperative and less upset than children in the other two groups, which suggests that medically related play can be more effective in alleviating stress than unrelated play.

Studies have shown that therapeutic play produces benefits not evidenced with alternative types of play or methods of preparation. Rae and colleagues compared the effects of play on the psychosocial adjustment of 46 children, aged 5 to 10 years, who were hospitalized for an acute illness. They randomly assigned the children to one of four groups: therapeutic play, diversionary play, verbal support, and no treatment. The therapeutic play consisted of playing with medical and non-medical materials as well as puppets, dolls and toy animals. During this non-directive play, the facilitator encouraged re-enactments of experiences while allowing the child to reflect and interpret feelings. Results showed that children who engaged in therapeutic, non-directive play showed a significant reduction in self-reported hospital fears in comparison with children from other groups[8].

Only one study did not show a statistically significant decrease in anxiety for children following therapeutic play. Fosson, Martin and Haley[6] investigated the effectiveness of guided medical play in reducing anxiety in latency-age children. Fifty children, aged 5 to 9 years, were randomly assigned to either the control group, where the child watched TV with a recreational therapist for 20 minutes, or the experimental group, where a recreational therapist facilitated medically-oriented play with the child. This study found that although the mean levels of anxiety of children in the experimental group decreased more than children in the control group, the difference was not sufficient to reach statistical significance. In order to explain these findings, the authors noted that the intervention consisted of only one 30-minute play session and the control group had access to other forms of play during hospitalization.

Physiological Outcomes

In addition to relieving psychological stress, therapeutic play is also effective in reducing apprehensive physiological responses, such as palm sweating, excessive body movement, escalating pulse rate and high blood pressure[5]. In two studies, children who were provided opportunities for therapeutic play showed less physiological distress, as indicated by lower blood pressure and pulse rate and shorter time between surgery and first voiding[3]. They also exhibited less palm sweating than children who did not have opportunities for therapeutic play[10].

Gaps in Current Literature

Although there is considerable literature concerning play in hospitals, much of this material is anecdotal and non-empirical. From an evidence-based practice perspective, this is problematic. For instance, little is known about the process and development of therapeutic play. How does play evolve over the course of a child's hospitalization, and should more complex forms of play (i.e. medically related) be offered only after a trusting relationship has been established with the child? Also, to what extent does therapeutic play rely on non-directive approaches? In terms of timing the introduction of therapeutic play, Young and Fu found that regardless of whether needle play took place before or after the blood test, children who received therapeutic play showed significantly lower pulse rate five minutes after the blood test when compared to those who did not[3]. Although the timing of medical play did not alter its effectiveness in reducing pulse rate, additional studies should be conducted in order to verify these findings across different forms of therapeutic play.

The majority of research in this area addresses the use of medically related play, while areas such as creative arts, body image activities and tension-release forms of play are understudied. Not only is the comparison of various forms of therapeutic play lacking, but also the suitability of specific types of play for particular age groups, gender types, or anxiety levels. As well, it is unclear whether group or individual therapeutic play is generally more effective for children in hospital.

Perhaps most importantly, there is a limited understanding of how children perceive therapeutic play through *their own descriptions and experiences*. The paucity of research **with children** (participatory) rather than **on children** (non-participatory) is recognized as problematic by those working in the field [18-21]. Inherent complexities also are associated with how play is studied and evaluated. For instance, the way in which a

6

child life specialist facilitates play can determine the degree of therapeutic value and the establishment of trust with the child. Qualitative studies which are more suitable for exploring health care issues with children should address the following questions: how do children experience therapeutic play with their CLS and what types of activities are most meaningful to them?

Summary

A central goal in pediatric health care is to facilitate the emotional and physical well-being of children in the hospital[16]. Research provides evidence for the effectiveness of therapeutic play in reducing psychological and physiological stress for children facing medical challenges. Therapeutic play offers long-term benefits by fostering more positive behavioral responses to future medical experiences. Since childhood play transcends cultural barriers, play opportunities should be provided for children of all ages and backgrounds.

Despite a large amount of literature purporting the value of play, research gaps exist regarding the evaluation of therapeutic play in health care settings. Future research must address the play preferences and perspectives of children if evidence-based practice is to reflect the needs of pediatric patients. Since therapeutic play embodies the essence of the child life profession, it should remain the focus of ongoing critical analysis and empirical investigation.

References

1. Gibbs LE. Quality of Study Rating Form: An Instrument for Synthesizing Evaluation Studies. *Journal of Social Work Education.* 1989;25(1):67.

2. Gibbs L. *Evidence-based practice for the helping professions: A practical guide with integrated media.* Pacific Grove, CA: Brooks/ Cole an Imprint of Wadsworth Publishers; 2003.

3. Young MR, Fu VR. Influence of play and temperament on the young child's response to pain. *Children's Health Care.* 1988;16(3):209-215.

4. Schwartz BH, Albino JE, Tedesco LA. Effects of psychological preparation on children hospitalized for dental operations. *Journal of Pediatrics.* 1983;102(4):634-638.

5. Zahr LK. Therapeutic play for hospitalized preschoolers in Lebanon. *Pediatric Nursing.* 1998;23(5):449-454.

6. Fosson A, Martin J, Haley J. Anxiety among hospitalized latency-age children. *Developmental and Behavioral Pediatrics.* 1990;11(6):324-327.

7. Cassell S. Effect of brief puppet therapy upon the emotional responses of children undergoing cardiac catheterization. *Journal of Consulting Psychology.* 1965;29(1):1-8.

8. Rae WA, Worchel FF, Upchurch J, Sanner JH, Daniel CA. The psychosocial impact of play on hospitalized children. *Journal of Pediatric Psychology.* 1989;14(4):617-627.

9. Clatworthy S. Therapeutic play: Effects on hospitalized children. *Journal of Association for Care of Children's Health.* 1981;9(4):108-113.

10. Johnson PA, Stockdale DF. Effects of puppet therapy on palmar sweating on hospitalized children. *The Johns Hopkins Medical Journal.* 1975;137:1-5.

11. Ellerton M-L, Caty S, Ritchie JA. Helping young children master intrusive procedures through play. *Children's Health Care.* 1985;13(4):167-173.

12. Wikstrom B-M. Communicating via expressive arts: The natural medium of self-expression for hospitalized children. *Pediatric Nursing.* 2005;31(6):480-485.

13. Institute of Medicine. *Crossing the quality chasm: A new health system for the 21st century.* Washington: DC: National Academy Press; 2001.

14. Schwartzman HB. *Transformations : the anthropology of children's play.* New York: Plenum Press; 1978.

15. Fisher EP. The Impact of Play on Development: A Meta-Analysis. *Play & Culture.* May 1992;5(2):159-181.

16. Vessey JA, Mahon MM. Therapeutic play and the hospitalized child. *Journal of Pediatric Nursing.* 1990;5(5):328-331.

17. Oremland EK, Oremland, J.D. Protecting the emotional development of the ill child. The essence of the child life profession. Madison, CT, Psychosocial Press; 2000.

18. Alderson P. *Children's consent to surgery.* Buckingham [England]: Open University Press; 1993.

19. Darbyshire P. Guest editorial: From research on children to research with children. *Neonatal, Paediatric and Child Health Nursing.* 2000;3(1):2-3.

20. Eiser C. *Chronic childhood disease: An introduction to psychological theory and research.* New York, NY, US: Cambridge University Press; 1990.

21. Morrow V, Richards M. The Ethics of Social Research with Children: An Overview. *Children & Society.* 6 1996;10(2):90-105.

8

Appendix

Table 1. List of keywords used to conduct literature search

PsycINFO

Category	Search Words
Therapeutic play	Play therapy, childhood play behavior, games, recreation, toys, pretend play, anatomically detailed dolls, childhood play development, children's recreation games, doll play, role playing
Hospitalized Children	Hospitalized patients (limit to childhood and adolescence)

MEDLINE

Category	Search Words
Therapeutic play	Art therapy, dance therapy, music therapy, play therapy, role playing, play and playthings, illustrated books, recreation, anatomic models
Hospitalized Children	Inpatient (limited to all child), hospitalized child, hospitalized adolescent

CINAHL

Category	Search Words
Therapeutic play	Art therapy, dance therapy, music therapy, pet therapy, play therapy, play and playthings, games, anatomic models, recreational therapy, role playing
Hospitalized Children	Hospitalized infant, hospitalized children, hospitalized adolescent, inpatients (limit age from 0 to 18)

9

Table 2. Final selection of studies included in this review

- Cassell, S. (1965). Effect of brief puppet therapy upon the emotional responses of children undergoing cardiac catheterization. *Journal of Consulting Psychology, 29*(1): 1-8.

- Clatworthy, S. (1981). Therapeutic play: Effects on hospitalized children. *Journal of Association for Care of Children's Health, 9*(4):108-113.

- Ellerton, M. L., Caty, S., & Ritchie, J. A. (1985). Helping young children master intrusive procedures through play. *Children's Health Care, 13*(4):167-173.

- Fosson, A., Martin, J., & Haley, J. (1990). Anxiety among hospitalized latency-age children. *Developmental and Behavioral Pediatrics, 11*(6):324-327.

- Johnson, P. A., & Stockdale, D. F. (1975). Effects of puppet therapy on palmar sweating of hospitalized children. *The Johns Hopkins Medical Journal, 137*, 1-5.

- Rae, W. A., Worchel, F. F., Upchurch, J., Sanner, J. H., & Daniel, C. A. (1989). The psychosocial impact of play on hospitalized children. *Journal of Pediatric Psychology, 14*(4):617-627.

- Schwartz, B. H., Albino, J. E., Tedesco, L. A. (1983). Effects of psychological preparation on children hospitalized for dental operations. *Journal of Pediatrics, 102*(4):634-638.

- Wikstrom, B-M. (2005). Communicating via expressive arts: The natural medium of self-expression for hospitalized children. *Pediatric Nursing, 31*(6):480-485.

- Young, M. R., & Fu, V. R. (1988). Influence of play and temperament on the young child's response to pain. *Children's Health Care, 16(3):* 209-215.

- Zahr, L.K. (1998). Therapeutic play for hospitalized preschoolers in Lebanon. *Pediatric Nursing, 23*(5), 449-454.

10

128

eCAM 2007; Page 1 of 9
doi:10.1093/ecam/nem033

Review

The Life Threatened Child and the Life Enhancing Clown: Towards a Model of Therapeutic Clowning

Donna Koller[1] and Camilla Gryski[2]

[1]Academic and Clinical Specialist, Department of Child Life, Hospital for Sick Children and [2]Therapeutic Clown, Therapeutic Clown Services, Toronto, Ontario, Canada

In the last decade, there has been a rapid growth in the presence of clowns in hospitals, particularly in pediatric settings. The proliferation of clowns in health care settings has resulted in varying levels of professionalism and accountability. For this reason, there is a need to examine various forms of clowning, in particular therapeutic clowning in pediatric settings. The purpose of this article is to address what therapeutic clowning is and to describe the extent to which it can provide a complementary form of health care. In an attempt to apply theory to practice, the article will draw upon the experiences of a therapeutic clown within a pediatric setting while providing a historical and theoretical account of how clowns came to be in hospitals. Toward this end, a proposed model of therapeutic clowning will be offered which can be adapted for a variety of settings where children require specialized forms of play in order to enhance their coping, development and adjustment to life changes. Finally, current research on clowning in children's hospitals will be reviewed including a summary of findings from surveys administered at the Hospital for Sick Children.

Keywords: child life – clowning – complementary care – hospitalized child – pediatric psychosocial care – therapeutic play

Introduction

In the last decade, there has been a rapid growth in the presence of clowns in hospitals, particularly in pediatric settings. Many thousands of children are exposed to clowns during their hospitalization. For example, six clowns from the Therapeutic Clown Program at the Hospital for Sick Children (Sick Kids) in Toronto, Ontario, Canada, see an average of 20 children 2 days per week, for a total of over 10 000 visits a year. Patients can range in age from infancy to adolescence.

The Theodora Foundation sponsors clowns in 82 hospitals on three continents, Europe, Africa and Asia. In the United States, 90 clown doctors from the Big Apple Circus Clown Care Units (CCU) provide 250 000 bedside visits yearly. Australia has the Humour Foundation Clown Doctor Programs, South America its *Doutores da Alegria (Doctors of Happiness)* and France, *Le Rire Médecin (Laughing Doctors)*. In addition, volunteer caring clowns visit countless hospitals and nursing homes, particularly in the United States and Canada.

This rapid expansion of clowns in health care settings has resulted in varying levels of professionalism and accountability. At their most professional, therapeutic clowns are respected complementary care providers who are able to articulate their role in the care of the patients as integral members of the health care team. At the other end of the spectrum, volunteer clowns, though well-intentioned, may be simply dressed-up people with little training and less understanding of the role and potential of the therapeutic clown. Therapeutic clowns in pediatric settings use gentle play and laughter to provide ill children with another avenue for emotional expression,

For reprints and all correspondence: Donna Koller, Child Life Department, Hospital for Sick Children, 555 University Avenue, Toronto, ON M5G 1X8, Tel: 416-813-8211; Fax: 416-813-5364; E-mail: donna.koller@sickkids.ca

control and social interaction during their hospitalization. The goal of therapeutic clowning is to minimize stress for patients and their families during hospitalization and treatment (1–3).

Since clowning in pediatric settings continues to grow, there is an urgent need to define the role of the therapeutic clown, particularly because this form of clowning can involve interactions with seriously ill or dying children. The purpose of this article is to address what therapeutic clowning is and to describe the extent to which it can provide a complementary form of health care. The aim is to offer an established model of therapeutic clowning upon which standards of practice can be developed and measured. In an attempt to apply theory to practice, the article will draw upon the experiences of a therapeutic clown within a pediatric setting while providing a historical and theoretical account of how clowns came to be in hospitals. Toward this end, a proposed model of therapeutic clowning will be offered which can be adapted for a variety of settings where children require specialized forms of play in order to enhance their coping, development and adjustment to life changes. Finally, current research on clowning in children's hospitals will be reviewed including a summary of findings from surveys administered at Sick Kids.

Clowns as Healers

Clown historian John Towsen (4) suggests that 'the clown's ability to evoke feelings of superiority in the spectator plays a hidden role in all clowning' (p. 206). Hoyle (5) calls clowns 'life-enhancing' and for Henderson (6), the clown is 'the embodiment of hope in the face of hopelessness, and possibility in the face of the impossible'.

However, the journey towards acceptance of therapeutic clowns by other health care professionals has not always been smooth, reflecting the ambivalent nature of the relationship between the clown and the society of which he or she is a part. Cline (7) offers a useful synthesis of this unsettled relationship. Speaking of the essence of the clown he says:

> He is our scapegoat, "he who gets slapped," suffering every indignity that the human mind can conceive. He is our alter-ego, vicariously acting out the unspoken desires that we could never hope to act on in reality. He is our critic, piercing through our cultural hypocrisies with well-aimed barbs. And he is our healer, enabling us to laugh at the realities that could too easily make us weep. (p. 8)

Recounting a now-famous incident from the early days of the Big Apple Circus' Clown Care Unit, founder Michael Christensen tells how his clown character, Dr Stubs, once had a doctor come up to him and say,

'"Clowns don't belong in hospitals." I told him, "Neither do children."' (8, p. 37). 'Clowns *here* are you joking?' (9, p. 9) was the apparent response of a physician to Caroline Simonds, Artistic Director of France's Le Rire Médecin, upon hearing her request to provide clown doctor services to children in his hospital with life-threatening illnesses. Yet the relationship between clowns and those in need of healing should not be so surprising. Historically and culturally, clowns have been associated with the well-being of society and the healing arts. It is believed that the hospital of Hippocrates kept troupes of players and clowns in the quadrangle, 'as the doctors of the day believed that mood influenced healing' (10, p. 202). The 12th century buffoon Rahere or Rayer, went on to found St Bartholomew's Priory and Hospital and Fair.

Clowns appear in the cultures of many First Nations peoples, functioning in ways similar to the saints, prophets and artists of the Western world (11). The sacred clowns of the Hopi serve as jesters, priests and shamans (12). This latter concept is taken up by Van Blerkom (13) who discusses the role of the Big Apple Circus CCU clowns in the context of shaman healers providing complementary therapy. To support her case, she cites the clowns' appearance, use of puppets, music, character and ritual, and their role as order-breakers.

Although many clowns have volunteered in hospitals as entertainers, and today's Caring Clowns continue to do so, the advent of the clown doctor and the therapeutic clown in health care settings can be traced back to 1986, when the two models in current hospital clowning originated independently. The following is a brief review of these models and their origins.

Clown Doctors

Michael Christensen, one of the founders of the Big Apple Circus, was asked to perform at an event at New York's Babies and Children's Hospital. Christensen, Dr Stubs, and his colleague Jeff Gordon presented a 20-min parody of the realities of hospital life to a delighted audience of patients, parents and staff. For Christensen, this was 'the most fulfilling twenty minutes of my professional career, and it was from that experience that the Clown Care Unit plan took root' (14).

All of the CCU clowns are professional artists who undergo a rigorous training program before working in the hospital. Their doctor characters evolved from the clown's natural relationship with authority figures: in the circus, the ringmaster; in the hospital, the doctor. It has also been suggested that the clown doctors' brightly-colored costumes and red noses paired with white coats help to make the 'institutional garment and the medical staff more "friendly" and less intimidating' (15, p. 1). In addition, clown doctors always work in pairs, to encourage creative performance, to free the child from pressure to participate, and to offer professional and emotional support (9). Simonds and Warren also suggest that a partner can indicate to a colleague the need to put on the brakes if a clown scenario is getting out of hand.

The CCU clowns use parody to demystify medicine and help children to cope with illness. Their 'clown medicine' includes red nose transplants, kitty cat scans and prescriptions for laughter. The CCU model has been both successful and influential. Clowns in programs from Paris to Montreal, Sao Paolo to Edinburgh as well as the clown doctors of the Theodora Children's Trust have adopted the doctor appellation and have donned white coats.

Therapeutic Clowns within Child Life Programs

In Canada, many programs follow the Therapeutic Clown/Child Life model. In 1986, professional clown Karen Ridd took her character Robo into the Children's Hospital of the Winnipeg Health Sciences Centre in Manitoba, Canada. Ridd joined the hospital's Child Life department, working both as a clown and a child life specialist. The aim of Child Life programs is to reduce the stress experienced by children and families while enhancing their abilities to cope effectively with stressful situations.

In her unpublished paper 'There Ought to Be Clowns', Ridd (2) sets the work of the clown in the context of humor and healing (i.e. Fry, Moody among others), the role of the clown in native societies, and the need for some creative order-breaking in the health care setting. She portrays the therapeutic clown as one who can change the child's perception of the hospital by her very presence while facilitating much needed stress release. Robo's ineptness allows the child to become the caregiver as well as the care-receiver, and enhances the child's sense of coping and control. Ridd portrays Robo as the child's friend, the encourager of play, imagination and creativity. Robo also provided support for patients during IV insertions and other procedures and starred as the patient in a series of short films designed to help children with medical procedures. Ridd summarizes Robo's work: 'Robo fulfills the clown's traditional role as healer by alleviating stress, raising spirits and abounding with love and joy' (p. 20).

Unlike clown doctors, therapeutic clowns usually work alone. It is not necessarily true that a single clown will put pressure on a child to respond as has been suggested in the literature (9). The therapeutic clown always asks permission before entering the room, and is trained to sensitively pick up cues from the child and family. The therapeutic clown interacts with the environment as well as the patient and family, and can use props or puppets as additional partners in play.

A single clown walking down the hospital corridor is out of place and vulnerable. The clown's vulnerability mirrors that of the child, who is also out of place in the health care environment, and who must ultimately, despite the support of family and friends, cope with his or her illness alone. In this respect, the clown and the child become allies. Cline (7) quotes Anthony Hippisley Coxe whose comments on the relationship between clowns and children are particularly applicable to the therapeutic clown: 'Children love him for a simpler reason. He expresses, loudly and eloquently, the bewilderment they feel when they find themselves in an adult world' (p. 19).

The Therapeutic Clown/Child Life Model has influenced programs across Canada, from Halifax to Vancouver. In 1993, Joan Barrington with the assistance of Ridd founded The Therapeutic Clown Program at The Hospital for Sick Children, Toronto, Canada. At Sick Kids, therapeutic clowns are considered staff of the Child Life department. As members of the larger health care team, therapeutic clowns provide a *complementary* form of care while sharing the goals and objectives of other professionals working with families.

Recently, efforts have been made to ensure that a level of professionalism and clinical standards exist among those who call themselves therapeutic clowns in Canada. Therapeutic clowns and clown doctors from across the country have joined together to form The Canadian Association of Therapeutic Clowns/L'Association Canadienne des Clowns Thérapeutiques (CATC/ACCT; 16). CATC/ACCT members agree to abide by the organization's Statement of Principles, Code of Ethics and By-Laws.

Case Study Example: The Magical Music Box

In order to further define the role of the therapeutic clown, the following case example illustrates three key concepts associated with this form of clowning: (i) empowerment, (ii) play and humor and (iii) supportive relationships.

This story is about an eight-year-old boy, a clown, and a game with a musical box:

At the time of this play, the child was comfortable with the clown, with whom he had played on and off for several months. His father was almost always present during the play, but usually chose not to be involved. The game with the music box had been developed and elaborated upon during several admissions. The tinkling notes played by the child always induced yawns and sleepiness in the clown, as her head slowly subsided onto her arms. When the music stopped, she sleepily raised her head and opened her eyes, only to subside again when the music began. The second or third time the child requested this game, he added the words, "You are getting very sleepy..."

The clown obliged and added some realistic snores. "When I snap my fingers twice," he added, "you will peck like a chicken." The clown was required to become a chicken, a dog, and to sing Twinkle, Twinkle Little Star, which she did in her most clown-like off-tune voice. There was always an expectant silence before the clown, eyes closed, became transformed and launched into her new persona, followed by gales of laughter from both the child and his father. After about three transformations, the clown was allowed to wake up. The clown always left the room commenting on how refreshed she felt, and how restful it was to play with this child.

Empowerment

Clearly, in a child's relationship with a clown, in this play space, the rules are different. The clown is a master at manipulating status (3). A clown, clearly an adult, can be hypnotized by a music box, and a child can require her to do silly or incomprehensible things. The child feels superior, and is empowered: a very tidy turning of the tables for a patient who must cope with rules and regulations that could seem arbitrary and incomprehensible. Therefore, the continuing evolution of this play scenario encourages the child to take control in a situation where little control is possible.

This story also illustrates the vulnerability of the clown. The clown mask requires that we *unmask*, that we drop all our other masks and increase our sensitivity to others (17–19). Many clowns have commented on the necessity of enhanced antennae as they travel from room to room in the hospital. The experienced therapeutic clown will understand the careful balance he or she must achieve between true skills—whether in music, juggling or improvisation—and the need for qualities of innocence and the willingness to relinquish control to the child.

Play and Humor

The therapeutic clown, in her interaction with a child and his father, uses gentle play and humor to relieve the stress of treatment for cancer. Both therapeutic clowns and clown doctors, create opportunities for humor and laughter in the health care setting. Many claims have been made for the physiological and psychological benefits of humor. Dr John M. Driscoll Jr, quoted in a press release from the Big Apple Circus CCU that was published in *The Hospital Clown Newsletter* (20), makes a simple and effective statement:

'Ministering to sick children goes beyond medication and technology. Children don't understand these things, but they do understand the reassurance and fun that the CCU provides.

When a child begins to laugh, it means he's probably beginning to feel better. I see the clowns as healers' (p. 2).

The clown is a 'standing joke': she carries incongruity within her person (21, p. 29). The clown's presence in the hospital setting adds yet another layer of incongruity. Both therapeutic clowns and clown doctors benefit from the humor they create by simply being there. Therapeutic clowns are out of place altogether. Clown doctors create humor by joining together the idea of the clown and the idea of the doctor, a concept that Arthur Koestler (22) calls bisociation. Provine (23) discusses Schopenhauer's theory of laughter: 'Our success at incongruity detection is celebrated with laughter' (p. 15).

Central to the concept of fun, and an important prerequisite for the enjoyment of humor is a playful frame of mind (24). For the child in the hospital, the clown comes to embody the spirit of playfulness. When she is invited to step over the threshold, the space is changed and charged with possibility. The room suddenly becomes a playground, and the child is invited to come out and play.

Supportive Relationship

Building supportive relationships with patients and families is an essential part of the work of the therapeutic clown. As the music box story shows, the therapeutic clown and the child have played together over a period of several months, thereby establishing a trusting and supportive relationship. The child and his clown friend have developed ways of playing together that are comforting and predictable. The therapeutic clown will always bring certain toys and the play will often unfold along familiar paths. It may be said that the therapeutic clown exists only in a state of potential, waiting to be fully realized in a relationship with a child or young person.

Despite the fact that the therapeutic clown is a health care professional, he or she is perceived as coming not from the world of medicine but, as the family does, from the world of biography, the world of story (25). In these ways, with bubbles and giggles, with face paints and wind-ups and pure play silliness, meaningful and supportive relationships are forged between the child and the therapeutic clown. As a member of the health care team, the therapeutic clown is aware of the needs of other staff members as they work with the child. When it is appropriate, the clown can be a helpful distractive presence during medical procedures. Sourkes (26) suggests, 'For the child who lives under threat, the establishment of a secure therapeutic alliance is an intervention in and of itself' (p. 11).

As the therapeutic clown works to support the child through play, humor and empowering friendship, it is important that he or she keep in mind the fact that some children, young people and adults are afraid of clowns, whether because of the unfamiliarity of the make-up and costuming, because of unfortunate incidents with unskilled and insensitive clowns or because of the fairly recent appearance of 'evil clowns' in the media—all of which are given ample play on numerous Internet sites. In order to address some of these issues, therapeutic clowns tend to present with minimal make-up and costuming. A red nose and a hat, and a visually pleasing costume are enough to communicate the clown's identity. Therapeutic clowns learn how to approach babies, children, young people and their parents, and the staff, sensitively—for all of these are their clientele. A well-trained therapeutic clown will watch for cues and react instantly if any sense of unease is present. For example, simple techniques can often reassure a patient or family member: keeping an appropriate distance, initially avoiding eye-contact, and minimizing physical presence by crouching down or turning sideways. In addition to respecting a 'No' from a patient or parent and leaving for that day, a clown might at first play at the doorway or send bubbles into the room without ever entering. Many therapeutic clowns use music as a way to bridge the gap between clown and patient or parent. However, therapeutic clowning is not a popularity contest, and the clown must realize that on occasion, despite his or her best efforts and for whatever reasons, it is not possible to establish a therapeutic relationship with a patient. In this case, the clown gracefully withdraws, which action in itself can be empowering for the child or young person.

Therapeutic Play and the Hospitalized Child

Since children from all cultures play, the universality of play suggests it is an essential human function. Even in cultures where young children are expected to assume adult work responsibilities, literature provides examples of how children manage to integrate play activities into their daily work tasks (27). Through play, children learn how to handle the world and the social roles in it. For this reason, play becomes the predominant context in which children interface with the environment.

In child development literature, the use of play as a therapeutic intervention is extensively supported where the benefits are shown to be profound and wide-ranging. Following a meta-analysis of 800 studies, Fisher (28) concluded there was cogent evidence for the positive impact of play on child development. *Play was found to significantly promote cognitive and social aspects of development and these effects were magnified when adults participated in play with children.*

In pediatrics, research consistently cites the value of incorporating *psychosocial care* in children's *health care* (29). Particularly in a pediatric context, play provides a protective factor against developmental delays, regressive behaviors and emotional withdrawal (30–32). For this reason, Child Life programs are essentially hospital play programs and they have become an integral part of pediatric psychosocial care. These programs provide opportunities for hospitalized children to engage in play and to build therapeutic relationships based on these interactions.

Within this context, several varieties of play can occur. For example, children traumatized by medical experiences require opportunities for both non-directive and directive forms of play. For the most part, child life philosophy supports a child-centered approach where the adult follows the child's lead during play, opting for more non-directive than directive experiences. Non-directive forms of play allow children to safely explore their environment at a time when they may perceive physical challenges and vulnerability. In this way, hospitalized children are afforded the opportunity to take 'control' over their play experience in an environment where limited control is available to them (33–34).

Distinctions also need to be made between *therapeutic play* and *play therapy*. According to Oremland and Oremland (29), the focus of therapeutic play in contrast to play therapy is on the promotion of continuing 'normal development' and enabling children to respond more effectively to difficult situations such as health care experiences. *Therapeutic play* is developmentally-supportive and can include forms of enactments related to illness and hospitalization issues. *Play therapy*, on the other hand, addresses basic and persistent psychological issues associated with how a child may interact with his or her world. Therefore, *therapeutic play*, in a less structured way, focuses on spontaneous phenomena as the child engages in play to aid mastery of developmental milestones and critical events such as illness and hospitalization.

For the therapeutic clown within a Child Life program, play is predominantly defined as 'therapeutic' in that the clown takes the lead from the children, allowing them to become creative partners in the play experience. In particular, clowns are poised to create forms of play that tend to invite children to participate. The therapeutic clown assists children in the creation of safe and imaginary spaces, 'magic circles' of play (35, p. 19) within stressful hospital environments. Writing of the life-threatened child, Barbara Sourkes (26) comments on the child's particular need for safety: 'In a sea of uncertainty, the child's ongoing quest is to find a "safe place" within the storm' (p. 81). For this reason, the presence of the clowns in this setting is extremely powerful, for clowns can go where other adults may hesitate.

Imaginary, story-filled spaces allow the emergence of play forms that may function as therapeutic metaphors for the child. A game of Hide and Seek may allow the life-threatened child to test whether or not he or she would be missed (26). For example, the swelling and bursting of bubbles may speak to a child about the presence, growth or absence of a tumor (36). A magic trick that transforms a small object into a larger one and back again may allow a child to express feelings about a changing body image during treatment (37). As the play unfolds, the child's often profound concerns can be explored in a creative space that is both safe and comforting.

For the hospitalized child, playing with a therapeutic clown can provide opportunities for creative self expression as well as a welcome refuge from the stresses and challenges associated with illness, both of which support the notion that therapeutic play is indeed a form of complementary health care.

Research on Clowning

Despite the growing number of clown programs, there exists a paucity of research on clowning. In particular, research is needed to evaluate the impact of clowning in health care settings, and more specifically how therapeutic clowns play a role in the well-being of pediatric patients, their families and health care providers. Furthermore, the few studies that have been carried out have not been widely disseminated.

Studies on 'Clown Therapy'

Two pilot studies at Columbia University (38,39), funded by the Richard and Hinda Rosenthal Center for Complementary and Alternative Medicine, focused on the effectiveness of clowns as distractive presences during cardiac catheterization and invasive procedures in a pediatric oncology day clinic. The research was conducted at Babies and Children's Hospital at Columbia-Presbyterian Medical Center in New York. Researchers at the hospital collaborated with specially trained clowns to study the medical significance of 'clown therapy'. Clinical researchers from a variety of disciplines hypothesized that humorous distraction provided by the clowns would increase patient cooperation, ameliorate parental anxiety and decrease the need for sedation. Results showed that during cardiac catheterization there were significant decreases in observed child distress, in child self-reported distress and parent-rated child distress with the clowns present. As a result, physicians found the procedure significantly easier to perform with the clowns present. Clown interventions were non-toxic, did not cause respiratory depression, sedation or gastric upset. In addition, positive changes in the behavior and mood of health care providers were observed when the clowns were around. Long-term outcomes of the research

included the successful implementation of clowns into medical settings in which there were no previous clown programs. In summary, this research showed how the presence of clowns can improve certain aspects of the pediatric experience. Authors call on the need for further research on the bio-psychological benefits of clowns with sick children in less frightening settings.

Children's, Parents' and Staff Perspectives on Clowns in Pediatric Settings

In a rare qualitative study, Aquino *et al.* (40) of Brazil asked children to describe their experiences with clown doctors. Twenty-seven pediatric patients between the ages of 4 and 12 participated in semi-structured individual interviews. Data analyses showed several important themes. Participants found the clowns to be humorous, which allowed the patients to laugh and be happy. In a review of the literature on laughter and humor, Bennett and Lengacher(41,42) note that humor acts as a coping mechanism to reduce stress and psychological symptoms related to negative situations. For this reason, participants associated the work of the clown with one of healing, 'clowns helped kids to forget about their pain'. Some children noted that the playfulness of the clown allowed for distraction in that some children stopped crying during their medical procedures.

Similar findings were cited in a recent Italian study by Vagnoli *et al.* (43). The aim of their study was to investigate the effects of the presence of clowns on a child's pre-operative anxiety during the induction of anesthesia and on the parent who accompanied the child. The sample comprised 40 children (5–12 years of age) who had to undergo minor day surgery. They were assigned randomly to the clown group ($N = 20$) in which children were accompanied in the pre-operative room by a clown and a parent. The control group ($N = 20$) consisted of children being accompanied by one parent without the clown. The anxiety of the children and parents was measured using standardized scales. The clown group was significantly less anxious during induction when compared with the control group. A questionnaire was also developed for health care professionals in order to ascertain their opinions regarding the presence of clowns during induction. The questionnaire data for health care professionals indicated that the clowns were a benefit to the child, but the majority of staff was opposed to continuing the program because of perceived interference with the procedures of the operating room. This study provides a valuable contribution to the literature in that it validates the therapeutic benefits of the clown in a pediatric setting. Perhaps more importantly, the study identifies key issues for further exploration; namely, the significance of supportive health care teams for the development of innovative programs. Similar findings were identified in a study by Caprilli and Messeri (44) where some staff were hesitant to fully support a pet visiting program for fear it would interfere with hospital policies around safety. Therefore, a critical aspect associated with the development and sustainability of new forms of complementary medicine rests on whether health care staff are well-informed and collaborative efforts are maximized.

Clown programs at the Winnipeg Health Sciences Centre, British Columbia Children's Hospital, and the Children's Hospital of Wisconsin, among others have surveyed children, families and staff in their institutions. None of this research has been published. Other research (45,46) examined therapeutic clowns and clown doctors and their programs rather than the specifics of their impact on the well-being of children.

Evaluating the Therapeutic Clown Program at Sick Kids

In 2004, at the Hospital for Sick Children (Sick Kids), the authors conducted a survey to address the impact of therapeutic clowning from the perspectives of pediatric health care professionals and parents of hospitalized children. Ethical approval was obtained by the hospital's Research Ethics Board. The purpose of the survey was 2-fold: (i) to provide an informal evaluation of the program and (ii) to obtain pilot data on the impact of therapeutic clowning with the objective of designing a future research study. Two quantitative surveys were created; one for staff and another for parents. Surveys were administered to staff and parents on five in-patient units. Both surveys addressed participants' understanding of the clown's role, how many clown visits per week were ideal, possible concerns regarding the program, to what extent they viewed clowns as part of the health care team and to what extent they valued the clown program. Questions provided participants with a variety of responses or they could indicate their own. Likert questions were also included. For example, participants could indicate the degree to which they viewed the therapeutic clown as part of the health care team. Survey questions were based on a careful review of existing literature on clowning in pediatric settings. The staff and parent surveys are included under Appendix 1 and 2 (published online as supplementary data).

A total of 330 surveys were randomly distributed to staff, of which, 143 (43%) were completed and returned. Surveys were kept at the nurses' station and child life specialists assisted in the recruitment of staff by providing information at unit meetings. Of the 143 respondents, 123 (86%) were nurses. Nurses included: bedside nurses, clinical nurse practitioners, nurse managers and discharge planners. Additional staff comprised: unit clerks (7%), child life specialists (2%), social workers (2%), occupational therapists (2%) and physiotherapists (1%). The greatest number of completed surveys was received from in-patient units where the role of the therapeutic clown was established, usually over a 2-year period.

Because some parents would be unfamiliar with the clown program, parent surveys were administered after a clown visit was made with a child. For each in-patient unit, a research assistant accompanied a clown as visits were made. Following a play session, the research assistant would inform the parent of the survey. Parents were told that the purpose of the survey was to help evaluate the clown program. They were also explained that participation was voluntary and that the surveys were anonymous in that no identifying information was asked. Only two parents refused participation; one based on limited English language skills and another for a lack of knowledge about the clown program. A total of 51 parent surveys were completed.

Frequencies were calculated on the raw data for each of the questions on the surveys. In terms of how staff viewed the work of the therapeutic clown, 88% believed it was to engage children in play. Almost half of the staff participants (47%) viewed the clowns as supportive of their work. For the most part, staff were comfortable with two clown visits per week on their units. With regard to the question: 'are there things about the therapeutic clown that concern you?' the vast majority (85%) had no concerns at all. Some staff indicated concerns regarding the fear of clowns, both from the staff and child's perspectives. Other issues addressed how clowns decide on which children to visit and that clowns were predominantly beneficial for younger children. A large number of staff (76%) also believed that clowns were a part of the health care team (i.e. definitely—45%, and very much so—31%). Similarly, 93% of staff believed that the clown program was beneficial to the hospital (i.e. definitely—34%, very much so—59%).

For parents, 88% viewed the role of the clown as making children happy. Only 22% of parents believed that the role of the clown was to help other professionals with the children. The majority of parents (80%) enjoyed the clown visits, and believed their children did too (i.e. always—78%). Ninety-four percent of parents acknowledged that their child was happier following a clown visit. In contrast to staff, the majority of parents (51%) believed they wanted more clown visits and 86% believed that the clown program was 'very good' for the hospital.

Although only frequency data were compiled, the results of these surveys show strong support for the role of the therapeutic clown. However, clear outcomes cannot be assessed from descriptive data obtained from one survey. Additional statistical analyses (i.e. inferential statistics) from a comprehensive study could yield a more in-depth examination of therapeutic clowning in pediatric settings. Because this area of research remains virtually unexplored, a mixed method approach may be most suitable. For example, qualitative interviews and focus groups could provide the basis upon which to create standardized measures that reflect key aspects of therapeutic clowning. Emerging themes from qualitative data may identify critical areas relating to child outcomes such as the impact of therapeutic clowning on pediatric anxiety.

In the meantime, the growing number of therapeutic clown programs suggests that the field is rapidly expanding despite a lack of clinical standardization and research. Additional research is necessary for the development of evidence-based practice, a prerequisite for establishing legitimacy within ever-changing and demanding health care environments. Future research must also include the perspectives and experiences of pediatric patients. The relationship between a therapeutic clown and a hospitalized child is complex, laden with inherent meanings and perceived benefits. Having children participate in such research as primary stake-holders assures them a voice in decision making around various aspects of their psychosocial and complementary forms of health care, which include opportunities for therapeutic play.

Conclusions

The purpose of this article was to elucidate the role of the therapeutic clown in a pediatric health care setting. The Therapeutic Clown Program at Sick Kids currently practices the Therapeutic Clown/Child Life model proposed here. Therapeutic clowns are most effective when they are specifically trained to work in health care settings, and when they function as members of the health care team, either under or working closely with the Child Life department. Ultimately, the professional clown working with therapeutic intent, no matter what the model, offers to the child a supportive, empowering relationship and opportunities for play and laughter in imaginative and safe play worlds. The creation of these valuable play spaces is made possible through the unique relationships established between clowns and hospitalized children.

Acknowledgments

We acknowledge the support of Joan Barrington, Coordinator, Therapeutic Clown Program at Sick Kids in the writing of this article, and the Palliative and Bereavement Care Service at Sick Kids. We also thank Lucia Cino, Therapeutic Clown, for her assistance in developing and administering the clown surveys.

Supplementary Data

Supplementary data are available at eCAM online.

References

1. Gryski C. Creating the magic circle: the child and the clown in the pediatric healthcare setting [master's research paper]. Ontario Institute for Studies in Education/University of Toronto. Unpublished 2002.
2. Ridd K. There ought to be clowns: child life therapy through the medium of a clown. Unpublished paper 1987.
3. Schwebke S, Gryski C. Gravity and levity – pain and play. In: Klein AJ (ed). *Humor in Children's Lives.* Westport (CT): Praeger, 2003, pp. 49–68.
4. Towsen J. *Clowns.* New York: Hawthorn Books, 1976.
5. Hoyle G. *The Fool Show [program notes].* Bayview Playhouse, Toronto, 1989.
6. Henderson J. Philosophy of clown. 2005 [cited August 16, 2005]. Available from: www.foolmoon.org/clown_mask_philosophy_of_clown.htm.
7. Cline P. *Fools, Clowns and Jesters.* La Jolla: Green Tiger Press, 1983.
8. Tedeschi B. Send in the clowns. *Hope Magazine* 1998;14:56–63.
9. Simonds C, Warren B. *The Clown Doctor Chronicles.* Amsterdam, New York: Rodopi, 2004.
10. Warren B. Treating wellness: how clown doctors help to humanize health care and promote good health. In: Twohig P (ed). *Making Sense of Health, Illness and Disease.* Amsterdam, New York: Rodopi, 2004, 201–16.
11. Herring R. The clown or contrary figure as a counseling intervention strategy with Native American Indian clients. *J Multicult Couns Devel* 1994;22:153–64.
12. Wright B. *Clowns of the Hopi.* Flagstaff (AZ): Northland, 1994.
13. Van Blerkom L. Clown doctors: shaman healers of western medicine. *Med Anthropol Q* 1995;9:462–75.
14. Williams L. Treating the funny bone. *Time* 1990;136:17–20.
15. Fools for Health [homepage on the Internet]. Windsor. c2005 [cited June 8, 2005] Available from: http://web2.uwindsor.ca/fools_for_health/index.html
16. The Canadian Association of Therapeutic Clowns/L'Association Canadienne des Clowns Thérapeutiques (CATC/ACCT) [homepage on the Internet]. [cited October 17, 2006] Available from: http://stw.ryerson.ca/~sgrove/index.htm
17. Grock [Adrien Wettach]. *Life's a Lark.* London: Heinemann, 1931.
18. Isaacson A. The way of the clown. *New Age J* 1995;59.
19. Meany A. Learning to be a fool. *The Irish Times.* 2002 [cited March 29, 2006]. Available from: http://scripts.ireland.com/se...r/features/2002/0307/88722148atclown.html
20. Big Apple Circus Clown Care Unit. Medical effects of Big Apple Circus Clown Care Unit to be studied by Columbia University's College of Physicians and Surgeons [press release]. *Hospital Clown Newsletter.* 1996;1(3:2).
21. Disher MW. *Clowns and Pantomimes.* London: Constable, 1925.
22. Koestler A. *The Act of Creation.* London, Arkana: Penguin, 1989.
23. Provine R. *Laughter: A Scientific Investigation.* New York: Viking, 2000.
24. McGhee PE. *Humor: Its Origin and Development.* San Francisco: W.H. Freeman, 1979.
25. Cribb A, Bignold S, Ball SJ. Linking the parts: an exemplar of philosophical and practice issues in holistic nursing. *J Adv Nurs* 1994;20:233–38.
26. Sourkes B. *Armfuls of Time: The Psychological Experience of the Child with a Life-Threatening Illness.* Pittsburgh: University of Pittsburgh Press, 1995.
27. Schwartzman H. *Transformations: The Anthropology of Children's Play.* New York: Plenum Press, 1978.
28. Fisher EP. The impact of play on development: a meta-analysis. *Play and Culture* 1992;5:159–81.
29. Oremland EK, Oremland JD. *Protecting the Emotional Development of the Ill Child. The Essence of the Child Life Profession.* Madison (CT): Psychosocial Press, 2000.
30. Pederson C. Effect of imagery on children's pain and anxiety during cardiac catheterization. *J Pediatr Nurs: Nurs Care Children Families* 1995;10:365–75.
31. Thompson RH, Stanford G. *Child Life in Hospitals: Theory and Practice.* Springfield (IL): Charles Thomas Publisher, 1981.
32. Vessey J, Carlson KL, McGill J. Use of distraction with children during an acute pain experience. *Nurs Res* 1994;43:369–81.

33. Bolig R, Fernie D, Klein E. Unstructured play in hospital settings: an internal locus of control rationale. *Children's Health Care* 1986;15:101–07.
34. Oremland E. Mastering developmental and critical experiences through play and other expressive behaviors in childhood. *Children's Health Care* 1988;16:150–56.
35. Huizinga J. *Homo Ludens*. Boston: The Beacon Press, 1955.
36. Oppenheim D, Simonds C, Hartmann O. Clowning on children's wards. *Lancet* 1997;350:1838–40.
37. Dumont N. L'enfant et la magie en oncologie pédiatrique [The child and pediatric oncology magic]. *Pratiques Psychologiques* 2002;3:69–77.
38. Slater J, Gorfinkle K, Bagiella E, Tager F, Labinsky E. *Child Behavioral Distress During Invasive Oncologic Procedures and Cardiac Catheterization with the Big Apple Circus Clown Care Unit*. Columbia University (NY): Rosenthal Center for Complementary and Alternative Medicine, 1998.
39. Smerling AJ, Skolnick E, Bagiella E, Rose C, Labinsky E, Tager F. Perioperative clown therapy for pediatric patients. *Anesth Analg* 1999;88:243–56.
40. Aquino RG, Bortolucci RZ, Marta IER. Doutores da graca: a crianca fala [Clown doctors: the child talks]. *Brazilian J Nursing* 2004;3(2). [cited June 16, 2005] Available from: www.uff.br/nepae/objn302aquinoetal.htm

41. Bennet MP, Lengacher CA. Humor and laughter may influence health: II Complementary therapies and humor in a clinical population. *Evid Based Alternat Complement Med* 2006;3:187–190.
42. Bennet MP, Lengacher CA. Humor and laughter may influence health. I. History and background. *Evid Based Alternat Complement Med* 2006;3:61–63.
43. Vagnoli L, Caprilli S, Robiglio A, Messeri A. Clown doctors as a treatment for preoperative anxiety in children: a randomized, prospective study. *Pediatrics* 2005;116:563–67.
44. Caprilli S, Messeri A. Animal-assisted activity at A. Meyer Children's Hospital: a pilot study. *Evid Based Complement Alternat Med* 2006;3:379–383.
45. Spitzer P. Clown doctors! e-Bility News. 2002 [cited March 8, 2006]. Available from: http://e-bility.com/articles/clowndoctors.shtml
46. Warren B. [homepage on the Internet]. Knowing laughter: what do clown doctors know and how do they learn to do what they do? [cited June 8, 2005]. Available from: http://www.oise.utoronto.ca/depts/sese/csew/nall/res/43knowinglaughter.htm

Received March 24, 2006; accepted March 3, 2007

Module 5:
Families in Crisis, Culture & Grief

Hmong leader to whom they made this proposition politely discouraged them, suspecting that Coelho, who is a Catholic of Portuguese descent, might not appreciate having chickens, and maybe a pig as well, sacrificed on his behalf.

On the other hand, the Hmong consider *qaug dab peg* to be an illness of some distinction. This fact might have surprised Tony Coelho no less than the dead chickens would have. Before he entered politics, Coelho planned to become a Jesuit priest, but was barred by a canon forbidding the ordination of epileptics. What was considered a disqualifying impairment by Coelho's church might have been seen by the Hmong as a sign that he was particularly fit for divine office. Hmong epileptics often become shamans. Their seizures are thought to be evidence that they have the power to perceive things other people cannot see, as well as facilitating their entry into trances, a prerequisite for their journeys into the realm of the unseen. The fact that they have been ill themselves gives them an intuitive sympathy for the suffering of others and lends them emotional credibility as healers. Becoming a *txiv neeb* is not a choice; it is a vocation. The calling is revealed when a person falls sick, either with *qaug dab peg* or with some other illness whose symptoms similarly include shivering and pain. An established *txiv neeb*, summoned to diagnose the problem, may conclude from these symptoms that the person (who is usually but not always male) has been chosen to be the host of a healing spirit, a *neeb*. (*Txiv neeb* means "person with a healing spirit.") It is an offer that the sick person cannot refuse, since if he rejects his vocation, he will die. In any case, few Hmong would choose to decline. Although shamanism is an arduous calling that requires years of training with a master in order to learn the ritual techniques and chants, it confers an enormous amount of social status in the community and publicly marks the *txiv neeb* as a person of high moral character, since a healing spirit would never choose a no-account host. Even if an epileptic turns out not to be elected to host a *neeb*, his illness, with its thrilling aura of the supramundane, singles him out as a person of consequence.

In their attitude toward Lia's seizures, the Lees reflected this mixture of concern and pride. The Hmong are known for the gentleness with which they treat their children. Hugo Adolf Bernatzik, a German ethnographer who lived with the Hmong of Thailand for several years during the 1930s, wrote that the Hmong he had studied regarded a

---

3

The Spirit Catches You and You Fall Down

When Lia was about three months old, her older sister Yer slammed the front door of the Lees' apartment. A few moments later, Lia's eyes rolled up, her arms jerked over her head, and she fainted. The Lees had little doubt what had happened. Despite the careful installation of Lia's soul during the *hu plig* ceremony, the noise of the door had been so profoundly frightening that her soul had fled her body and become lost. They recognized the resulting symptoms as *qaug dab peg*, which means "the spirit catches you and you fall down." The spirit referred to in this phrase is a soul-stealing *dab*; *peg* means to catch or hit; and *qaug* means to fall over with one's roots still in the ground, as grain might be beaten down by wind or rain.

In Hmong-English dictionaries, *qaug dab peg* is generally translated as epilepsy. It is an illness well known to the Hmong, who regard it with ambivalence. On the one hand, it is acknowledged to be a serious and potentially dangerous condition. Tony Coelho, who was Merced's congressman from 1979 to 1989, is an epileptic. Coelho is a popular figure among the Hmong, and a few years ago, some local Hmong men were sufficiently concerned when they learned he suffered from *qaug dab peg* that they volunteered the services of a shaman, a *txiv neeb*, to perform a ceremony that would retrieve Coelho's errant soul. The

child as "the most treasured possession a person can have." In Laos, a baby was never apart from its mother, sleeping in her arms all night and riding on her back all day. Small children were rarely abused; it was believed that a *dab* who witnessed mistreatment might take the child, assuming it was not wanted. The Hmong who live in the United States have continued to be unusually attentive parents. A study conducted at the University of Minnesota found Hmong infants in the first month of life to be less irritable and more securely attached to their mothers than Caucasian infants, a difference the researcher attributed to the fact that the Hmong mothers were, without exception, more sensitive, more accepting, and more responsive, as well as "exquisitely attuned" to their children's signals. Another study, conducted in Portland, Oregon, found that Hmong mothers held and touched their babies far more frequently than Caucasian mothers. In a third study, conducted at the Hennepin County Medical Center in Minnesota, a group of Hmong mothers of toddlers surpassed a group of Caucasian mothers of similar socioeconomic status in every one of fourteen categories selected from the Egeland Mother-Child Rating Scale, ranging from "Speed of Responsiveness to Fussing and Crying" to "Delight."

Foua and Nao Kao had nurtured Lia in typical Hmong fashion (on the Egeland Scale, they would have scored especially high in Delight), and they were naturally distressed to think that anything might compromise her health and happiness. They therefore hoped, at least most of the time, that the *qaug dab peg* could be healed. Yet they also considered the illness an honor. Jeanine Hilt, a social worker who knew the Lees well, told me, "They felt Lia was kind of an anointed one, like a member of royalty. She was a very special person in their culture because she had these spirits in her and she might grow up to be a shaman, and so sometimes their thinking was that this was not so much a medical problem as it was a blessing." (Of the forty or so American doctors, nurses, and Merced County agency employees I spoke with who had dealt with Lia and her family, several had a vague idea that "spirits" were somehow involved, but Jeanine Hilt was the only one who had actually asked the Lees what they thought was the cause of their daughter's illness.)

Within the Lee family, in one of those unconscious processes of

selection that are as mysterious as any other form of falling in love, it was obvious that Lia was her parents' favorite, the child they considered the most beautiful, the one who was most extravagantly hugged and kissed, the one who was dressed in the most exquisite garments (embroidered by Foua, wearing dime-store glasses to work her almost microscopic stitches). Whether Lia occupied this position from the moment of her birth, whether it was a result of her spiritually distinguished illness, or whether it came from the special tenderness any parent feels for a sick child, is not a matter Foua and Nao Kao wish, or are able, to analyze. One thing that is clear is that for many years the cost of that extra love was partially borne by her sister Yer. "They blamed Yer for slamming the door," said Jeanine Hilt. "I tried many times to explain that the door had nothing to do with it, but they didn't believe me. Lia's illness made them so sad that I think for a long time they treated Yer differently from their other children."

During the next few months of her life, Lia had at least twenty more seizures. On two occasions, Foua and Nao Kao were worried enough to carry her in their arms to the emergency room at Merced Community Medical Center, which was three blocks from their apartment. Like most Hmong refugees, they had their doubts about the efficacy of Western medical techniques. However, when they were living in the Mae Jarim refugee camp in Thailand, their only surviving son, Cheng, and three of their six surviving daughters, Ge, May, and True, had been seriously ill. Ge died. They took Cheng, May, and True to the camp hospital; Cheng and May recovered rapidly, and True was sent to another, larger hospital, where she eventually recovered as well. (The Lees also concurrently addressed the possible spiritual origins of their children's illnesses by moving to a new hut. A dead person had been buried beneath their old one, and his soul might have wished to harm the new residents.) This experience did nothing to shake their faith in traditional Hmong beliefs about the causes and cures of illness, but it did convince them that on some occasions Western doctors could be of additional help, and that it would do no harm to hedge their bets.

County hospitals have a reputation for being crowded, dilapidated, and dingy. Merced's county hospital, with which the Lees would become all too familiar over the next few years, is none of these. The

MCMC complex includes a modern, 42,000-square-foot wing—it looks sort of like an art moderne ocean liner—that houses coronary care, intensive care, and transitional care units; 154 medical and surgical beds; medical and radiology laboratories outfitted with the-the-art diagnostic equipment; and a blood bank. The waiting rooms in the hospital and its attached clinic have unshredded magazines, unsmelly bathrooms, and floors that have been scrubbed to an aseptic gloss. MCMC is a teaching hospital, staffed in part by the faculty and residents of the Family Practice Residency, which is affiliated with the University of California at Davis. The residency program is nationally known, and receives at least 150 applications annually for its six first-year positions.

Like many other rural county hospitals, which were likely to feel the health care crunch before it reached urban hospitals, MCMC has been plagued with financial problems throughout the last twenty years. It accepts all patients, whether or not they can pay; only twenty percent are privately insured, with most of the rest receiving aid from California's Medi-Cal, Medicare, or Medically Indigent Adult programs, and a small (but to the hospital, costly) percentage neither insured nor covered by any federal or state program. The hospital receives reimbursements from the public programs, but many of those reimbursements have been lowered or restricted in recent years. Although the private patients are far more profitable, MCMC's efforts to attract what its administrator has called "an improved payer mix" have not been very successful. (Merced's wealthier residents often choose either a private Catholic hospital three miles north of MCMC or a larger hospital in a nearby city such as Fresno.) MCMC went through a particularly rough period during the late eighties, hitting bottom in 1988, when it had a $3.1 million deficit.

During this same period, MCMC also experienced an expensive change in its patient population. Starting in the late seventies, Southeast Asian refugees began to move to Merced in large numbers. The city of Merced, which has a population of about 61,000, now has just over 12,000 Hmong. That is to say, one in five residents of Merced is Hmong. Because many Hmong fear and shun the hospital, MCMC's patient rolls reflect a somewhat lower ratio, but on any given day there are still Hmong patients in almost every unit. Not only do

the Hmong fail resoundingly to improve the payer mix—more than eighty percent are on Medi-Cal—but they have proved even more costly than other indigent patients, because they generally require more time and attention, and because there are so many of them that MCMC has had to hire bilingual staff members to mediate between patients and providers.

There are no funds in the hospital budget specifically earmarked for interpreters, so the administration has detoured around that technicality by hiring Hmong lab assistants, nurse's aides, and transporters, who are called upon to translate in the scarce interstices between analyzing blood, emptying bedpans, and rolling postoperative patients around on gurneys. In 1991, a short-term federal grant enabled MCMC to put skilled interpreters on call around the clock, but the program expired the following year. Except during that brief hiatus, there have often been no Hmong-speaking employees of any kind present in the hospital at night. Obstetricians have had to obtain consent for cesarean sections or episiotomies using embarrassed teenaged sons, who have learned English in school, as translators. Ten-year-old girls have had to translate discussions of whether or not a dying family member should be resuscitated. Sometimes not even a child is available. Doctors on the late shift in the emergency room have often had no way of taking a patient's medical history, or of asking such questions as Where do you hurt? How long have you been hurting? What does it feel like? Have you had an accident? Have you vomited? Have you had a fever? Have you lost consciousness? Are you pregnant? Have you taken any medications? Are you allergic to any medications? Have you recently eaten? (The last question is of great importance if emergency surgery is being contemplated, since anesthetized patients with full stomachs can aspirate the partially digested food into their lungs, and may die if they choke or if their bronchial linings are badly burned by stomach acid.) I asked one doctor what he did in such cases. He said, "Practice veterinary medicine."

On October 24, 1982, the first time that Foua and Nao Kao carried Lia to the emergency room, MCMC had not yet hired any interpreters, de jure or de facto, for any shift. At that time, the only hospital employee who sometimes translated for Hmong patients was a janitor, a Laotian immigrant fluent in his own language, Lao, which few

Hmong understand; halting in English; and even more halting in Hmong. On that day either the janitor was unavailable or the emergency room staff didn't think of calling him. The resident on duty practiced veterinary medicine. Foua and Nao Kao had no way of explaining what had happened, since Lia's seizures had stopped by the time they reached the hospital. Her only obvious symptoms were a cough and a congested chest. The resident ordered an X ray, which led the radiologist to conclude that Lia had "early bronchiopneumonia or tracheobronchitis." As he had no way of knowing that the bronchial congestion was probably caused by aspiration of saliva or vomit during her seizure (a common problem for epileptics), she was routinely dismissed with a prescription for ampicillin, an antibiotic. Her emergency room Registration Record lists her father's last name as Yang, her mother's maiden name as Foua, and her "primary spoken language" as "Mong." When Lia was discharged, Nao Kao (who knows the alphabet but does not speak or read English) signed a piece of paper that said, "I hereby acknowledge receipt of the instructions indicated above," to wit: "Take ampicillin as directed. Vaporizer at cribside. Clinic reached as needed 383-7007 ten days." The "ten days" meant that Nao Kao was supposed to call the Family Practice Center in ten days for a follow-up appointment. Not surprisingly, since he had no idea what he had agreed to, he didn't. But when Lia had another bad seizure on November 11, he and Foua carried her to the emergency room again, where the same scene was repeated, and the same misdiagnosis made.

On March 3, 1983, Foua and Nao Kao carried Lia to the emergency room a third time. On this occasion, three circumstances were different: Lia was still seizing when they arrived, they were accompanied by a cousin who spoke some English, and one of the doctors on duty was a family practice resident named Dan Murphy. Of all the doctors who have worked at MCMC, Dan Murphy is generally acknowledged to be the one most interested in and knowledgeable about the Hmong. At that time, he had been living in Merced for only seven months, so his interest still exceeded his knowledge. When he and his wife, Cindy, moved to Merced, they had never heard the word "Hmong." Several years later, Cindy was teaching English to Hmong adults and Dan was inviting Hmong leaders to the hospital to tell the

residents about their experiences as refugees. Most important, the Murphys counted a Hmong family, the Xiongs, among their closest friends. When one of the Xiong daughters wanted to spend the summer working in Yosemite National Park, Chaly Xiong, her father, initially refused because he was afraid she might get eaten by a lion. Dan personally escorted Chaly to Yosemite to verify the absence of lions, and persuaded him the job would do his daughter good. Four months later, Chaly was killed in an automobile accident. Cindy Murphy arranged the funeral, calling around until she found a funeral parlor that was willing to accommodate three days of incense burning, drum beating, and *qeej* playing. She also bought several live chickens, which were sacrificed in the parking lot of the funeral parlor, as well as a calf and a pig, which were sacrificed elsewhere. When Dan first saw the Lees, he instantly registered that they were Hmong, and he thought to himself: "This won't be boring."

Many years later, Dan, who is a short, genial man with an Amish-style beard and an incandescent smile, recalled the encounter. "I have this memory of Lia's parents standing just inside the door to the ER, holding a chubby little round-faced baby. She was having a generalized seizure. Her eyes were rolled back, she was unconscious, her arms and legs were kind of jerking back and forth, and she didn't breathe much—every once in a while, there would be no movement of the chest wall and you couldn't hear any breath sounds. That was definitely anxiety-producing. She was the youngest patient I had ever dealt with who was seizing. The parents seemed frightened, not terribly frightened though, not as frightened as I would have been if it was my kid. I thought it might be meningitis, so Lia had to have a spinal tap, and the parents were real resistant to that. I don't remember how I convinced them. I remember feeling very anxious because they had a real sick kid and I felt a big need to explain to these people, through their relative who was a not-very-good translator, what was going on, but I felt like I had no time, because we had to put an IV in her scalp with Valium to stop the seizures, but then Lia started seizing again and the IV went into the skin instead of the vein, and I had a hard time getting another one started. Later on, when I figured out what had happened, or not happened, on the earlier visits to the ER, I felt good. It's kind of a thrill to find something someone else has missed, especially when you're a resident and you are looking for excuses to make yourself feel smarter than the other physicians."

Among Dan's notes in Lia's History and Physical Examination record were:

HISTORY OF PRESENT ILLNESS: The patient is an 8 month, Hmong female, whose family brought her to the emergency room after they had noticed her shaking and not breathing very well for a 20-minute period of time. According to the family the patient has had multiple like episodes in the past, but have never been able to communicate this to emergency room doctors on previous visits secondary to a language barrier. An english speaking relative available tonight, stated that the patient had intermittent fever and cough for 2-3 days prior to being admitted.

FAMILY & SOCIAL HISTORY: Unobtainable secondary to language difficulties.

NEUROLOGICAL: The child was unresponsive to pain or sound. The head was held to the left with intermittent tonic-clonic [first rigid, then jerking] movements of the upper extremities. Respirations were suppressed during these periods of clonic movement. Grunting respirations persisted until the patient was given 3 mg. of Valium I.V.

Dan had no way of knowing that Foua and Nao Kao had already diagnosed their daughter's problem as the illness where the spirit catches you and you fall down. Foua and Nao Kao had no way of knowing that Dan had diagnosed it as epilepsy, the most common of all neurological disorders. Each had accurately noted the same symptoms, but Dan would have been surprised to hear that they were caused by soul loss, and Lia's parents would have been surprised to hear that they were caused by an electrochemical storm inside their daughter's head that had been stirred up by the misfiring of aberrant brain cells.

Dan had learned in medical school that epilepsy is a sporadic malfunction of the brain, sometimes mild and sometimes severe, sometimes progressive and sometimes self-limiting, which can be traced to oxygen deprivation during gestation, labor, or birth; a head injury; a tumor; an infection; a high fever; a stroke; a metabolic disturbance; a

drug allergy; a toxic reaction to a poison. Sometimes the source is obvious—the patient had a brain tumor or swallowed strychnine or crashed through a windshield—but in about seven out of ten cases, the cause is never determined. During an epileptic episode, instead of following their usual orderly protocol, the damaged cells in the cerebral cortex transmit neural impulses simultaneously and chaotically. When only a small area of the brain is involved—in a "focal" seizure—an epileptic may hallucinate or twitch or tingle but retain consciousness. When the electrical disturbance extends to a wide area—in a "generalized" seizure—consciousness is lost, either for the brief episodes called petit mal or "absence" seizures, or for the full-blown attacks known as grand mal. Except through surgery, whose risks consign it to the category of last resort, epilepsy cannot be cured, but it can be completely or partially controlled in most cases by anti-convulsant drugs.

The Hmong are not the only people who might have good reason to feel ambivalent about suppressing the symptoms. The Greeks called epilepsy "the sacred disease." Dan Murphy's diagnosis added Lia Lee to a distinguished line of epileptics that has included Søren Kierkegaard, Vincent van Gogh, Gustave Flaubert, Lewis Carroll, and Fyodor Dostoyevsky, all of whom, like many Hmong shamans, experienced powerful senses of grandeur and spiritual passion during their seizures, and powerful creative urges in their wake. As Dostoyevsky's Prince Myshkin asked, "What if it is a disease? What does it matter that it is an abnormal tension, if the result, if the moment of sensation, remembered and analysed in a state of health, turns out to be harmony and beauty brought to their highest point of perfection, and gives a feeling, undivined and undreamt of till then, of completeness, proportion, reconciliation, and an ecstatic and prayerful fusion in the highest synthesis of life?"

Although the inklings Dan had gathered of the transcendental Hmong worldview seemed to him to possess both power and beauty, his own view of medicine in general, and of epilepsy in particular, was, like that of his colleagues at MCMC, essentially rationalist. Hippocrates' skeptical commentary on the nature of epilepsy, made around 400 B.C., pretty much sums up Dan's own frame of reference: "It seems to me that the disease is no more divine than any other. It has a natural cause just as other diseases have. Men think it is divine merely because they don't understand it. But if they called everything divine which they do not understand, why, there would be no end of divine things."*

Lia's seizure was a grand mal episode, and Dan had no desire to do anything but stop it. He admitted her to MCMC as an inpatient. Among the tests she had during the three days she spent there were a spinal tap, a CT scan, an EEG, a chest X ray, and extensive blood work. Foua and Nao Kao signed "Authorization for and Consent to Surgery or Special Diagnostic or Therapeutic Procedures" forms, each several hundred words long, for the first two of these. It is not known whether anyone attempted to translate them, or, if so, how "Your physician has requested a brain scan utilizing computerized tomography," was rendered in Hmong. None of the tests revealed any apparent cause for the seizures. The doctors classified Lia's epilepsy as "idiopathic": cause unknown. Lia was found to have consolidation in her right lung, which this time was correctly diagnosed as aspiration pneumonia resulting from the seizure. Foua and Nao Kao alternated nights at the hospital, sleeping in a cot next to Lia's bed. Among the Nurse's Notes for Lia's last night at the hospital were: "0001. Skin cool and dry to touch, color good & pink. Mom is with babe at this time & is breastfeeding. Mom informed to keep babe covered with a blanket for the babe is a little cool." "0400. Babe resting quietly

with no acute distress noted. Mom breast feeds off & on." "0600. Sleeping." "0730. Awake, color good. Mother fed." "1200. Held by mother."

Lia was discharged on March 11, 1983. Her parents were instructed, via an English-speaking relative, to give her 250 milligrams of ampicillin twice a day, to clear up her aspiration pneumonia, and twenty milligrams of Dilantin elixir, an anticonvulsant, twice a day, to suppress any further grand mal seizures.

---

* Despite this early attempt by Hippocrates (or perhaps by one of the anonymous physicians whose writings are attributed to Hippocrates) to remove the "divine" label, epilepsy continued, more than any other disease, to be ascribed to supernatural causes. The medical historian Owsei Temkin has noted that epilepsy has held a key position historically in "the struggle between magic and the scientific conception." Many treatments for epilepsy have had occult associations. Greek magicians forbade epileptics to eat mint, garlic, and onion, as well as the flesh of goats, pigs, deer, dogs, cocks, turtledoves, bustards, mullets, and eels; to wear black garments and goatskins; and to cross their hands and feet: taboos that were all connected, in various ways, with chthonic deities. Roman epileptics were advised to swallow morsels cut from the livers of stabbed gladiators. During the Middle Ages, when epilepsy was attributed to demonic possession, treatments included prayer, fasting, wearing amulets, lighting candles, visiting the graves of saints, and writing the names of the Three Wise Men with blood taken from the patient's little finger. These spiritual remedies were far safer than the "medical" therapies of the time—still practiced as late as the seventeenth century—which included cauterizing the head with a hot iron and boring a hole in the skull to release peccant vapors.